LAN SECURITY
HANDBOOK

ELLEN DUTTON

M&T BOOKS

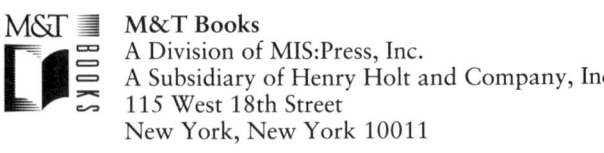

M&T Books
A Division of MIS:Press, Inc.
A Subsidiary of Henry Holt and Company, Inc.
115 West 18th Street
New York, New York 10011

Copyright © 1994 by M&T Books

Printed in the United States of America

Library of Congress Cataloging-in-Publication Data

Dutton, Ellen.
    LAN security handbook / Ellen Dutton.
      p. cm.
    Includes index.
    ISBN 1-55851-387-6 : $39.95
    1. Local area networks (Computer networks)—Security measures.   I. Title.
TK5105.7.D89   1994
005.8--dc20
                                            94-19132
                                                CIP

97 96 95 94   4 3 2 1

Copy Editors: Jessica Boria
Technical Editor: Ted Needleman
Production Editor: Patricia Wallenburg

DEDICATION

To my Mother, who encourages her children to be all they can be
and does what she can to make their dreams come true.

To the memory of my Father, who would have been proud of this book
because of its subject and because I wrote it.

Acknowledgments

I apologize for having so many people to thank, but I have been blessed with a great number of friends, mentors, and supporters throughout a long career. Everyone wants to write a book. In awe of the accomplishment, first time authors feel enormous gratitude towards those who helped make it possible, so their thank yous are, understandably, longer than most.

First of all, I am grateful to Brenda McLaughlin for asking me to write a book on LAN security for M&T Books and to Patty Wallenburg, Production Editor, for her determination to overcome the difficulties of an "all electronic" edit and make the book a reality.

I wish to thank Joseph C. Cruden for his encouragement and good ideas. He helped me keep the big picture in view from the start.

The contributions of Dr. David A. Harris, Lieutenant-Colonel U.S. Army, and professor in communications, quantitative studies, computer science, and MIS at George Washington University and the American University graduate schools, were many. The book is better because he reviewed it and offered his expertise and excellent suggestions throughout. In fact, it would take a great many books to do justice to all of his suggestions and ideas.

A sincere thank you to Wayne Rash for doing a marvelous and thorough final technical review.

Many thanks to a few more very special people for their help:

- My daughter, Bethany Dutton, for her work on the graphics, the Glossary, the Product appendix, photography, and general readability.

- Mona Clements Hunt, literary editor (and my mother), who contributed by reading, editing, offering thoughtful feedback, and working through the Fourth of July weekend to complete the final edit.

■ Dave Cruden for taking pictures of the White House and other secure sites around town.

■ Peter Hunt, my brother, who expertly created original graphics.

■ Austin Dutton, my son, who allowed his Rottweiler, Condor, to be photographed for the book.

■ Arch C. Davis, III, Electrical Engineer and systems integrator, for adding disk hardware terms to a 1990 revision of my glossary which help explain concepts important to performance in disk hardware.

State-of-the-art LAN security products are at the very heart of this book. I wish to express thanks to the product experts, technicians, and public relations people who went out of their way to locate the information and pictures I requested.

The M&T editors Jules Gilder, Margo Pagan, Dawn Erdos, and the many people behind the book production scenes deserve a special note of thanks for their hard work.

TABLE OF CONTENTS

■ CHAPTER 4

Electronic Network Access Control 69

■ CHAPTER 5

Encryption and Other Useful Disguises 87

■ CHAPTER 6

■ CHAPTER 7

■ CHAPTER 9

■ CHAPTER 10

■ CHAPTER 11

INTRODUCTION

"Life is a series of problems. Do we want to moan about them or solve them?...Discipline is the basic set of tools were require to solve life's problems. Without discipline we can solve nothing."

The Road Less Travelled
—M. Scott Peck, M.D.

In a perfect electronic world our relationships with our networks and computers will be very different from what they are today. Instead of spending our time pounding away on a keyboard most of us will communicate the way we do best, verbally. A simple, "Good morning, Cyber" will alert the computer that we are ready to start the day. As a result of asking the simple question, "What's new?" we will expect the information which interests us most to be given to us immediately—verbally, visually, or in hard copy—depending on our established preferences and habits. Our personal data bank will no longer consist of filing cabinets containing paper transactions, shelves of books, and hard drives full of text, spreadsheets, and graphics. Instead, our data bank will consist of our unique filters and views of most of the readable data ever gathered and compiled and most of the words ever written. Worries about data privacy will be unknown because all communications will be perfectly secure.

Unfortunately, that is still the dream not the reality. A John Burgess article in the *Washington Post* indicates that great forward strides are being made towards the ultimate use of computers as true electronic servants. IBM's three-dimensional personal software agent "Charlie" has a human image and can shop electronic malls and make dinner and airline reservations. The ideal agent according to an executive of General Magic, a software developer, will be "more intelligent than a dog, but clearly subhuman...dutiful but uncreative."

The *Corporation for National Research Initiatives* has created an agent—they call it a "knowbot", for knowledge robot—that travels from database to database in Europe and the United States in search of specific names in hopes of locating their Internet addresses. (There is no directory for the large Internet user community.)

A mobile *PersonalLink* network designed to support roaming personal software agents between hand-held devices is promised in 1994 by an AT&T, Motorola, Apple, Sony, and Nippon T&T partnership.

Technology still has a long way to go before the evolution of our perfect electronic world is complete. Many information security issues such as agent authentication, message privacy, assigning privileges and limits, and the legality and recognition of liabilities created by agents acting on behalf of individuals will have to be addressed along the way. This book is intended to help network managers thrive until then.

When Brenda Mcloughlin invited me to write this book, I thought it would be professionally satisfying. It has been that. It has also been exciting in a way I never imagined. For months now, the network security topics I am busy writing about keep appearing on the front page of the *Washington Post*. Stories appear with regularity on such topics as the Clipper Chip, the need for new management methods and controls for keeping secret information private and intact, Internet break-ins, the Information Superhighway, new products and technology, and so on. Now that the writing is over I am more excited about the work that needs to be done than I was before I started.

This is, surely, the decade of information security.

Why This Book Is For You

LAN Security was written for practicing LAN managers, administrators, and support persons. However, since it presents a great quantity of information in an organized easy-to-read, easy-to-locate manner, it is also a useful reference tool for LAN designers, engineers, installers, value added resellers, as well as systems professionals who develop applications for

LANs. Users with an interest in their networks will gain knowledge from a technical management perspective. Senior managers who are also users will appreciate this concise treatment of a subject which represents an increasingly significant asset, risk, and responsibility to the organization as a whole. A short list of the topics and perspectives presented include the following:

- The power of LANs to change or destroy organizations is little appreciated
- "LAN" applies to any type of PC network but LAN issues require distinction based on network type, size, data sensitivity, connections to computers and other networks, performance requirements, and nature and criticality of applications
- LANs and LAN technologies evolve too quickly for busy managers to stay current
- Security management is difficult, time consuming, invisible, and unpopular; thus it takes a back seat to implementing new LAN features and user applications
- Varied threats against networks and data are little understood
- Users often lack basic security awareness
- LAN evolution has increased complexity of security management and now requires considerable technical expertise
- While LAN security needs have increased, the policies and practices of day-to-day LAN security have not kept pace
- LAN security awareness lags the availability of solutions
- Interconnected LANs increase vulnerability to intrusion, hackers, viruses, etc. (a LAN is only as secure as its weakest link)

Students will find reading this book an easy way to quickly absorb LAN security concepts and to appreciate the realities and difficulties of securing networks.

LAN technology evolves so quickly that few managers can keep their fingers on its pulse. Little formal education is available on the full spectrum of security issues related to network management. Even the content of university programs can trail the use of LAN technology in organizations. As a result, LAN managers rely on trade journals to guide them through the uncharted waters of planning, installing, upgrading, administering, and securing their LANs. LAN magazines understandably focus on the hottest topics, which do not necessarily give LAN managers, administrators, and users the fundamentals and specifics of LAN network and application system security knowledge which they require.

Recognizing that it is impossible to completely protect any network, I intended only to identify the relevant issues and clarify the state-of-the-art of LAN security for those responsible for managing and protecting LANs. This book offers a baseline for LAN security, practical solutions which managers can employ now, and other valuable insights and resources for meeting your LAN security needs. Managing the security of Local Area Networks is one of the most important efforts an organization can undertake, yet the implications and complexity of the task are often minimized or misunderstood. This book will be invaluable to you in meeting your obligation to manage and protect your LAN.

Purpose of This Book

The challenge of managing network security is to provide the greatest possible function and flexibility to the broadest set of users while safeguarding network assets, particularly shared data. The ease of network use and the costs of networking must constantly be balanced against the need to effectively manage and protect network assets. The purpose of this book is to clarify the issues, threats, and available solutions for network managers so they can more easily balance the risks associated with the threats against their LANs with the costs (measured in dollars and user convenience) of installing safeguards.

CHAPTER 1

LAN SECURITY: LANS AT RISK

*L*ocal Area Network (LAN) security is interesting, technical, sophisticated, and challenging. Because this is so, it is easy to become caught up with the high-tech aspects and forget that there is more to LAN security than viruses and hackers. Much more.

For example, the employees at Ontrack Data Recovery, Inc. arrived at work one morning to find a nervous Japanese man waiting outside their offices clutching a damaged hard disk drive. He said he had neglected to back up the system for which he was responsible. He had been told not to come back unless he was able to retrieve the data. Happily, Ontrack *did* retrieve the data, and he was able to go home to Japan. This is an example of what can happen if you neglect basic computer and network security until a disaster occurs. It also illustrates the tendency of individuals to neglect their responsibility to secure and protect LAN assets, until their jobs are on the line.

1

What would you have done if that had happened to you before you learned about Ontrack's data recovery expertise? Would you have had a solution ready and waiting, or would you have just quietly lost your job, and resolved to take care of basic security the next time around?

We can be sure the replacement for the damaged hard disk has been backed up regularly since the disaster occurred. It is doubtful that the LAN manager continues to take unnecessary security risks.

Security-Aware LAN Management

You do not have to have all the latest high-tech security products to be an effective LAN manager. You do have to plan effectively, have the right products and tools, use them wisely and diligently, and know what to do and where to go to get help in an emergency. Even the best surgeon is useless in the operating room without adequate tools and competent support.

Low-Tech Threats and Common-Sense Solutions

Quite frankly, many LAN security problems have nothing to do with high technology and only require solutions as simple as locking a door or a drawer.

This occurred at an art gallery plagued by the loss of valuable works of art. A security review showed that the installed high-tech surveillance and security equipment was highly effective in protecting the works on display. The problem was that valuable prints and paintings were being taken out of completely unprotected drawers in the rear of the gallery when no one was around. A few simple drawer locks, with sound and flashing light alarms, and the installation of a secure back door was all it took to stop the losses.

Who knows how many LANs have sophisticated (and expensive) safeguards, yet are not at all secure because network passwords are left in plain sight. Security can also be compromised when visitors are allowed to wander in areas where LAN workstation PCs are left logged into the LAN, completely unattended and vulnerable. If you walked by a LAN workstation and saw a stranger diligently working away on it, would you question the person's right to have access to that computer? Or would you just think it was a repair person or temporary employee? Too many people would just assume the person was authorized.

I am reminded of the movie, *War Games*, where a student accessed the computer at school by using the school secretary's password. She changed her password religiously, but, unfortunately, posted it neatly on an unlocked pull-out shelf in her desk. Using her authorized user ID and password, the student simply logged onto the system and changed his grades. He was also able to access any other information he cared to see. The most sophisticated barriers to LAN hackers could not keep this young man out, because he had the information he needed to masquerade as the secretary—a bona fide user ID and password.

This LAN could have been protected by password generators, LAN management software, audit software systems, monitoring procedures, tap and intruder detectors, etc., yet no security problem would be indicated. All the audit reports would show is that a duly authorized secretary in the Dean of Students' office made adjustments to student data, a fairly routine occurrence.

Since the secretary has the necessary access rights to modify student data, no exception report would be generated, no intruder alarm would sound, and no one would ever know the grades had been changed. The solution to the problem is obvious. There is nothing high-tech about guarding your password.

Four LAN Security Sins

The four unforgivable LAN security sins are easily avoided by taking common-sense precautions. They are:

■   Failure to make appropriate, routine backups.

■ Using easy-to-guess passwords, no passwords, or not protecting passwords.

■ Failure to fully protect data by not implementing basic Network Operating System security features.

■ Failure to train users and make them accountable for their actions.

Virus and Hacker Hype

With LAN security it is easy to lose sight of the forest for the trees. The LAN manager who is hit with a virus that takes his system down will probably protect the LAN vigorously against viruses in the future, even at the expense of other simple safeguards. The hype surrounding viruses and hackers creates an unrealistic picture for computer users. Indeed, they are more likely to have unprotected PCs stolen and many times more likely to lose valuable data through errors or faulty software, than they are to have a major loss caused by a virus. The bottom line is that virus attacks make good scare stories; petty theft and pilferage do not. We need to put computer and LAN security into proper perspective so that everyone who uses a computer realizes that common sense security measures are just as important as the sophisticated, high-tech kind.

A communications company experienced losses from insider theft from time to time, like many other companies. They were zealous about protecting against outsiders by using uniformed security guards, visitor logs, escorts for visitors, etc. Yet they failed to secure their computers and other valuable equipment within their offices. Even after they discovered that some PCs had been lowered to the ground from the office windows during off hours, the company still took no action to lock their equipment in place!

High-tech Solutions

High-tech safeguards and countermeasures such as LAN analyzers, electronic asset protection, and encryption certainly have their place in the

LAN security portfolio, and get their share of attention in this book. Intrusion methods such as passive wiretapping, intruder-friendly physical wiretaps and targeted electronic penetration attacks, or *network cracking*, are described here along with appropriate high-tech defenses.

The defenses include wiretap detector and alarm systems, encryption, compression, password generators, password checker products, and dial-in protection techniques used to disguise or otherwise protect LAN data from intruders.

From Secure Mainframe to Risky LAN

Valuable data is typically protected in traditional mainframe systems. However, the same data is often highly vulnerable in LANs that lack the most rudimentary security safeguards. The importance and complexity of LAN security is still largely unappreciated. Even when it is recognized, the issues seem so complex that they are frequently ignored. Not having the time to do a thorough job of understanding the threats and devising workable safeguards, LAN managers often do little or nothing. That practice must change.

LANs were not originally designed to support the mission-critical data and information processing applications that are routinely installed on them today. Instead, LANs evolved slowly from peer-to-peer links, which did little more than permit printer sharing, to become the present day communications hub of the organization. The emergence of reliable LAN technology enabled the business world to downsize by converting information processing applications, previously run on mainframe computers, to microcomputers and LANs. When LAN-based systems proved to be viable low-cost alternatives to those run on more expensive processors, vital business operations were restructured to use the new information-sharing resource. By the mid '80s, when LANs began to proliferate, security management was well established in centralized data processing installations. The high value of the total IS resource—hardware, software, engineers, and support personnel—had earned risk management and security attention. LANs by contrast receive little such attention even now and are unnecessarily vulnerable to loss of service and loss of net-worked data. Too many LANs are managed without sufficient attention to security issues such as reliability, availability, integrity, accuracy, and disaster recovery. Without security they are not a safe platform for mission-critical data processing applications.

LANs: Unprecedented Opportunity, Greater Vulnerability

Networking solves some of the security problems associated with PCs and exacerbates others. On the positive side, LANs permit the protection and management of PC data when it is stored on servers. They also offer unprecedented opportunities for users to access, use, disclose, modify, and process shared data, and to make mistakes that can compromise the privacy, integrity, and overall security of the data they contain. Through the interconnection of PCs and networked resources, LANs also present greater vulnerability in terms of exposure to external threats, such as intrusion, viruses, damage, theft, or destruction caused by hackers or other wrongdoers.

Why LANs Are at Risk

There are three main causes of lax security which result in the vulnerability of today's LANs. They are:

1. **User Management**—LANs are often managed exclusively by end-users with no technical expertise.

2. **Complexity**—They are technically complex, increasingly intercon-nected, and change constantly.

3. **Ignorance and Inattention**—Organizations frequently are unaware of or fail to address LAN security issues.

User Management

LANs evolved as an end user solution to the growing backlog of computer application systems and what users perceived to be a lack of responsiveness of traditional IS organizations. They were originally planned and managed by an end user community that lacks the systems management techniques and traditions which would provide a desirable level of security awareness.

Many LANs are still managed by end users at arm's length from traditional IS management. While this arrangement gives end users the responsiveness and flexibility they want, and absolves IS of the risk of operating highly vulnerable resources, the organizations are not being well-served. Organizations need dependable access to increasingly vital network services and to have their data resources protected to the full extent of their value.

Complexity

Management and security of networks is far more complex than management and security of traditional centralized data processing. A favorite saying is that the only thing you can count on in managing a network is that it will change. Changes occur so rapidly on LANs that they need the *most* expert (not least expert) management.

Ignorance and Inattention

LANs offer unique security problems which are ignored to a great extent. Security-aware managers may want to work at the issues, but they have no constituency calling for more security. Users want more services; business units want more applications; and executives want to generate ever greater returns on investments in technology. In effect, LAN managers—who are usually responsible for LAN security by default—are under attack on all sides. While they stay current with the technology and keep everyone happy by delivering desired results, no one is watching the store. We are not giving security the attention it deserves.

It is difficult for a manager to stand back and look at the big LAN picture in the midst of the pressure to provide and support ever more sophisticated LAN applications, interconnections, and network services. It is particularly unrewarding to address LAN security since security measures are generally costly and can make a system both more difficult to use and less responsive. Yet that is what must be done if the billions of dollars of LAN resources presently at risk are to be properly protected.

The Importance of Security Planning

When a LAN is in the planning stage, it is useful to create long-term security plans with budget forecasts. This should be done to anticipate the expense of providing contingencies long before they are mandated by essential applications being installed on the LAN. Once a critical mass of applications (or even one sensitive or essential application) has been implemented, your security portfolio must be upgraded to incorporate new and appropriate safeguards. It is good strategy to have a plan at hand when the facts and figures are needed. A comprehensive and dynamic security plan is an asset for a harried LAN manager, because LANs tend to grow rapidly in size and complexity. Once they start to expand throughout an organization there is no stopping them, and no going back. If you have not invested time in security planning up front, it is doubly difficult to go back later, after crucial decisions have been made, and do a thorough job.

Government tends to be far more security-aware than the private sector (except for financial institutions and certain strategic industries). Even so, a 1990 survey of 22 federal agencies by the U.S. General Accounting office showed that only 38 percent of security controls scheduled to be implemented were actually in place. Budget constraints and lack of management support were cited as reasons for the failure to protect government assets and resources. In the 1993 Computer Crime Survey by COM-SEC, 43 percent of the organizations admitted that they have security incidents at least once a month and 1 in 7 losses amounts to more than $100,000. About 40 percent of the managers believe their network security is inadequate and more than one-fourth say their security is "lax" or "reactionary."

One survey respondent volunteered, "My company suffered a $580,000 (U.S.) loss in a computer fraud incident. Management decided to cover it up and not tell anyone because of the possible negative publicity."

So the picture of our network security nationwide is pretty bleak, and steps must be taken to correct the situation.

Electronic Crime Threatens National Security

If you think that our national security problems are over because the cold war has ended, guess again. The cold war may be over, but the global economic war is not. We are engaged in economic combat with other nations, which is a struggle of a different kind. For national economic security reasons, we need to protect strategic industries and those where we maintain a strong competitive edge such as energy and computer software, from industrial espionage.

Michelle Van Cleave, *White House Assistant Director* for National Security Affairs during the Bush administration, called electronic crime, and the theft of business data in particular, "...as serious a strategic threat to national security" as it is to the survival of the firms that have been the targets of attacks. Not too many years ago a Japanese company was found guilty of stealing trade secrets from IBM. An international industrial spy ring was recently found to be bribing U.S. and British oil company employees for inside information on large, lucrative contracts. Since businesses, the underworld, and even some nations seem willing— even determined—to take illegally what they cannot win fairly, we are being forced to keep tabs simultaneously on a thousand points of darkness. With the electronic theft of data having become a national security issue, network security deserves more than passing attention.

Terrorism and the Underworld

Our peace and well-being are more precarious now than ever before. When the U.S. and the U.S.S.R. were in balance, neither country would risk making the first strike. Aggressors and terrorist groups previously held in check around the world by the super powers have been unleashed. Instead of just one major military threat we now have many and the horror of terrorism to deal with in this country.

If global economic war, terrorism, aggressor nations, and industrial espionage are not enough reason to take precautions, then there is organized crime. The underworld is looking for new profit centers now that legalized gambling is cutting into their revenues. Organized crime is taking advantage of new opportunities offered by the sophisticated techniques used to penetrate networks and computer systems.

The criminal element is becoming more high-tech in their growing use of digital technology and the more secure forms of encryption, thwarting government and police efforts to keep tabs on them. They can afford the cutting edge technology (LAN professionals refer to it as bleeding edge technology), and the brightest people to support their efforts, which police and government often cannot. Other countries are well aware of the threats and have been actively working to protect themselves.

Well, aren't we doing the same, you ask? No. Surprisingly enough, we are not. Security is such a hard sell in this country it is almost unbelievable. We play down and ignore security incidents to such a degree that it essentially deprives us of the information we need to appreciate our vulnerability.

Challenges of a New World Order

The world is changing rapidly as a result of unseen and seemingly uncontrollable forces. As a result we need to take a broader, even global, view of business trends and such economic realities as the needs of workers for productive, fairly paid employment. Employees have many new concerns: fear of falling wages from the unleashing of workforce "wannabes" at all skill levels in the Soviet bloc, poorly paid workers in the third world countries, new technologies, higher taxes, fewer employer-provided benefits, and the down-sizing layoffs that eliminate entire layers of management and clerical workers. Workers have little or no incentive to put the good of the company before self-interest. Employee honesty has often been relied on by organizations in the past; that may be a head-in-the-sand attitude given current realities. Employees cannot count on their employers, so why should employers think they can count on their employees?

The Risk of Downplaying Computer Crime

Stockholders tend to hold managers and executives accountable when they suffer large losses, whatever the reason. Large losses and other operating difficulties are routinely explained in financial statements and at shareholders' meetings; but you rarely come across references to losses from computer and other white-collar crimes. It's as though there is a "datacrime" conspiracy to keep these losses, crimes, and other security incidents a secret. When businesses suffer LAN penetration and electronic fraud, they prefer to sweep the problem under the rug, and take corrective action quietly. Then, and only then, do they put safeguards in place to protect the company's assets. This silence makes sense for the company because when a business is thought to be vulnerable—as a result of having poor controls or a major security loss—the stock plummets, the executives are embarrassed, and everyone feels their jobs are at risk. The problem with this approach is that the businesses down the street could very well be victimized tomorrow. Why? Because they don't realize how common computer crimes and other security problems are, or how vulnerable they are to a wide range of threats, or how great their losses can be when they are victimized.

Downplaying computer crime lends itself to outrageously destructive activity such as the recent publication of a CD-ROM called the *Hacker*

Chronicles, which contains 600 MB of underground utilities for LAN crackers including programs for penetrating Novell LANs. The product is likely to appeal to adventurous, curious youngsters (who may become the Lan crackers of tomorrow) and make a great deal of money for the authors and sellers. We need to stop reinforcing negative behavior and instead, require those who sell tools for destruction to be accountable for the losses they cause.

Quality Then, Security Now

That other countries are willing to deal with security issues, when we are not, reminds me of the way U.S. businesses stonewalled W. Edwards Deming's ideas about continuous quality improvement. Tired of having doors slammed in his face in this country, he eventually went to Japan. The Japanese, still reeling from their devastating losses in WWII, welcomed Deming's fresh ideas about rebuilding their industrial base, and their will to win.

We lost whole industries to the Japanese because we would not take a realistic look at the diminishing quality of our products compared to theirs. We did not begin to realize that their successful manufacturing operations were the result of revolutionary quality improvement programs until the early 80's, when it was nearly too late for the American automobile industry.

Internet Incidents

There are hundreds of security incidents every day on the *Internet*, the network that was originated to link government and the research community. It now provides about 20 million users with electronic mail and other services, as well as access to many other networks. The increasingly common penetration of Internet computers, which has been going on for about a year, is being investigated by the FBI. Some incidents consist of "sniffer" programs being installed illegally on computers that are connected to the Internet. These unauthorized rogue programs have captured user information, including passwords, from unsuspecting users. Sniffer programs were originally designed to monitor network message traffic and to collect various data and statistics for troubleshooting and network tuning purposes. Breaches of the Internet are increasingly common to the point where tens of thousands of passwords may already have been compromised.

Managers and administrators of the Internet do a credible job of policing and securing it. But the recent surge in connection gateway businesses that do not have security-aware experts and programmers on staff has placed an additional burden on Internet security. Tighter security measures, including programs to identify and prevent the introduction of sniffer programs on vulnerable computers, were recently announced by Internet administrators. When a rogue sniffer was discovered at *Panix*, an Internet gateway service, *Panix* alerted users and connecting networks, but many other affected networks chose to handle their incidents quietly. No system was shut down, so there was very little fuss or press coverage, despite the possibility that the magnitude of the loss could have exceeded the *Morris worm* incident. The loss caused by the Morris worm (which spread through the Internet, infecting and shutting down university, business, and government networks and computers) was estimated to be as much as $100 million.

Unfortunately, organizations are generally in a state of denial concerning security problems from within and from without. We do not want to admit that the problems exist, but unaddressed, they can only get worse.

Threats to the Information Superhighway

With our computers and networks so vulnerable, what risks are we taking by relying on an electronic information superhighway? What steps are we taking to ensure the privacy and security of the information it will hold and transport? How will we know for certain that the billions of dollars to be paid out electronically will not wind up in underground hands? How will we know that the votes we cast in the electronic town halls of the future are not altered by a subversive element?

There is much work to be done to secure our networks and computers, and a great deal still has to be learned.

Time For Action

Let this be a call to action. We must not wait until we have been humbled throughout the world because no one would point to the Emperor and say he is naked. Look at the statistics and you will know you cannot afford to do nothing. If you need more data after reading this book, contact one of the organizations given in the Appendix. If your organization is not already taking appropriate steps to plug the holes in your LAN security, then use the information in this book to get started—today.

How This Book Can Help

The diversity of backgrounds, training, and skills of today's LAN managers makes the task of addressing their security issues, in one book, a challenge. This book is intended to encourage LAN managers and others to give LAN security a priority equal to user's demands for new software and services. Lack of support for security in the executive suite is a major roadblock to securing LANs and is another focus of this book. It is intended to enlighten LAN managers and—through risk assessment and other techniques—give them a framework for analyzing security requirements and presenting compelling security proposals.

The solutions to LAN security problems are as numerous as the threats. Solutions, as well as threats, are presented with just as much attention given the common-sense, practical, and low-cost variety as to more high-tech solutions. Particularly helpful to LAN managers is the information found throughout on LAN safeguard products, security organizations, hotlines, and other resources. The products mentioned in the text are listed by product and cross-referenced to suppliers in the Appendix. There are resources such as the *Computer Security Institute* and the COM-SEC bulletin board, a forum where LAN managers with day-to-day security problems can find information and solutions. There are tips, hints, and useful material such as the *Baseline for LAN Security, Disaster Recovery* and *Continuation Of Operation* contingency plans, a risk assessment methodology. A case study at the end of the book pulls the information together.

Real life stories are used throughout to make you aware of the dangers and help you to avoid making the same mistakes.

The "computer book" style does not allow for page references. The authors and publications referred to in this book are listed in Appendix F, "For Further Reading."

CHAPTER 2

A BASELINE
FOR LAN SECURITY

There are many ways you can begin to look at LAN security. You can explore one topic at a time in detail, and gradually build your understanding of the subject. The LAN Baseline, on the other hand, looks at the subject through a panoramic lens. The full range of LAN security issues is addressed and each threat is viewed in relation to the whole. This makes the daunting task of balancing conflicting needs a little easier to manage.

There is a wide range of issues and concerns, vast numbers of threats, and countless solutions to cover. Do not be overwhelmed. This chapter is designed to whet your interest in the many aspects of LAN security before you begin your adventure through the detail. The Baseline is a road map for the journey before you.

The Baseline is a useful way of viewing LAN security because it brings order to the chaos of LAN security solutions for LAN managers, who need to understand them all. It identifies the safeguards and counter-measures designed to recognize, control, contain, reduce, correct, or even eliminate threats from insiders, outsiders, and natural forces that might cause loss of LAN service, data, or privacy. It puts the threats into per-spective for the manager who must constantly evaluate ease of use and performance against security needs. The Baseline is a useful reference tool for LAN managers and administrators, as well as planners and designers. In summary form, it can be used as a checklist by reviewers, security peo-ple, and auditors. It can be an asset to you in reviewing and evaluating the security of a LAN in any stage of development, but is indispensible for long-range planning for LAN security.

In the Baseline for LAN security, safeguards and countermeasures are categorized by type of control and by the methods used to implement them. The type of control is determined by the way a safeguard is used. The five types of control are as follows:

1. Prevention
2. Detection
3. Containment
4. Correction
5. Establishment of accountability

There are three main methods used to implement LAN security measures. The methods are:

1. Physical access safeguards and countermeasures.
2. Electronic network hardware and software security features.
3. Management controls in the form of policies, standards, plans, systems, and procedures.

No security measure or combination of measures is completely foolproof. Just as we use a variety of security measures to safeguard ourselves, our homes and our cars against possible threats, we can employ multiple safe-guards to secure our networks and to deter wrongdoers. Many important safeguards are identified in this chapter. If you cannot justify or afford a full suite of LAN safeguards now, do not despair. Just learning about the solutions and how they can help is a giant step forward.

This chapter describes, briefly, each of the safeguards presented in the Baseline, Figure 2.1. The remainder of the book elaborates further on many of these security measures. A number of useful LAN security products are also discussed in these pages.

The safeguards and countermeasures are grouped by type of control within the three methods of implementation: physical, electronic network, and management controls.

Physical Access Safeguards and Countermeasures

Barriers to physical access to the LAN prevent unauthorized persons from coming in contact with network servers, cabling, and other components such as workstations, jacks, and connectors. Locked server rooms, LAN wiring closets, and network control rooms can help to prevent physical access. The walls and doors that prevent unauthorized persons from entering the area served by the LAN and viewing or using information on the LAN server, LAN analyzer or workstation screens, are also physical barriers. Likewise are the guards who check employee and visitor identification before granting entrance to buildings and secure floors.

At high security locations such as the CIA and many military installations, armed guards challenge visitors at gates sufficiently far from the perimeter of the building to prevent unauthorized persons from getting close. Attended stations are used in both public and private locations such as airports, the Capitol, schools in high-risk areas, and office buildings to detect weapons and bombs and counteract the threat of terrorist attacks. Americans have little first-hand experience with terrorism; thus we have little fear of it. The threat of terrorism is being taken seriously in the wake of the bombing of the World Trade Center (WTC). The public can no longer park in the WTC and heavy steel plates now present a

SAFEGUARDS AND COUNTERMEASURES

TYPE OF CONTROL	PHYSICAL	NETWORK	MANAGEMENT CONTROLS
Prevention	Guards Card key systems Lock and key Equipment lock-down cables Non-standard PC screws Electronic Asset Protection Security-aware LAN design Climate control Safety standards	Security-friendly LAN components User IDs Passwords Password expiration Lockout after failed login Secure dial-in Data coding Encryption Data compression Anti-virus software	Quality programs Administrative LAN policies, procedures, and training Security-aware management systems for LANs Pre-employment screening and security checks Security awareness training Separation of duties and cross-training Surveillance and "sweeps" Testing plan LAN Certification
Detection	Smoke detectors Heat and cold detectors Moisture detectors Intruder detectors Power trouble detector Tap detector Surveillance	Network monitoring and management tools Electronic surveillance Internal system controls Exception reports	LAN security plans, methods, and procedures Security reviews Change control Software walk-through Testing plan Surveillance Required vacations

SAFEGUARDS AND COUNTERMEASURES

TYPE OF CONTROL	PHYSICAL	NETWORK	MANAGEMENT CONTROLS
Containment/ Correction	Fire suppressants Water sprinklers Intruder traps Uninterruptible Power Supply (UPS) Exception reports and alarms Threat removal Contingency plan for emergencies	Transmission control and error checking Server backup File recovery Exception reports and alarms Contingency plan for emergencies	Administrative LAN policies, standards, and procedures Contingency plans for emergencies (DRP, COOP) Exception reports and alarms
Establish Accountability/ Audit Trails	LAN security plans, methods, and procedures Security-aware management systems Area access logs Exception reports	User ID and password Workstation (node) ID Network access logs Transaction trace logs Network management and monitoring software	LAN roles and responsibilities, job descriptions, organization charts Data Administration: data dictionary, published data transfer requests and schedules Checklists, logs, duty rosters, and approvals Exception reports

FIGURE 2.1   BASELINE FOR **LAN** SECURITY SAFEGUARD SUMMARY.

physical barrier to unauthorized vehicles. The security of public buildings is being completely re-thought because of the $550 million disaster and many new buildings are being designed with security in mind.

Gates, walls, fences, and concrete pillars are barriers that are used in support of the high-profile armed guards who protect important locations. Government buildings are attractive targets and vulnerable to attack because crowds and traffic surge around them routinely.

Locks are still important deterrents to theft. Should a wrongdoer get near enough to LAN equipment to pose a threat, a security breach may still be prevented if the equipment is rendered useless by locks or other means. Workstations and other equipment can be "locked down" in areas with minimal physical security and no guards at exits to prevent the theft of LAN components. Few organizations use this low-cost measure to protect their investment in equipment, despite what may be a fairly routine disappearance of expensive assets.

An alternative to locking-down vulnerable networked computers is to place them in attractive computer furniture which can be closed up and locked. Locked furniture is not impenetrable but it is a deterrent. A thief cannot *see* the contents of the locked furniture, which makes it a less interesting target, and the encased equipment is too large to surreptitiously carry away.

The safeguards are grouped by type of control: prevention, detection, containment or correction, and establishment of accountability.

Threat Prevention

Physical access safeguards and countermeasures that prevent threats from resulting in loss are the first line of defense. Some preventive measures such as locked doors and building guards are in effect because they are standard security practice and are not in place specifically to secure a LAN. The more vulnerable and valuable the LAN and data are perceived to be, the more likely extensive safeguards are to be used. A quick look at physical access threat prevention safeguards follows.

- **Guards** are often a physical presence at building and secure area entrances and security control locations, which serves to deter wrongdoers. Guards often restrict building entrants to employees and bona fide visitors and may check suspicious packages and require authorization before allowing the removal of equipment. Guards may be responsible for visitor and employee time-in/time-out logs and may patrol secure areas during off hours.

- **Card key systems** are magnetic cards encoded with employee identification information that trigger the release of door locks when inserted into a wall slot near the door. Cardkey systems often secure unattended building entrances and interior doors that open into public hallways. Cardkeys can also secure LAN workstations and servers against unauthorized use.

- **Traditional key locks** safeguard offices and buildings after business hours. They also lock PC furniture, file cabinets and desk drawers, disable PC keyboards and hard disk drives, and prevent unauthorized removal of server disk drives and system unit covers.

- **Lock-down cable systems** prevent the theft of valuable equipment such as computers by attaching it to heavy or immovable furniture. To lock down computer equipment, secure both ends of a thick cable together after threading it through loops attached to the components and a large piece of furniture. If you find the cables unsightly and awkward to work around on a desktop you might consider locking pads to lock equipment in place on the desktop. Lock-down is a constant, highly visible reminder that a security control problem exists, thus is rarely used except in schools and other places with public access.

- **Non-standard screws** in PC system unit cases are a simple deterrent to the theft of LAN network interface cards and other PC boards. Traditional flat-head or Phillips-head screwdrivers cannot remove non-standard screws.

- **Security-aware LAN design** is needed. Many existing LANs were designed without consideration of security. Now that organizations are firmly committed to LAN technology and many security features are available, these LANs are being reviewed. Giving high priority to LAN security in requirements definition obligates designers to balance ease-of-use and cost against the protection of valuable data and other LAN assets.

■ **Climate control** must be maintained at a sufficiently moderate level to permit the server and other LAN components to operate without malfunctioning. Thermostats and air conditioning regulators that keep offices comfortable for humans are quite sufficient to keep LAN components running smoothly. When the climate is uncomfortable for people it is usually unsuitable for sensitive electronic equipment such as servers. If this situation occurs, shut the server down to avoid losing or damaging data. The equipment specifications contain operating temperature and humidity range information.

SAFETY STANDARDS

When it comes to PCs and LANs, office workers seem to forget that there are safety standards and regulations in effect designed specifically to protect employees. Unqualified people often open their PCs with little regard for the danger of electrocution. Users need to know this danger is all too real. As the power requirements of PCs and LAN components increase, the danger increases accordingly as well.

The tangle of wires in and around computer components is a constant threat. People can be disabled by falls caused by computer wires in disarray. Your safety standards should address these and other safety issues. You should charge each employee with the responsibility for looking for safety problems in your security-awareness training programs.

Threat Detection

Threat detection is the crux of LAN security. Detection of environmental hazards such as fire or excessive heat, or unauthorized physical devices attached to LAN components is crucial. When detection measures come into play, the unthinkable has already happened; LAN security has been breached. Quick action is in order to contain the damage and begin corrective action. Speedy detection may prevent devastating damage or loss from occurring. A suite of threat detection safeguards is affordable, especially when compared to the cost of a serious LAN failure.

- **Smoke detectors** sense the presence of smoke and immediately sound an alarm to alert the staff to the possibility of a fire. Heat and cold detector thermostat devices can trigger an alarm or other action when the temperature of the server or network control room is outside established limits.

- **Moisture detectors** measure the humidity in the air and can trigger an alarm when the level of moisture exceeds acceptable limits.

- **Intruder sensors** that can detect motion and trigger security alarms are effective in securing offices and buildings after hours. Guards and guard dogs are also useful for this purpose and after detecting intruders, may be able to contain them until authorities can respond to an alarm.

- **Power trouble detectors,** like intelligent Uninterruptible Power Supply (UPS) units are usually connected to essential equipment such as LAN servers. They can sound an alarm when power problems occur (or when their own batteries are low).

- **Tap (intrusion) detectors** sense unauthorized nodes on LAN cables and can trigger an alarm or an exception report. Taps on fiber optic cable are easier to detect than on twisted pair or coaxial cable.

- **Surveillance,** or physical inspection of LAN components including cabling, is verification that no unauthorized nodes or taps are currently on the LAN.

Containment and Correction

Containment measures prevent a problem from continuing or spreading and causing further damage and loss. The idea is to learn of the problem through detection measures, then attempt to contain or control the threat, thereby reducing the overall loss. When the threat is under control, the correction process can begin. Some noteworthy physical access containment and correction safeguards and countermeasures follow.

- **Fire suppressants** are chemicals used to retard and extinguish fire. Special chemicals are used in computer and network control rooms where moisture would cause excessive damage. *Halon* gas was used widely for this purpose before it was found to deplete ozone in the atmosphere. Environmentally safe gasses are used today.

- **Automatic water sprinklers** extinguish fires detected by alarms in many offices and are usually turned on by smoke or heat detectors.

- **Intruder traps** such as interlocking doors can isolate intruders to prevent them from getting away before authorities arrive. An intruder who follows an employee through one door and does not have the correct key for the second door will be trapped between interlocking doors. Working dogs can also sound an alert and trap and contain intruders until authorities arrive. Dogs are very effective when intruders are caught unaware but are vulnerable to physical harm.

- **Uninterruptible Power Supply (UPS)** hardware devices prevent system crashes and damage to sensitive electronic parts caused by power losses. Some UPS units also condition power and protect against power problems such as dips, surges, and spikes, which shorten the life of electronic equipment. They either provide power from the electrical supply on a continuous basis (absorbing spikes, surges, etc.) or they provide auxiliary power only when a power failure occurs.

  Some UPS devices provide battery service that may bridge brief electrical power outage and shortage periods, thereby sparing users the inconvenience of an unscheduled LAN shutdown altogether. Low-end products typically supply sufficient energy to permit an orderly network shutdown when a power problem occurs.

- **Exception reports and alarms** are produced by the Network Operating System (NOS) and by add-on network monitors, analyzers testers, and management systems. Examples of useful exception reports are notices of security violations such as repeated login attempts with an incorrect user ID or password or unusual transmissions that may indicate communications malfunctions.

■ **Threat removal** may be required to maintain safe operation of the LAN in some situations. Security plans and procedures should specify what action to take to contain and remove threats. For example, "notify local police by dialing 911 when an intruder is found," and steps to take in a virus, worm, or other rogue program attack are specific actions that may be included in security procedures.

■ **Contingency plans for emergencies** contain policies, methods, and procedures for employees to follow in emergencies so losses and disruption may be minimized and LAN operations quickly resumed.

The Disaster Recovery Plan (DRP) should contain sufficient information for you to be able to contain and correct disaster situations that affect the LAN and eventually return to normal LAN operations.

The Continuation Of Operations Plan (COOP) should contain instructions for operations at an alternate location until disaster recovery is complete.

Establishment of Accountability and Audit Trails

Accountability, that is, being held responsible for something you did (or something you should have done), is a vital aspect of securing physical access to the LAN. Security measures take time from other duties and may be shirked completely unless some mechanism is in effect to enforce them. The combination of accountability and audit trails help accomplish this.

An audit trail documents events and shows when practices differ from policy. Analysis of audit trails permits the LAN manager to take corrective action when needed.

Accountability control measures try to link specific actions to individuals and can be quite useful in deterring potential wrongdoers as well as motivating employees to perform their assigned duties. Accountability controls also help to identify individuals who inadvertently breach security, so that their security training may be refreshed. Accountability for physical LAN access can be established by:

- Formal security plans.
- Management systems designed for LAN protection.
- Audit trails, including logs of various kinds.
- Exception reports.

LAN SECURITY PLANS, SYSTEMS, PROCEDURES, AND TRAINING

LAN security plans, systems, procedures, and training inform employees of security issues and their responsibilities regarding physical access and security. Employees should complete *Responsible LAN User Agreements* before being granted a user ID to ensure they will actively participate in securing their LAN. After agreeing to be responsible, employees should be required to account for breaches of LAN security.

SECURITY-AWARE MANAGEMENT SYSTEMS

Security-aware management systems are necessary to protect LANs and minimize risks, including the risk of physical access and threats against the LAN. LAN management must devise new solutions to old problems and anticipate new problems before they occur. New security management processes are needed for LANs.

ACCESS LOGS

Access logs identify individuals entering buildings and restricted areas by name and by purpose (identification is usually required).

VISITOR LOGS

Visitor logs commonly identify individuals other than the employees who work at a particular location. Employees should sign the log and be responsible for the actions of visitors during their stay.

EXCEPTION REPORTS

Exception reports may be produced by the NOS, report utilities, or network management software. Exception reports can be prepared to show any deviation from policy or expected results. These can include a listing of employees who neglect to escort and sign out visitors or an audit report of attempts to access another employee's electronic mailbox. Exception reports should notify LAN administration and/or security with sufficient information about the user, workstation, and attempted activity to permit investigation and corrective action of LAN security violations.

Electronic Network Safeguards and Countermeasures

Component failure sometimes causes LAN disasters. Equipment manufacturers have made great strides in developing reliable, resilient, fault tolerant, easy-to-service hardware, and our LANs are more secure and useful as a result.

Network hardware offers a great variety of useful security features. Servers have redundancy in CPUs, controllers, disk drives, and LAN boards. Intelligent LAN hubs trap LAN traffic and other data that can be analyzed for performance flaws, bottlenecks, and other possible problems.

Network analyzers intercept LAN communications and provide information about:

■   Noise

- Crosstalk

- Attenuation

- Continuity

- Polarity

- Distance-to-fault measurements

- Traffic

Such information is vital for identifying and correcting LAN transmission and line problems. The safeguards in this category follow.

Electronic network safeguards are described below and are ordered by type of control.

Prevention

Electronic network safeguards and countermeasures that prevent threats from resulting in loss exist in either hardware or software form. Some are always present. Others come into play only when needed, for instance, when someone attempts an electronic penetration of the network. Some safeguards which can prevent electronic network security incidents follow.

- **Security-friendly LAN components** can be selected by LAN designers. For example, fiber optic cabling is difficult to tap and offers considerable performance advantages over other cable media. It is the LAN cabling of choice when either security or wide band-width is a particularly high priority, such as in the financial industries. Fault tolerant, reliable components, with high availability characteristics, are most desirable for LANs.

    Intelligent hubs offer LAN management and analysis features which track traffic, errors, and even broken cables without the overhead penalty of server-based software or the expense of separate hardware devices. This is not a standards-based technology, however; as a result, these features are not always compatible with equipment from other manufacturers of LAN communications equipment.

- **User IDs** should identify an individual to the network and LAN applications. User IDs are usually published information and follow a naming pattern within a given organization or workgroup.

- **Passwords** are unique code words or phrases known only to an individual LAN user. The NOS verifies passwords to authenticate LAN users (that is, certify that the LAN user is the owner of the user ID). Choosing a hard-to-guess but easily remembered password is the key in thwarting network penetration attempts. Some LAN applications including WordPerfect permit password protection of individual files. Application level IDs and passwords are required by some groupware, e-mail, calendar and scheduling LAN applications as an additional level of user identification.

  Take care to standardize password restrictions, expirations, and other requirements across the LAN and enterprise network. This will allow users to use one password for all systems. It is difficult for users to manage multiple passwords that expire at different times and have different lengths, uniqueness, construction rules, grace logins and other restrictions.

- **Password expirations** should be set to force LAN users to change their passwords periodically. Frequent password changes reduce the risk of password guessing and the related risk of successful LAN penetration attempts. The vulnerability of the LAN dictates the frequency of change. Users of highly vulnerable LANs should change their passwords often.

- **Lockout after failed login** disallows further attempts after some fixed number of failed logins. This reduces the likelihood that a network cracker—a specialist in penetrating networks—will successfully penetrate a given LAN. A lockout may inconvenience users after they forget their passwords, or type them carelessly, but the LAN administrator can easily correct the situation.

- **Secure dial-in** will make penetration of your LAN more difficult. The LAN should not offer dial-in access to users unless safeguards are used. To do otherwise invites attack by hackers and network crackers. Mainframe systems and secure LANs use authenticated call-in or call-back systems to prevent unauthorized access to their LANs. Secure or "authenticated" call-in can require devices at both server and remote workstations, and authenticates both the remote user and the remote device. Audit trails may be maintained.

Call-backs usually pre-authorize calling phone lists, thus are less flexible. When a call comes from an approved number (the system may also require entry of an access code), the system hangs up and dials the number back. Only then is a user allowed to log in. In more secure systems, dial-in users get blank screens and no assistance, and must identify themselves before the call-back and login system will work.

■ **Data coding** either secures information or saves file storage space. It is used less often now that storage is cheap and designers realize there are better methods to secure data. Excessive coding complicates system development, and causes errors and makes systems difficult to use.

■ **Encryption** algorithms change data so it becomes unintelligible until decoded. Encryption protects LAN data from misuse in the event it is intercepted during transmission.

■ **Data compression** reduces the physical storage space a file requires by removing spaces and redundant characters, and other methods. Besides saving storage space, compression makes data unreadable in its compressed form. Compressed data can, however, be decompressed quickly and easily.

Threat Detection

Electronic threats are detected by administration, management, analysis, and testing tools. State-of-the-art network management, analysis, and surveillance tools were not in wide use until recently when easy-to-use, low-cost software-only tools became available. Other detection measures are system controls and exception reports. Descriptions of electronic network threat detection safeguards follow.

■ **Network management tools** include the software used by the LAN administrator to set up new users and applications as well as monitor and maintain an efficient, reliable, secure network. The NOS provides internal network management tools. There are add-on products, utilities, and hardware and software-based network analyzers.

The most widely used network utility is anti-virus software. It is now used on 80 percent of data networks in this country (and should be on *every* LAN as well as every PC with a floppy disk drive). It is difficult to eliminate a virus from an organization because they spread quickly, so users must take precautions to avoid introducing them and be held accountable when they do. To avoid introducing viruses into LANs, users should scan questionable diskettes for viruses before they are used on a LAN workstation. Virus detection programs that scan existing files and memory should be run periodically or as part of the computer boot process. TSR (Terminate and Stay Resident) programs look for virus-like behavior (as well as other problems that are even more likely to damage your data) as you use your computer.

■ **Routine electronic surveillance** or inspection will detect many LAN security problems. At a minimum, this inspection should include:

■ server program size, changes, and usage;

■ files and resources in use and those used within a certain time;

■ network traffic; and security violations.

■ **Internal system controls** routinely verify the accuracy and completeness of data processed in mainframe computer applications. User-controlled LAN applications rarely use internal controls and rely instead on the software, users, and operators to store and process data accurately and completely. These controls should be built into applications and may need to be specified in system requirements.

■ **Exception reports** notify LAN administration (and possibly the security of staff) unusual occurrences and attended security violations such as unsuccessful login attempts and new unaccounted-for network nodes that may indicate penetration attempts by network crackers or unauthorized physical wire taps. Operational problems, warnings, and system error messages may also be reported as exceptions to permit preventive action.

Threat Containment and Correction

Electronic network safeguards for threat containment and correction include security features such as server backups, file recovery, transmission control and error checking, and exception reports of security violations such as lockouts, indicating the possibility of an electronic presence of a network cracker or unaccounted-for nodes.

A description of electronic network containment and correction safeguards follows.

- **Transmission control and error checking** are performed by the NOS and are a function of the LAN protocol (such as *Ethernet*). The more transmission control, error checking, and error correction services are performed, the more error-free data will be after transmission. However, there is a corresponding increase in processing overhead at the server and in processing time, which can mean slower overall network performance. The need for transmission control, error checking, and error correction must be balanced against the need for fast network transmission of messages and high throughput.

- **File recovery** reinstates deleted and corrupted LAN files. This is a utility function performed by some NOSs and LAN utilities including backup and recovery systems. If the NOS has already reclaimed the space occupied by a deleted file, the NOS cannot salvage "undelete" it. In that case, the file should be recovered from the server backup systems files.

- **Server backups** offer protection against loss of data. Servers are repositories for LAN data and should be backed up routinely. Some backup systems enable user workstations to be backed up through the LAN as well. Taking regular, periodic backups is the most essential, fundamental LAN security safeguard known. Individual files can be restored from backup copies using most backup and retrieval software. Copies of backup files should be secured offsite so LAN operations can continue elsewhere if the LAN becomes inoperable in an emergency.

Responsibility for backing up large, multiple LAN servers at the enterprise level rests with the central IS organization in half of the organizations with larger LANs. Some LANs are being backed up quickly, easily, and reliably using mainframe computers. Mainframe systems can reduce restore time for backed up files from five hours to as little as five minutes. Server and NOS manufacturers are including more backup features in their products.

- **Exception reports and alarms** notify LAN administration and/or security staff of security violations so immediate action can be taken to contain, control and correct security incidents.

- **Contingency plans** for emergencies contain policies, methods, and procedures for employees to follow in emergency situations to minimize losses and disruption and to resume operations as soon as possible.

  The Disaster Recovery Plan (DRP) includes sufficient information for containing and correcting disaster situations that affect the LAN in preparation for a return to normal LAN operations.

  The Continuation Of Operations Plan (COOP) contains instructions for operating the LAN at an alternate location until disaster recovery is complete.

Establishment of Accountability

This section covers the establishment of accountability for protecting the LAN against electronic threats by means of:

- Formal security plans.
- Management systems designed for LAN protection.

■ Audit trails using LAN node (workstation) and user IDs.

■ Logs of various kinds, exception reports, and network management and monitoring software.

These are vital aspects of LAN security. Accountability measures try to link specific action to an individual or specific workstation, which is why they are useful in deterring potential wrongdoers and motivating LAN staff to perform their duties as assigned. Accountability measures also identify individuals who breach security by introducing a virus or attempting access of restricted data, for example. Management use this information to identify employees who require re-training or disciplinary action.

The NOS supplies basic network management software. Several highly functional and easy-to-use add-on tools are now available from NOS and other software manufacturers. All LAN managers and administrators use network management and monitoring tools, but some have superior tools and are more expert at using them than others.

These are electronic network safeguards for establishing accountability:

■ **User IDs and passwords,** in combination, identify an individual who becomes a user of a NOS (or secure LAN application). User IDs are generally public information, whereas only an individual knows his or her password. Individuals are held responsible for action taken by anyone signing onto the LAN with their unique user ID and password.

■ **LAN workstation (node) identifiers** are useful in tracking resource usage and isolating security violations and other troublesome activity to a particular workstation. LAN workstation (node) IDs on the server reference the LAN interface card installed in the workstation. A cable connects the interface card to the network wiring.

■ **Network access logs** are audit trail features of NOS and LAN audit utilities. The logs contain LAN access information as well as user and workstation information to establish accountability. They inform the LAN administrator of the actions of selected users as well as activity against selected files and directories.

- **Transaction Trace Logs** are audit trails that detail the LAN usage activity of selected users and are useful in establishing responsibility for security violations and troubleshooting LAN problems.

- **Network monitoring and management software** is used by the LAN administrator to give users unique user IDs, which are then used to monitor LAN activity.

Virus protection is an example of a network threat that can be lessened in part by establishing accountability. If a virus is introduced and your controls are adequate you will know:

a) who was responsible

b) that management control procedures are not being followed

c) that further security training is needed.

When they detect a virus, some security-conscious organizations remove the floppy diskette drives from the workstation of the offending employee. Less severe measures include retraining in LAN security for the careless individual, or instituting a system of controlled diskettes.

Management Control—Policies, Standards, Plans, Systems, and Procedures

Management controls are essential in instituting LAN security and can be extremely effective. "Internal controls" is the term often used for the controls used to protect against waste, fraud, and abuse from *within* the organization. Management controls encompass measures to protect against other threats as well and address risks which might prevent a fair return on the investment in LAN resources.

Management controls that affect security are specified in the policies and procedures of an organization. The *LAN Security Plan* is an example that greatly influences LAN security. Among other things it contains contingency plans for disaster recovery which are essential for restoring LAN operations after a prolonged disruption of service or other disaster.

Use of management controls for loss prevention is another prime concern since insiders are responsible for about three-fourths of all threats to information security. At least half of information losses are the result of human error.

Management systems include strategy, control, organization, motivation, leadership—all the elements of good management. They are a critical tool for protecting LANs and avoiding or reducing risk, yet are rarely designed just for LANs.

Many organizations have emergency plans but few have disaster plans for their LANs and fewer still have tested them, as evidenced by the havoc caused by major disasters such as the World Trade Center bombing.

Ninety percent (90%) of companies that suffered from the World Trade Center bombing had *no* disaster contingency plans. Studies show that companies unable to resume normal computer operations soon after a disaster find it increasingly difficult to operate and usually fail. Data loss is a growing problem that costs U.S. businesses more than $4 billion a year. Considering the negative impact of a disaster on a computerized, networked business, it is hard to imagine what could have a higher priority than security and emergency planning. Management controls must be extended to the LAN.

Ideally, management should provide LAN security policies, plans, and procedures in written form and impress them upon employees through training so that everyone knows their duties concerning security and the LAN. It is up to LAN managers to see that they do.

LAN managers often involve their staff and users to devise the best plans they can and to gain acceptance for the plans within the LAN community.

To be effective, a security plan must be a formal one and be observed by the entire staff.

Threat Prevention

This section will discuss the prevention of LAN security problems by means of management controls.

One pervasive information security problem is viruses. Viruses can be avoided altogether with good management systems and controls. This is preferable to relying on virus detection and removal software to deal with viruses (although it is an excellent fallback when an infection occurs).

Management systems control safeguards and countermeasures for the prevention of loss are as follows.

■ **Quality programs** are key threat prevention measures. An involved, aware, security-conscious attitude by employees can do more to deter threats than any piece of software known. Quality improvement programs such as Total Quality Management (TQM) foster employee empowerment, awareness, and the concept of employee responsibility for the well-being of the organization as a whole.

■ **Administrative LAN policies, plans, procedures, and training** give employees information about their responsibilities as users of the network. They are the written guidelines which employees must follow as they use the network in performance of their duties. Training helps employees learn how to use the LAN and to meet their responsibilities as LAN users.

LAN server backup may be the most critical administrative responsibility. As LANs expand and mature, server backup often emerges as a critical issue. Backup systems may lag the expansion of the network, leaving assets unprotected unless specific backup policies exist.

Administrative LAN policies address preventative security measures such as cancelling user IDs for former employees on their last day of work. Administrators may neglect such important tasks if they are not stated LAN security policies.

■ **Security-aware management systems** must meet the new security challenges afforded by LANs. Change is the order of the day for LANs; therefore it is necessary to protect against chaos and resulting loss. LAN management must be zealously proactive and clever at anticipating new problems and changing user needs, as well as devising new solutions to old problems.

Data administration, database administration, change management, and security management are needed for LANs just as for traditional IS. However, these roles rarely exist outside of organizations with large, mature LANs.

■ **Pre-employment screening and security checks** verify that information on job applications is truthful and, in general, ensure the stability and good character of the applicant.

■ **Security awareness training** acquaints employees with network vulnerabilities and the variety of threats they must guard against. LANs are new and relatively vulnerable, unprotected resources. Employees have little knowledge of computer and network security issues and concerns, and must be trained to protect data and other LAN assets. Security awareness training is required for federal government employees and is addressed in other security-conscious organizations as well.

■ **Separation of duties and cross training** promote security and are particularly important regarding computers and LANs. White-collar crime has had a boost from computers and LAN technology and the downsizing trend. Today's lean organizations do not always protect vulnerable computer-assisted business processes with the same rigor they use for manual business processes. Managers should structure jobs to separate duties that could result in collusion or fraud by employees or groups of employees. Cross training restricts opportunities for fraud and abuse, increases team spirit, and provides backup for key positions.

■ **Surveillance and "sweeps"** can identify taps (in wiring closets and on cables), vulnerabilities, and lapses in security which invite breaches. LANs that have obvious surveillance (and good security in general) are less likely to be penetration targets. Surveillance, including physical and electronic examination of the cabling, server, and other LAN components is a good management safeguard and can also identify potential points of failure from wear, age or environmental factors.

A *sweep* is the use of gear that detects eavesdropping bugs and taps that intercept voice and data, as well as devices used to

transmit data to unauthorized recipients. Security-conscious organizations and individuals sweep facilities routinely to locate taps
and bugs placed for purposes of industrial, military, or political
espionage. New digital network communication makes the task of
locating penetration and interception equipment more difficult.
LAN managers rarely do sweeps because special electronic surveillance equipment and experience are required. Only professionals should conduct electronic surveillance.

■ **Testing plan** specifies the tests to be run on the LAN to prevent
trouble during operation. Since most start-up LAN problems are
cable-related, Testing Plans should require a complete cable plant
check to verify that cable, lines, jacks, and connectors are functional for all nodes, and no unidentified nodes or lines are connected.

■ **Certification** offers assurance that the LAN meets your established security and performance criteria. Networks are often
installed in segments and can be expected to change rapidly for
some time. LAN managers are advised to view the installation as
a project that has as its end-point, a viable and fully operational
LAN, or users may start to rely on it while it is still in a highly
vulnerable state.

Network certification should mark the end of the installation
and precede or coincide with formal user acceptance of the LAN.
After that point, change control procedures should be used. LAN
Certification states that the initial requirements for security, performance, and applications have been met, and should be conducted by experts in these areas.

In the Federal government, accreditation, or verification that
the LAN has been Certified by the ranking Network Security
Official, is the final step in the implementation process.

Threat Detection

Widely publicized network break-ins, worm attacks, and virus threats
have helped to call attention to the need for threat detection safeguards,

but many threats are still largely ignored. A discussion of management control safeguards for detecting threats follows.

■ **LAN security plans, methods, and procedures** are the responsibility of LAN managers, the LAN administrative staff, and the security staff. Written plans, methods, and procedures inform employees of security issues and of their responsibilities in detecting threats against the LAN and preventing losses.

■ **Security reviews** by security or audit staff are useful for identifying potential LAN security problems. Unannounced reviews are effective in identifying practices that differ from formal security policies, plans, and procedures.

■ **Formal change control** procedures protect LANs from threats by ensuring that approved, tested programs are used, and a stable LAN operating environment is maintained. Change control may force the testing of applications and programs by a unit separate from the one that installed the change. Multiple versions of software offer protection in the event of program failures. If a new program fails, you may be able to revert to the previous version for use on the LAN.

■ **Software walk-through,** or peer review, of software programs developed in-house encourages programmers to produce well structured, easily maintained software. The practice also uncovers logic bombs (destructive code), illegal acts, and other threats embedded in program code. Threats of this type are usually eliminated in organizations known to use software quality assurance methods.

■ **Testing plan** specifies the tests that should run on the LAN before full operation to detect problems before they inconvenience users or cause damage. The Testing Plan can be used in subsequent routine surveillances of the hardware and cabling, and for regression testing after major network expansions.

■ **Surveillance** detects security breaches such as taps in wiring closets and other locations on LAN cables, penetrations, and rogue programs on the server.

■ **Required vacations** should be enforced for employees with responsible LAN-related jobs so that in their absence other employees are obliged to perform their duties. Fraud, theft, and other white-collar crimes committed by long-term, seemingly model employees are often uncovered because of a forced employee vacation policy.

Threat Containment and Correction

Management control safeguards for containment and correction of LAN security problems such as Disaster Recovery Plans (DRP), Continuation of Operation Plans (COOP), exception reports, and administrative policies and procedures are not yet in wide use for LANs.

DRP and COOPs are presented in Chapter 10 of this book, which is intended to help fill this void. You can adapt the plans for your unique LAN environment, test them thoroughly, and include them in your LAN Security Plan documentation. You may be glad you did!

Some useful management control safeguards follow.

■ **Administrative LAN policies, standards, and procedures** should encompass the following LAN administrator, and user, responsibilities: track, resolve, report trouble; backup server; secure LAN environment, LAN data, and backup tapes; store and secure backups off-site; manage network activity, traffic, performance, and server capacity; manage user IDs, changes, expansions, and data access rights.

■ **Contingency plans** for emergencies include the DRP and COOP. The DRP contains detailed instructions for the disaster recovery team to follow if there is an emergency that causes serious loss of LAN data or service. The objective is to contain and correct the problem, limiting the loss as far as possible. The DRP, backup files, and operating instructions should be secured off-site and the Plan should be tested under simulated emergency conditions prior to user acceptance, and periodically thereafter. A disaster causing substantial loss of service might require use of the COOP while disaster recovery is underway.

The COOP goes into effect when the LAN is expected to be out of service longer than the organization can tolerate the absence of LAN data, service, and processing capabilities. A COOP team follows the Plan to provide LAN resources to business units according to preset priority, urgency, and timing constraints, thus limiting the detrimental effects of the disaster.

The COOP typically identifies an alternate processing location, server, workstation equipment, and facilities so that essential business and LAN data processing operations can continue off-site until disaster recovery is complete.

An Emergency Response Plan (ERP) is usually prepared for the unit as a whole. Thus, the ERP is not totally the responsibility of the LAN manager; however, the LAN manager will generally play a significant role in its preparation.

■ **Exception reports and alarms** may be produced by the NOS, by utilities, or by hardware/software network analyzers.

Establishment of Accountability

Accountability of both users and support staff is a prime concern for LAN managers. The reasons for this are that virtually every employee is involved with the LAN, there are so many threats to LANs, and employee error is the single greatest cause of information security loss. Management systems are a critical tool for avoiding or reducing risk, thus management systems should be devised which address accountability in the LAN environment.

Roles and responsibilities should be formalized and documented for data administration, database administration, change control management, and security management, as well as LAN management and LAN administration, even when a position is held part-time. Managers who assign responsibility for a task should hold the control individual accountable for their performance or the management control system will not have the desired effect.

Other management control safeguards based on accountability that can reduce the risk of loss of service, data, or other LAN resources include formal, documented procedures and logs of several kinds. Management control safeguards and countermeasures based on establishment of accountability follow.

■ **LAN roles and responsibilities, job descriptions, and organization charts** provide the clear accountability for LAN duties that is essential to dependable LAN operation and LAN security. LAN support roles are often filled by users who have other primary positions. Formal job descriptions should specify LAN roles and responsibilities for user support as well as LAN administration and LAN management. Individuals having other primary roles should be evaluated on and held accountable for their LAN responsibilities as well.

■ **Data administration** is required to protect the integrity of data on a LAN. Data transfer, file replication, file version control, and data integrity problems can easily occur. Simultaneous data access by many people magnifies such problems. To avoid the problems of misleading and inaccurate data and reports, redundant file transfer requests, and poor data controls, formal Data Administration is required. Data Administration manages the Data Dictionary, coordinates with users and change management, coordinates with LAN administration to schedule approved data transfer requests, publishes transfer schedules, and generally oversees the protection of the data in the LAN.

■ **Checklists, logs, duty rosters, and approvals** are useful LAN management control tools and serve to add structure to LAN management responsibilities. Checklists may include LAN-related activities and tasks for managers, administrators, and support staff. Logs may include:

   ■ Equipment maintenance logs

   ■ Routine server software maintenance logs

   ■ Change request logs

   ■ Trouble logs

   ■ Documentation sign out logs

Duty rosters formalize the responsibilities of LAN staff members and formal approval processes clarify and help control and prioritize change requests.

Change Request Logs are a function of Change Management. Change requests can affect LAN software, hardware, data, schedules, and staff and should be carefully controlled and publicized to avoid wasting resources through redundancy, misunderstandings, and people working at cross purposes.

Software program and application documentation, training materials, and LAN hardware and equipment should be tracked through Sign Out Logs so that the material can be located in an emergency, and unnecessary loss minimized.

■ **Exception reports** notify LAN administration (and possibly security) staff of LAN trouble and security violations. Potential performance problems affecting the availability of the LAN may also be identified in exception reports.

Where Do We Go From Here?

The LAN security Baseline overview is now complete. If you have more questions than answers about LAN security, then the overview was effective. Having enough knowledge to ask the right questions about the security of your LAN is a very big first step and it is all you should expect of yourself at this point.

What about my specific LAN, you ask? Of all of the threats and possible solutions and safeguards, which should I choose to address first? Second? Third? There is no one correct answer to these questions because every organization is different and most LANs change constantly anyway so that the best answer today might not be the best one tomorrow. In the remaining chapters, many of the important topics presented in the Baseline will be covered in more detail. Specific products will be used to illustrate the benefits of employing safeguards which are available to those who wish to work on securing their LANs. The case study in the chapter on *Managing Threats* illustrates how one security-aware LAN manager on a budget plans to protect his LAN. By the time you have finished with the book you should have your own ideas about what steps to take to secure your specific LAN.

CHAPTER 3

PHYSICAL ACCESS CONTROL

*T*he point of controlling physical access to the various components of a LAN is to prevent unauthorized persons from getting near enough to exploit vulnerability. Giving someone an opportunity to cause a LAN security incident is likely to result in some form of loss and is poor management practice. This is the situation you have heard about so often, where an ounce of prevention is worth a pound of cure.

There are two kinds of access control: physical and electronic. Both kinds of access control are essential to a secure LAN. Physical access control tries to prevent unauthorized people from coming in contact with LAN components and LAN data. Electronic network access control seeks to prevent unauthorized people (such as hackers and network crackers), from gaining access to LAN data. These hackers and crackers may even be geographically far away from the physical LAN, but by using electronic communications they are able to penetrate it and retrieve, damage, or destroy data. This aspect is addressed in the next chapter, *Electronic Network Access Control*.

Why Control Physical Access?

One might ask why we should bother with physical access at all. Why not just encrypt the data while it is stored in the server and as it travels through the network, so that no one can read it, and eliminate all the rest? A few good reasons for providing physical access protection for LANs are:

■ Devastating damage can be wrought against LAN data in seconds through an attached server keyboard, regardless of how the data is stored.

■ Unattended workstations logged into the LAN give full access to a user's private information, shared LAN files, and unrestricted directories, programs, and files. Encryption offers no protection against unauthorized users at logged-in workstations since data is automatically unencrypted for authorized LAN users.

■ Theft of workstations and components such as network interface cards, (which connect workstations to the LAN), provide a perfect means of LAN access—until they are reported missing and removed from the authorized workstation list.

■ Theft of servers or workstations that contain valuable LAN data could compromise data privacy, integrity, and availability.

Controlling physical access is meant to provide a relatively secure perimeter area designed to protect the LAN in much the same way that moats protect castles. This secure perimeter should prevent unauthorized persons, including employees, from coming in contact with LAN equipment. This helps prevent theft as well as access to data and network services through the workstations, cables, and connections. By controlling access, you can reduce the likelihood that an authorized user's ID and password will be compromised by someone watching them sign onto the network. It will also help to prevent confidential information displayed on workstation screens from being read without permission. The nine key elements of physical LAN security are shown in Figure 3.1.

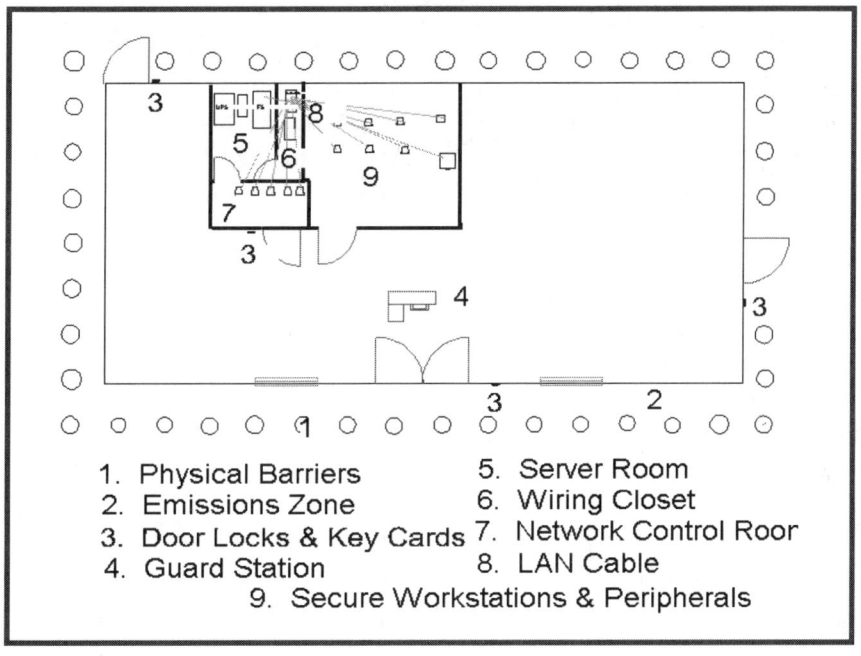

1. Physical Barriers
2. Emissions Zone
3. Door Locks & Key Cards
4. Guard Station
5. Server Room
6. Wiring Closet
7. Network Control Roor
8. LAN Cable
9. Secure Workstations & Peripherals

FIGURE 3.1   ELEMENTS OF LAN PHYSICAL SECURITY.

External Barriers

External barriers are used to make large-scale physical attacks (such as terrorists might attempt), difficult if not impossible. Concrete pillar barriers outside the White House, are shown in Figure 3.2. The use of large physical barriers has increased for important and vulnerable buildings, including the World Trade Center, since the bombing took place.

FIGURE 3.2   CONCRETE BARRIERS IN FRONT OF THE WHITE HOUSE.

Emanations Control Zone

One reason knowledgeable people say that no network is completely secure is that a determined network attacker can "passively tap" almost any LAN. A passive tap requires the purchase of low-cost equipment (at almost any local electronics store) which looks like a Walkman™, but is capable of capturing electronic signal emanations from nearby electronic equipment. The signals can easily be recorded for later analysis.

Highly security-conscious organizations are already concerned about their electronic emanations. For many others this will seem too high-tech to present an imminent danger. The problem with dismissing emanations as a threat is that you will never know if your LAN security is breached in this fashion. There will be no tap to detect, no active network intrusion, no alarm, and no audit trail of any kind.

Safeguard products that reduce the threat of invasion of LAN privacy through captured signal emanations include specially designed and highly secure *Tempest* products, fiber optic cable, Thin Film Transistor (TFT) computer screens which do not emit electronic signals, and paint and fabrics which are specially formulated to absorb electronic signal emissions.

 Tempest products are developed to meet government requirements to control electromagnetic emanations and are not available to the public *per se*. This equipment is used less often these days because of its high cost and technology lag that results from additional product engineering.

These products are discussed further in the chapter on LAN hardware.

Door Locks and Card Keys

A security system that is easily breached is the LAN manager's nightmare. All exterior and public area doors should be locked to permit only authorized persons to enter the area where the LAN is in operation. Facilities management staff generally have expertise in planning and contracting for the various kinds of locking systems required.

Traditional door locks and high-tech card key systems are available to suit any requirement. Several suppliers are listed in Appendix C, *Safeguard Products*. Of course, *you* have the most expert knowledge of the security requirements of your particular LAN.

As with any aspect of security management that may ultimately affect the LAN, you should get involved. Ask questions, make sure you understand the building security plan and the necessary decisions before they go into effect. A simple question asked in the planning stage can eliminate the potential for problems later on, but corrections *after* security systems are installed can be very costly.

Sometimes we go to great lengths to install expensive security equipment. Twenty years ago one such security system seemed impressive. There were card keys for employees, and special card keys and passcodes for the data entry, production control, and computer rooms. Employees who found themselves locked out without their card keys found, however, that they could move the tile in the false ceiling aside in the employee's entrance and hop over the wall to get into the building. It was an example of a good idea poorly implemented!

Once inside, a person could fit through the shelves built for data entry input to gain access to the production control area. The doubly-protected computer room doors opened easily when hit sharply where they met. Inside the computer room there were no deterrents to powering on the mainframe and accessing network and other data. One could just as easily have pressed the emergency shutdown switch which had no cover and no identifier of any kind. Pressing the emergency switch by mistake would have caused a wide range of hard to diagnose malfunctions and data integrity problems. This illustrates that security plans must be addressed *as a whole* and need to be reviewed and tested. Don't assume that expensive high technology safeguards will save you if your locks and basic barriers don't work.

Intruder Traps

Interlocking doors can isolate intruders to prevent them from getting away before authorities can be summoned. An intruder who follows an employee through one door and does not have the correct key for the second door will be trapped between interlocking doors.

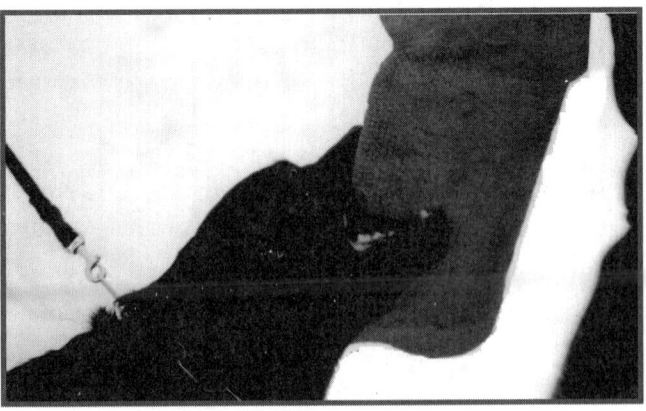

FIGURE 3.3   WORKING DOG IN TRAINING.

Building Access Guards

Guards, especially those who work during off-hours, may be assisted by dogs who are trained for security work and can sense intruders, explosives, fire, and other threats even before their human handlers do. These working dogs also provide loyal companionship for guards on patrol and during long shifts on duty. Dogs used for protection are vulnerable to physical harm, just as people are, and can be protected by bullet-proof vests when the situation calls for it. For their sake, these dogs must be thoroughly trained to refuse food from strangers and to obey their handlers without hesitation.

The three-year-old Rottweiler, *Rhonseiger* champion in '93, *V-1 Condor Vom Aachener Tor*—who answers to Condor—is a five-time *Schutzhund* (German for working dog) champion. He has already proven his basic soundness and good temperament as well as his tracking, obedience, and protection skills. In the picture in Figure 3.3, Condor demonstrates his willingness to defend and protect himself and his owner by biting when necessary.

Server Room

The server room, wiring closet, and network control room are designed to contain servers, UPSs, backup unit, LAN hub, cable connections, routers, bridges, modem pools, server consoles and monitor workstations, and LAN troubleshooting hardware. Depending on the size of the LAN and your space, your site may have everything in one all-purpose room or in as many as three. Regardless of physical layout, the security requirements are stringent; the rooms that house this equipment must be as secure as possible and climate-controlled.

I have seen spacious, new facilities in which the server room (far too small to begin with), served all three functions, and had environmental problems besides. If you cannot justify a separate control room for managing and administering the network, try to make the server room large enough to contain comfortable workstations for several people, as well as your servers, backup stations and other equipment. You will need considerable space for spare parts and equipment as well.

Several low-cost add-on devices that can simplify the job of securing LAN servers follow.

Power Switch Covers

Power switch covers prevent equipment from accidentally being turned off and are essential for LAN servers and any other equipment that must be kept running. When the server, UPS, printer, or other equipment is turned off the switch cover may be locked to protect against unauthorized use.

The PC-LOK, shown in Figure 3.4, covers the power switch and will also prevent the removal of the system unit cover with the addition of a CABLE-LOK device.

FIGURE 3.4   PC-LOK POWER SWITCH LOCK.

Locked Cabinets for Servers

If the server room cannot be kept locked, or is not sufficiently secure, the server(s) can be housed in a locking cabinet or piece of furniture. An example of a server cabinet is the Data-Mate Locking Fileserver Security Station, shown in Figure 3.5.

FIGURE 3.5   LOCKING FILESERVER STATION.

Wiring Closet

The wiring closet usually contains the following LAN components and equipment:

- **LAN hub**—the network communications controller.
- **Punchdown block**—provides connection between ports on the LAN hub and the LAN cables to each of the workstations.
- **Routers**—links between LANs with different protocols and LAN-WAN (Wide Area Network) gateways .
- **Bridges**—links between LANs with like protocols.
- LAN testing and troubleshooting equipment.

These components may be located in the telephone wiring closet, or there may be a separate wiring closet for the LAN. Anyone who has seen the inside of a wiring closet appreciates the importance of a well-organized, labeled, and documented cable plant. The *AccuTrack* system (described in the chapter on hardware) will identify each cable and organize the cables to keep them from resembling cooked spaghetti. This will make your trips into the wiring closet less of a challenge. Clearly marked cables also make unauthorized wiring more noticeable. However, clearly marked cables do present a more vulnerable target to wiretappers and wrongdoers intent on disrupting LAN operations.

All components and equipment in the wiring closet must be maintained in a completely secure state. The smallest event, such as switching two cables or turning a switch off on a router, can cause havoc on the network, and can be time-consuming to diagnose.

LAN testing and analysis equipment is particularly vulnerable to misuse since private LAN message traffic may be intercepted, captured, and analyzed with these devices. To protect the privacy of messages transmitted on the network you can encrypt them so the message characteristics can be analyzed, but the message contents will be unreadable.

Network Control Room

The network control room usually contains server console screens and keyboards, LAN monitor workstations and analyzer units, screens and keyboards, various control mechanisms, visual light and audio alarms, and backup units. The room must be completely secured with locks and other deterrents to unauthorized entry and equipment access, since the LAN servers and the data they contain are completely vulnerable through much of this equipment.

LAN Cabling

LAN wiring, also called the LAN cabling plant, is vulnerable to wiretap along every inch of its path. Twisted pair, which is the LAN wiring most often installed these days, is particularly susceptible to wiretap (the physical attachment of an unauthorized listening device on the LAN) and passive wire tap (interception of the electromagnetic emanations from communications signals traveling over the wires).

Wiring can be physically examined to detect taps and potentially vulnerable spots, but most LAN wiring is not visible in offices because it is placed inside ceilings and walls. The most popular safeguards for protecting LAN cabling from intrusion are to use fiber optic cable or to establish secure communication links with penetration-attempt detection and alarms. Fiber optic cable is difficult to tap and possible taps are easy to detect. It eliminates concerns about emanations and is the cabling of choice in security-conscious organizations.

Fiber optic cable is becoming more widely used, especially for LAN backbones where broad bandwidth is essential. Too many decision-makers still do not seriously evaluate taking fiber optic cable to the desktop because they ignore the security aspects of their LANs and twisted pair wiring is still cheaper and easier to install. For the security-aware, who still think fiber is too expensive or too esoteric a solution, you can learn a lot by talking to industry experts. *FiberWave Technologies*, the low-cost fiber optic cable and connector supplier to Wall Street provides a catalogue with large pictures in color and an informative glossary.

For twisted pair devotees, there is a little-known safeguard for trapping electromagnetic emanations. New wall covering fabrics and paints are specially formulated to absorb stray electromagnetic signals.

LAN Workstations and Peripherals

Hardware locking devices are relatively inexpensive safeguards that can pay big dividends in protecting LAN assets and individual PCs. However, when you have many workstations to secure, it pays to compare prices and ask about volume discounts for the products you choose. Locking devices deter opportunistic thefts, but can be defeated by determined thieves who are equipped with burglar tools such as cable cutters.

Some physical access safeguards for LAN workstations and their approximate prices (where available) follow.

■ Lock down plates and discs, such as with the LOK-KIT product shown in Figure 3.6, adhere to the surface of PCs and other valuable equipment. The lock down plates come in a variety of sizes, shapes, colors, and cable thicknesses. The kits cost approximately $30 with the key lock included.

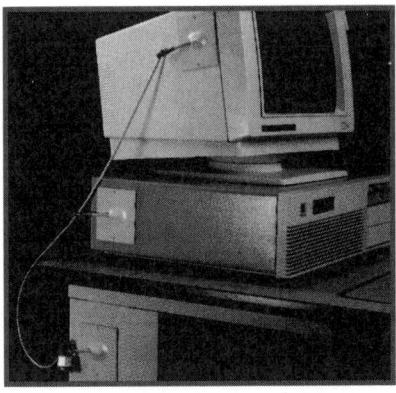

FIGURE 3.6   LOK-KIT LOCK DOWN SECURITY KIT.

■ Locking pads secure workstations to desks or tabletops. Optional cables can be used to secure monitors and printers to the locking pad. Approximate cost is under $100. Locking pads such as the *Secure-It* model, shown in Figure 3.7, are also available to secure laser printers to work desks in remote or vulnerable locations.

■ Cable traps can secure up to five cables for input devices such as mice, keyboards, trackballs, and scanners, as shown in Figure 3.8.

■ Mouse tethers can secure a mouse (by its cable) without limiting its mobility. Five tethers cost under $70.

■ Slotted cases on some computers and peripherals accept brackets which cannot be removed, and hold security cables in place. Slotted case security kits are priced in the $20–$35 range.

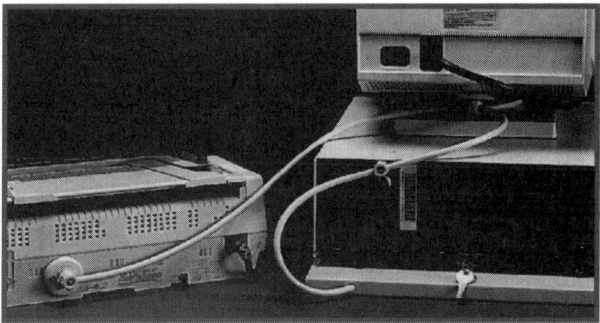

FIGURE 3.7 LOCKING PAD.

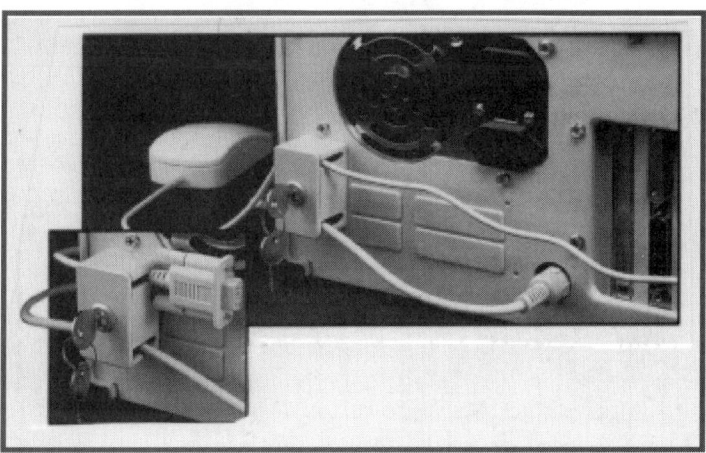

FIGURE 3.8 CABLE TRAPS.

■ Mobile (notebook, portable, and laptop) PC cable locking devices have a cable that loops around a desk or table leg and an end that slides into a floppy drive and locks in place, as shown in Figure 3.9. This device secures portable computers against theft and also locks the floppy disk drive. Some laptops have special metal brackets built into the case for use with a security cable. The devices are similar to those used to secure removable car radio and tape/CD players. Mobile PC cable locks can be used with any

PC with a 3.5-inch floppy disk drive. The approximate cost is $50.

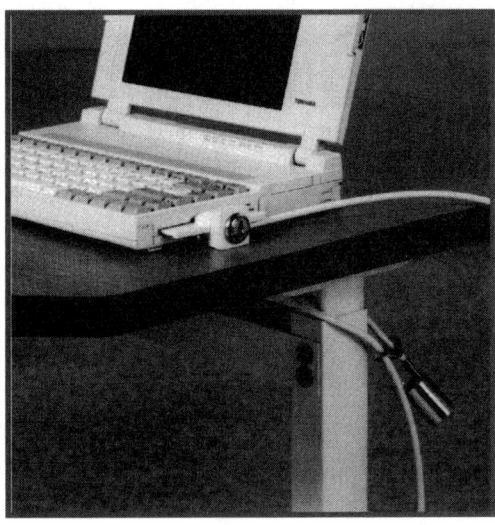

FIGURE 3.9 · NOTEBOOK CABLE LOCK.

■ Floppy disk drive locks are inserted into the floppy disk drive slot and locked in place with a key, as illustrated in Figure 3.10. These locks prevent intruders from booting the computer from the floppy drive to access an otherwise protected hard disk drive. Floppy disk drive locks also prevent the use of floppies in attempts to pirate data or software and will not allow the insertion of a diskette containing a virus. The approximate cost is in the $18–$25 range.

■ Port locks protect parallel, serial, and SCSI ports from intrusion. Metal plate covers are placed over the port on the back of the computer and are secured with non-standard, tamper-proof screws. A matching security screwdriver is included. The PORT-LOK, as shown in Figure 3.11, is approximately $20.

FIGURE 3.10   FLOPPY DISK DRIVE LOCK.

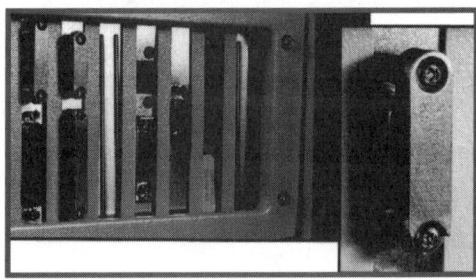

FIGURE 3.11   PORT-LOK.

■ Non-standard PC screws (such as in the PORT-LOK above) are another deterrent that can prevent spontaneous thefts of boards and other components from system units, because they require a special screwdriver. They are at the opposite end of the security spectrum from the new plastic screws, which can be removed by hand and require no tools at all, not even a screwdriver.

Surveillance

Being aware of your surroundings, observing the activities of people in your work area, and questioning strangers can be enough to ward off a theft or intrusion. Looking at the physical LAN cabling, connections, and other components is one way of locating taps. It is also useful for locating vulnerabilities, which could invite network intrusions or untimely equipment failures in the future.

Alarms

Network management is a time-consuming and tedious activity if the LAN administrator has no LAN management software and no alternative to spending great amounts of time scanning audit reports, error messages, and other LAN diagnostics, which can indicate the presence of a physical threat. Alarms are the most effective devices for calling attention to network problems. Alarms may be pop-ups on a workstation screen, audible sounds at varying noise levels, flashing lights, phone or pager messages, and the like. Ideally, both alarms and exception reports are used to alert the LAN administration and security people when a problem is suspected. In general, the easier these tools are to use the higher their price tag, which can make them difficult to justify for the smaller LAN.

Exception Reports

Exception reports are also very effective, and may be produced by the NOS, utilities, and network analyzers. Exception reports notify LAN administration (and possibly security), of LAN security violations such as lockouts (unsuccessful login attempts), which may indicate a security incident, and undocumented, unaccounted-for nodes, which may be unauthorized taps. Operational problems, warnings, and system error messages may also be reported.

Telecommuting Risk: Using Sensitive Data at Home

Physical access control is an important issue for organizations that permit employees to work at home. Telecommuters may be less zealous about securing their workstations, backups, and offsite storage of files, unless they have agreed in advance to observe strict security measures as a condition of working at home.

A therapist with a home office and a custom configured system with network links—set up with great effort on his part—finally decided to protect his system after his first computer was stolen. The first PC was taken, data and all, in a routine 10-minute burglary in which everything of value was dragged out the back door.

This time a more secure perimeter was established around the computer by installing deadbolts in the doors and locks on the windows. Unfortunately, burglars got in through a window he thought was too high to be vulnerable. The computer was not taken the second time thanks to the *Secure-It* locking cable he used to lock the system unit, VGA monitor, and HP printer to his desk. His criteria for choosing a locking cable system included:

- A large padlock.
- Thick cables.
- Reasonable flexibility of movement on the desktop.
- Easy removal (by the owner, who has the key).
- A reasonable price (the locking cable actually costs under $50).

Most burglars care nothing about the valuable information on your computer or that it may provide easy access to your LAN at work. They are simply looking for items of value that they can quickly exchange for cash. But, you should consider the value of the information you work with. The replacement cost of a burglarized PC or laptop may be insignificant compared to the cost of doing without the data on the hard drive or recreating the data. Do you backup your files often and store backup copies at the office or other secure location? Is there any reason you would not want someone to have the use of the contents of your hard drive?

Do you work in a highly competitive industry, with sensitive, classified, private data, or in a professional capacity? Might a highly motivated person target you for a burglary at home, because of the data on your computer? Has that possibility been fully considered in the preparation of your company's security plan? What precautions do you take, if any, to prevent loss due to such a targeted attack? Can an intruder get to your PC? Can they boot the PC and access the files on your hard drive? Can they use your floppy disk drive to remove data from your computer?

Computer controlled *smart house* products are available for everything from electronic premises alarm systems to energy management. Installing such a system in a house under construction can provide considerable protection at a reasonable cost.

The Real Loss Is in Data, Time, and Effort

Where computers and networks are involved, the loss of the physical equipment is usually insignificant. The effort and expertise it took to purchase, set up and resolve interface problems, and finally to create the records and establish data and operating environment integrity, represent the real loss. In fact, it is so costly to recover from a disaster that you may find business loss insurance coverage, other than for replacement of the physical equipment itself, to be prohibitively expensive. If you add in the time required to arrive at a fair insurance claims settlement, you begin to realize why network security incidents are to be avoided at all reasonable cost.

Document Classification and Marking

Security-aware organizations categorize written and computerized information by an information classification to assist employees in protecting valuable information assets including trade secrets, plans, and other proprietary, sensitive, and private information. Government agencies classify data as to its secrecy or sensitivity and have iron-clad rules about handling classified data. Many private companies do not have such precautions and are extremely vulnerable as a result.

Notices are prepared which identify each classification used in the organization and may include guidance for handling the information. The appropriate notice is then printed on every written page and is attached to every computer file. Some possible classifications are:

- Confidential
- Company confidential
- Proprietary
- Private
- Sensitive
- Unclassified

Employees must be trained to recognize each classification they will encounter in their work and to observe any special requirements for handling each kind of information.

Seemingly open and shut cases of industrial espionage have been lost because employees were able to convince a jury that they did not know they were doing anything wrong when they sold company information to outsiders. Employee training in security matters and establishing accountability are essential aspects of protecting valuable information. Had clear written policies and procedures been in effect in those organizations, the outcome of the espionage trials might have been different.

Controlling Climate and Atmospheric Threats

The *Inergen* fire suppressant system uses natural, environmentally safe gasses found in the air itself to smother a fire to reduce the losses which might otherwise occur. The oxygen content of the air is reduced to make combustion impossible. Sufficient oxygen is left in the Inergen atmosphere so that it is completely safe for humans to breathe. Inergen causes no damage to computers, networks, or other electronic components.

Halon can no longer be used as a fire suppressant because of its ozone depleting properties, thus organizations must employ other measures, such as using Inergen, to retard and extinguish fires.

When Your Facilities are Inadequate

In a leased office space the LAN server room was tiny and hot and wound up doing double duty as a LAN wiring closet. The appropriate space and HVAC (heating, ventilation, and air conditioning) for the communications equipment was misunderstood. The server room door had to be kept open so fans could circulate the air from a larger outer room to keep the temperature around the server within an acceptable range. Thus, the LAN had to remain in test mode until the problem could be corrected and the server secured in a locked room. The most cost-effective solution was to install a thermostat in the server room. The thermostat triggered a fan in the duct work that increased the air circulation into the room whenever the temperature began to rise.

As a temporary measure, a *FanCard* was installed in the server. FanCards were used en masse in Desert Storm. They have 2 fans installed that run on the PC's power. One card cooled the server enough to prevent heat related errors until the air cooling system could be modified. The LAN Manager was then able to close and lock the server room door, and convert the LAN to an operational mode.

ELECTRONIC NETWORK ACCESS CONTROL

*E*lectronic network access control is intended to safeguard data—while stored in the server or traveling through LAN cables—from penetration attempts through electronic channels. Electronic network access controls are more difficult to envision than physical access controls because they are largely enabled by software and the electronic circuits in LAN communications hardware. This is where LAN security becomes interesting and technically challenging. It is the realm of the telecommunications professional and computer scientist.

Electronic access network safeguard products must be in place, ready to perform when the need arises, for instance when the security of the LAN is breached or challenged in a penetration attempt.

The LAN manager has a responsibility to employ all reasonable safeguards to protect LAN resources. Regarding electronic access safeguards, there is no clear distinction between those that are lax, reasonable, and excessive. Electronic network safeguards consist of the software, hardware, NOS features, and add-on products that fall into the following categories:

- User identification and authentication.
- Electronic network access control products.
- Encryption and other data disguises (covered in Chapter 5).
- Virus (rogue program) detection and removal.
- Transmission control and error checking.
- LAN monitoring, management, and analysis.

User Identification and Authentication

LAN users are most often identified by a user ID that is assigned by the LAN administrator prior to the user's first use. User IDs generally follow a pattern for a LAN or an enterprise, so that if you know one user ID, you can usually determine the others. In most LANs, the user IDs are some variation of the names listed in the employee telephone book. Since anyone can type any user ID, further proof is required to establish that the person attempting to gain access is indeed the owner of the ID. *CompuServe*, for example, assigns its electronic mail users unique 10-digit user IDs.

User authentication is intended to thwart unauthorized network access by challenging would-be LAN users to prove their identity. Authentication techniques and schemes vary widely. In general, the proof of a user's identity to a NOS, LAN application, or authentication agent or device can be any combination of things the user has or knows, such as:

- User IDs and passwords.
- Smartcards (and other intelligent devices).
- Biometric identifiers.

User IDs and Passwords

NOSs grant permission to use the network only to authorized users, who identify themselves during a login process. A user ID is typically requested first, followed by a password. Users who type valid user ID-password combinations are *logged on* and given access to LAN files and network services. A network cracker wanting access to your LAN would get the names of your employees and try the obvious user ID patterns until one was found to work. Although passwords are usually optional in NOSs, all users should be required to provide them.

Weak Passwords: The Network Crackers Dream

Password generators and password checkers are available for those who wish to avoid the network crackers dream, the weak password. An organization can invest millions of dollars in safeguards and still be completely vulnerable to electronic attack because one user chooses a dictionary word or a common name for an easy to remember password. To penetrate LANs, network crackers set up automated dialing systems, which use a dictionary of popular passwords, a range of likely phone numbers, and a list of user IDs. The system keeps dialing until it connects to a modem, then tries to log on with one user ID password combination after another until it hits one that works.

To foil network crackers, LAN administrators can require passwords and take the following precautions against password guessing:

■ Long passwords or passphrases.

■ Hard-to-guess passwords.

■ Password generators.

■ Password checkers.

LAN users should be taught (encouraged, reminded, or forced, as required) to create passwords that cannot be guessed or dictionary-dialed.

Misspelling, placing special characters within a word, and using multiple words called *passphrases* produces good passwords. Phrases can meet the criteria for acceptable passwords, since they can be hard to guess and easier to remember than single words. However, if your system can only accommodate short passwords, your choice of possible words for passphrases may be limited to such a degree that the phrase may be easier to guess than a single password of the same length.

To ensure hard-to-guess passwords, some security-conscious organizations use password generators. The passwords they generate are secure compared to user-chosen passwords. However, when generated passwords consist of meaningless character strings, they are hard to remember and are considered to be extremely user unfriendly.

CompuServe uses a password generator to ensure unique guess-proof passwords for e-mail users. It currently assigns passwords consisting of two words and a special character. These system-generated passwords are easier to remember than the 10-digit user IDs.

For those who must put the convenience of their users before the security of their LANs, password checkers are available that identify weak passwords. Password checkers permit the users to continue to devise the passwords or pass phrases they find easy to remember. This allows the LAN administrator to routinely verify that the passwords, or phrases, are effective in safeguarding the LAN.

Password Coach is a password checker safeguard product that works on Novell LANs. It intercepts new passwords as users enter their password changes. Password Coach identifies weak passwords, and gives an immediate response to the user, including the reasons why a particular password is a poor choice. Only acceptable passwords are passed to the NOS.

It is unfortunate that no matter how often you explain to some users that their choice of weak passwords jeopardizes the security of the LAN, some will still choose poorly. After stressing the importance of the password issue in every conceivable way, I invariably find that some still use family first names and pet names. Since password guessing by hackers and network crackers is at the root of most LAN penetrations, a product like Password Coach seems a worthwhile investment at $395 for a single server.

Optional NOS Password Features

Besides providing for basic user ID and password protection, other password safeguard features are included in NOSs at no additional cost. The problem is that they are optional features and offer no protection at all unless they are implemented. The additional password safeguard features in *NetWare 3.x* are typical of NOSs in general and are described below:

- Minimum password length.
- Forced periodic password change.
- Unique passwords.
- User lockout after failed login.

MINIMUM PASSWORD LENGTH

Users are forced to select passwords that are some minimum number of characters. A good rule of thumb is to create long passwords. If you choose to use passphrases instead of passwords, the minimum length should be large enough to accommodate two or more words and some special characters. A long minimum password of 12 or more characters encourages (if not forces) users to use multiple words and to extend their passwords with special characters. It also increases the number of words that might be chosen.

FORCED PERIODIC PASSWORD CHANGE

This feature requires users to change their passwords periodically. This parameter can be set for anything ranging from very frequent changes for LANs that are considered to be highly vulnerable, to infrequent changes for the least vulnerable.

UNIQUE PASSWORDS

Unique passwords may be specified to prevent users from reusing their previous password. A related parameter specifies how many times the password must be changed before an old password can be reused.

USER LOCKOUT AFTER FAILED LOGIN

The NOS prevents a particular user from logging into the LAN, for some preset period of time, after a failed login attempt. The criteria for a failed login is the number of times a user is permitted to type in a user ID and password combination. When that limit is reached, the NOS will lock the user out. User lockout can be compared to locking a door to thwart a potential burglary attempt. If a thief tries one door and finds it locked, he progresses to the windows, then moves on to try the next door. A network cracker will usually proceed to the next user ID once a user ID lockout has occurred. However, the cracker may wait awhile and try again! A total of three unsuccessful login tries followed by a 30-minute lockout period offers some protection against penetration for the average LAN. More protection is gained by locking the user out until the LAN administrator verifies the identity of the user and re-enables the login.

A LAN cracker will not ask your LAN administrator to reset a password The *Banyan Vines* NOS locks the workstation rather than the user's login ID after a specified number of failed login attempts. Locking the workstation is an effective way of keeping network crackers out. However, an unauthorized person trying to gain access from inside the building can simply go to another workstation.

GRACE LOGINS

An optional feature that permits a user to bypass the forced password change some specific number of times is called *grace logins*. One or two grace logins permits users to reset their passwords even after they have expired. This is useful for users who travel and when the system fails during a password change. It is easy to lose track of how many grace logins have expired and NetWare users are not warned when they have reached their last grace login. Instead, they are locked out if their passwords are not changed before their last grace login is used. The LAN administrator must manually reset the passwords of locked-out users, so passwords should be changed as soon as possible and grace logins not used without a good reason.

SmartCards (and Other Intelligent Devices)

This category includes any intelligent physical device used to identify the carrier as a user of the system. A SmartCard, a floppy disk containing an encrypted key, or another intelligent hardware unit which carries secret information may be used in combination with a user ID and password to positively identify a user. Security concerns about this method are:

- User IDs are easily discovered.
- Physical devices may be lost or stolen.
- Passwords can be guessed or compromised.

If you rely on a physical device for user authentication and the device is lost, stolen, or fails to work, the user is prevented from accessing the network until the device is replaced. If replacement is managed efficiently, the units are kept safe, *and* long, secure passwords are used, the method can be highly effective.

A *SmartCard* device, the *SafeBoot* SmartDisk is shown in Figure 4.1.

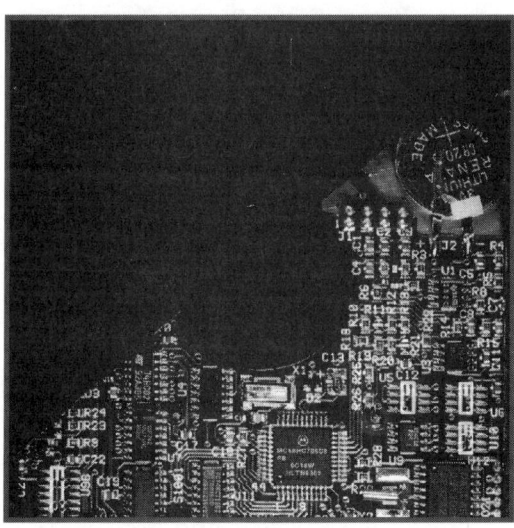

FIGURE 4.1   THE SAFEBOOT SMARTDISK.

Biometric Identifiers

Fingerprint, signature, voice print, palm print, retina pattern, and hand geometry are biometric characteristics that may be used for positive identification of network users. There is usually a small margin of error in biometric systems so that a person could theoretically be positively identified in error and granted access when it should be denied. Employees with limited mobility might find it difficult to reach a biometric reader device. Likewise a voice recognition system might reject a bonafide user who has a cold. Thus, backup identification systems are needed to avoid the risk of violating ADA rules for handicapped employees. Biometric authentication systems tend to be expensive, and the use of body parts for routine identification purposes is somewhat intrusive.

Combinations of identification methods such as user ID, secure password, and an intelligent device or biometric feature are the most foolproof authenticators. As one might expect, combined methods are used in financial systems where large amounts of money or other financial assets are at risk.

Electronic Network Access Control Products

Add on products that help to prevent unauthorized individuals from penetrating your LAN security generally intercept and validate the source of communications originating outside the local network area.

Secure Dial-in for Remote Users

Secure access to LANs for dial-in users requires that users be positively identified before allowing them to connect to the server and log into the LAN. The most secure dial-in requires devices at both server and remote workstations, as well as a password to authenticate remote users. For example, the *LeeMah* system for secure dial-in, uses a system that contains both hardware and software components and is completely independent of the LAN. Before a LAN connection is established and a user login is permitted with a LeeMah system, DES encryption is used to verify the authenticity of both the remote user and a keydisk, keycard, or *InfoKey* hardware device. The LeeMah system permits either secure, remote user dial-in, or a call-back to a preauthorized remote user's phone number by the secure device at the host computer. The LeeMah system is shown in Figure 4.2.

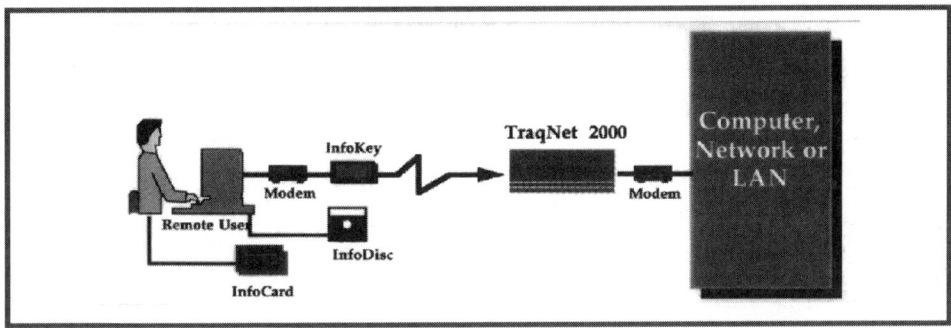

FIGURE 4.2   LEEMAH DATACOM SECURE DIAL-IN SYSTEM.

Call-back systems are a less stringent form of LAN access control for remote users. They usually require pre-authorized lists of remote users and approved phone numbers to prevent successful penetration attempts by people masquerading as authorized users. Thus, call-back systems are less flexible than some users might wish. Although the scenarios can vary, in general when a call is received from an approved number (an access code may also be required), the call-back system hangs up and dials the number back. Only then is a user allowed to log into the LAN.

Caller ID services make it easier to identify remote users and some systems permit calls from only pre-approved numbers.

In the more secure call-back systems, remote users get blank screens and no on-line assistance, and must identify themselves before the call-back and login system will work. The blank-screen method is only considered if access control security has a higher priority than ease-of-use. This method originated in the days of mainframe computer systems and relies on users having the login information on a need-to-know basis. LAN login and access audit trails may be maintained for most call-back or secure dial-in access systems.

Virus (Rogue Program) Detection and Removal

Rogue programs include viruses, Trojan horses, logic bombs, and worms that are introduced into computers and LANs for fraudulent or destructive purposes. Virus has come to stand, somewhat incorrectly, for the entire class of rogue programs. A *virus* is any malicious software, which spreads by attaching itself or replicating a copy of itself to other software programs. A human virus spreads from one person to the other in similar fashion.

A *Trojan horse* is software that seems to be benign—and may well have a useful function—but contains destructive program code.

A *logic bomb* is software that is designed to execute when it is triggered by some event which is expected to take place in the future. A *time bomb* is a kind of logic bomb which will be executed on a certain date. For example, if the programmers altered the payroll programs so payroll checks would be issued to them when they terminated their employment, that would be a logic bomb. The code would only be executed when the programmers' termination transactions entered the payroll system. If the same programmers inserted software that began to issue bogus salary checks on a particular date (without respect to any transactions processed), the payroll program would then contain a time bomb. The Friday the 13th "virus" is an example of a time bomb.

A *worm* is a rogue program that *replicates* itself until it uses up all available disk space or all available memory. The infamous Morris Internet worm replicated itself across many government and university networks through a connection to the Internet. Attentive network managers who noticed a slowdown of resources which is a characteristic of systems infected with worms, shut their networks and computers down. The estimated $100 million loss which resulted was from loss of service rather than intentional damage to data or resources.

There are three main kinds of anti-virus programs. Virus scanners search for known virus signatures, and rule-based TSR (Terminate and Stay Resident) programs recognize and report suspicious virus-like activity. Once a virus has been identified, a virus removal utility program can usually eradicate it. Virus scanners can only identify the viruses they are specifically programmed to find and rule-based TSRs often identify "suspicious" program behavior that is caused not by viruses or rogue programs, but by the software and utilities you use every day. This forces the administrator and users to respond to many false alerts. Custom designed virus protection can avoid these problems.

Excellent work has been done in making LAN managers virus-aware. In fact, the most widely-used network utility today is virus protection software, which is now on about 80 percent of networks in this country (and should be on *all* LANs). This number attests to the havoc rogue programs cause and the importance of identifying and eliminating them before they have a chance to execute their destructive code and spread themselves further.

It is difficult to eliminate viruses (because they do spread), so users should avoid introducing them and should be held accountable when they do. Diskettes should be scanned for viruses before use on LAN workstations.

Virus protection software utility programs are increasingly preloaded on new PC hardware and bundled with operating systems, including Novell's DOS 7.X and MS-DOS 6.X. Virus protection is also included in many general purpose utility programs including:

- Integrity Master
- Norton Utilities
- Disk Technician Gold
- PC-Tools

Integrity Master identifies and removes viruses and calls attention to virus-like behavior while your system is running. it keeps track of programs and alerts you to changes on your hard drive. Integrity Master is included on the attached disk.

F-Prot is an easy-to-use shareware product, which is highly rated for virus detection and removal. The cost is minimal—at one time it cost $1 per node for business users and it was free to private individual users.

Readers who wish to delve into the subject of rogue programs in greater detail will find interesting books on the subject in the suggested reading list.

Transmission Control and Error Checking

Transmission control and error checking are essential for maintaining accuracy and integrity in LAN communications.

While the topic is of great importance to LAN security because it directly affects message integrity, network performance throughput, and dependability, transmission control and error checking is entirely determined by your LAN protocol and controlled by your NOS. Protocol selection is the most fundamental decision you will make in designing your LAN and should not be taken lightly. All LAN protocols have transmission control and error checking mechanisms built in. LAN managers can do little to improve either once the protocol has been established, other than to keep the network well-tuned and operating efficiently.

The popular Ethernet protocol based on IEEE standard 802.3 implements CSMA/CD (Carrier Sense Multiple Access with Collision Detection) for transmission control and CRC (Cyclic Redundancy Check) methods for error checking and correction.

LAN Monitoring, Management, and Analysis

Network management is a time consuming, difficult activity. Great amounts of time can be spent scanning audit reports, reviewing errors and performance statistics, and examining other LAN diagnostic information to determine whether the LAN is functioning properly. Network monitoring and management software provide the needed information on a timely basis and free the staff from the task of searching endlessly for relevant information. Add-on LAN monitoring, management, and analysis products are available which identify existing as well as potential problems and call attention to situations requiring analysis or corrective action with various kinds of alarms. Visual screen displays and pop-ups, audible sounds, pager alerts, and other active alarms are the most effective means of calling attention to network problems. Exception reports provide necessary documentation and backup to supplement the more active alerts and alarms. LAN management tools are prized by busy LAN managers and administrators. Some highly functional and feature-rich systems may still be too high priced for use on the average LAN but several software-only products are now available to permit intelligent LAN management by everyone.

Network management tools include the software used by the LAN administrator to set up new users and applications, as well as monitor and maintain an efficient, reliable, secure network. The tools are provided as part of the NOS, as NOS-supplied and third-party add-ons, and by hardware- or software-based network analyzers.

LAN administrators set up, maintain, and manage users, workstations, printers, and software on the LAN. They benefit from any utility that makes it easier to track and change any of the things for which they are responsible. An example of an add-on tool that is useful for LAN administration is the BindView utility. *BindView* tracks workstation hardware, software, and security information such as user rights, configuration files, server time, and hardware changes. It also analyzes passwords, meters licensed software, and produces reports for subsequent network analysis and follow-up.

Monitoring, management, and analysis tools assist LAN managers by providing the following essential services:

- Data integrity verification.
- Routine electronic surveillance.
- Internal system controls..
- Exception alarms and reports.

In general, a small stand-alone LAN is relatively easy to maintain with few additional LAN management tools; large interconnected LANs are not.

Data Integrity Verification

Data integrity verification on LANs is performed by a wide range of utilities and other products. Some of these are:

- Server backup, restore, and recovery systems.
- Various performance optimizers.
- Repair programs (such as DOS CHKDSK and NetWare Bindfix).
- LAN analyzer programs.

The NOS is responsible for overall integrity of the LAN. It supplies the necessary basic utilities to manage the LAN, including maintaining LAN integrity and responsiveness. For instance, the programs provided with Novell's NetWare include BINDFIX, which maintains the integrity of the NetWare bindery, and VREPAIR, which corrects volume problems after many additions and deletions. These programs are generally run during routine server maintenance. They often improve server performance when errors begin to occur or LAN response time slows. "Post office" integrity and reorganization utilities are also useful to maintain peak e-mail performance.

There are many third-party products that specialize in verifying and maintaining LAN data integrity. Four such products are:

- *LT-Auditor 4.0+* is designed to perform the following data security and integrity tasks on NetWare LANs:
  - Notify the LAN administrator of attempts to breach LAN security.
  - Monitor local drives for data copied to and from the LAN.
  - Identify the source of viruses.
  - Meter software and notify users when limited software licenses become available on the network.
  - Generate tailored reports using a custom report generator.

(LT-Auditor is also discussed in the chapter on LAN Hardware.)

- *LT-Stat* provides LAN administrators with tools to manage users, monitor performance and utilization, report problems, and document changes to the bindery on NetWare LANs.

- *Integrity Master* (IM) gives you diagnosis and recovery information on your system including:

  - File or program corruption from software, hardware failure, bugs, and sabotage

  - Changes to data

  - Hardware malfunctions

  - Viruses

Integrity Master is ready to use with online documentation included. If you have wondered what files are damaged after CHKDSK finishes "fixing" disk errors, you can run Integrity Master to answer that question among others. Integrity Master is included on the attached disk in a shareware version. There is also a Pro version available that comes with additional utilities, a full year of the *Integrity Pro* newsletter, and new software releases for 12 months.

- *Disk Technician Gold* is a hard disk drive utility which:

  - Establishes a baseline on the state of a given physical hard disk.

  - Scans and reviews disk integrity.

  - Reports disk problems, potential disk problems, and programs that exhibit virus-like behavior.

  - Uses a TSR to continuously gauge the physical condition of a hard disk by intercepting and monitoring each hard disk access.

LAN Monitoring, Management, and Analysis Products

LT-Auditor 4.0+ was used to identify the corporate espionage culprit in an oil and gas company whose proprietary data, designs, and methods began to surface overseas. The audit tool provides electronic surveillance of selected LAN resources, and provides integrity assurance and controls on LAN resources. Limits can be set to issue real-time security alerts to catch intruders in the act and identify internal security breaches. In addition to monitoring LAN access and reasons for failed logins, it tracks:

■ File access with user-filtering of operations and directories (real-time alerts).

■ Bindery updates.

■ Workstation hardware inventory.

■ System files inventory (with alerts provided).

It is a *NetWare Loadable Module* (NLM), which means it is tightly integrated with the NOS and can operate efficiently and conserve memory as well.

The following products are other examples of network management software currently in use on Novell LANs. Prices are given for the initial server(s) where available.

■ *NetWare Early Warning System* from Frye monitors 50 statistics and notifies the administrator by pager, e-mail, or voice when an event occurs that requires management action. It fixes problems and responds to events automatically and can be used to automate many small but essential tasks. The cost is $495.

■ *LAN Server Watch* from Brightwork Development runs under Windows and manages servers. It gives onscreen, e-mail, and pager event notification of conditions that require immediate or administrative action. It performs configuration, fault-management, and usage monitoring functions. The cost is $695 for 100 users.

Other products are described in the chapters on LAN hardware and LAN software.

Exception Reports and Alarms

Exception reports and alarms may be produced by the NOS, LAN utilities, and hardware/software network analyzers. Exception reports notify LAN administration, and possibly security, of LAN security violations such as unsuccessful login attempts, indicating attempted network penetration, and/or the appearance of new, or unaccounted-for nodes on the network, indicating unauthorized physical taps.

Routine Electronic Surveillance

Routine electronic surveillance or inspection will detect many LAN security problems. At a minimum, this inspection should include:

- Server program size.
- Changes and usage.
- Files and resources in use.
- Those used within a previous period of time.
- Network traffic.
- Violation exception reports.

Internal System Controls

Controls are routinely used in mainframe applications to verify the accuracy and integrity of data processed by the system. User controlled LAN applications rarely use internal controls and rely instead on software, users, and system operators to store and process data accurately and completely. Whoever controls an application has a need to know what controls are in place on the data and when they are out of balance. This does not mean you should completely mistrust the LAN and its applications, or keep a set of manual books and records in your desk drawer (as accountants did when computers were new and systems were somewhat unreliable). But, there is still a need to know the number of records on a file or database, the number of records added, changed, and deleted each period, etc. The need for basic accounting and system controls continues, regardless of how many computers or networks you use, or how reliable you think they are.

CHAPTER 5

ENCRYPTION AND
OTHER USEFUL DISGUISES

P eople have been encoding messages to keep their contents private since civilization began. With the increasing use of computers and the need to transmit messages over electronic networks and communication channels that are inherently insecure, the task of maintaining information security has become an enormous technological challenge.

The wider the distribution of information, the more difficult it is to protect it without making the underlying systems cumbersome or hard to use. Attempts to protect the privacy of computerized and networked information have taken three main thrusts:

1. Physical security designed to limit access to computerized information to authorized individuals.

2. Safeguards to thwart network attacks through electronic communication channels.

3. Disguising data to make it unreadable should either the physical or network security safeguards fail.

This chapter covers techniques for disguising data including encryption, coding, compression, or padding of messages. Disguising the information stored in network servers and transmitted over LAN communication channels and connected networks helps to guarantee its privacy and overall security.

Data Coding

One means of disguising information is to code it. Before the microcomputer revolution when computer storage space was very expensive, data coding was extremely common as a means of reducing the size of computerized records and resulting files. For example, storing a field containing employee job titles, which were up to 20 characters in length, required that 20 characters be reserved for every record. The same data might be recorded in the computer in only one character by allowing each of the letter codes A though J to represent—and be substituted for—one particular job title. Thus 19 bytes of storage space could be saved in every record. In a file of 100,000 records, 1.9 million bytes of storage space would be saved.

It took considerable time for programmers and systems analysts to code the data and even more time for business analysts to decode it for everyday use. Since computer file storage resources were far more expensive than the relative cost of the alternative expenditure of human—computer programmer and analyst—resources, the practice was cost-effective. Some aviation and weather data is coded because it was originally transmitted over low-speed teletype lines and had to be compressed.

Coding data also happens to improve the security of data. A set of obscure codes, such as:

```
A1 .... J10
```

would have little meaning to someone who saw the data. Whereas the job title and annual salary data:

```
Chairman $203,000 .... Clerk $10,000
```

which the codes were created to represent, would have meaning for even the most casual observer. As with any good idea, data coding was occasionally carried to such an extreme that codes were used inappropriately and some coded data was almost impossibly complicated to use. In addition, the code translations introduced errors into data during the coding and decoding processes. One such system was designed and programmed by a genius who had been well trained as a physicist to manipulate data. He devised such clever and intricate code systems, and such thorough error-checking routines, that the users were virtually unable to get data into the system. It had to be abandoned.

In general, excessive coding of data complicates all aspects of system analysis and development and data administration. It also violates the principles of human factors engineering which attempts to make computers easy to use.

Fortunately, the evolution of microcomputer technology reduced the cost of storing data on disks, which eliminated the need to drastically conserve storage space with extensive data coding. While many *legacy systems* (that is, older systems created specifically to run on mainframe computers) still contain coded data, the practice is much less common today.

Encryption is a more effective method of disguising information than is data coding.

Encryption

Encryption is the transformation of information into something that no one but the intended receiver of the message can interpret correctly. Encryption is not the same as *scrambling*, which suggests randomness and unpredictable results. In encryption, a formula and a key are used to encrypt data to disguise it, so it cannot be used as it is. The process must be reversed to decrypt encrypted data. To complete the secure transmission of encrypted messages, the formula used to encrypt the message and the coordinated key must be used at the receiving end. This is necessary so that the process can be reversed and the message restored to its original form. The two factors that affect the degree of security of a given encryption method follow:

1. The complexity of the formula used to encrypt the data.
2. The length of the keys used.

The more complicated the encryption formula and the longer the keys, the longer it will take to break a given key in order to restore the original information.

The more sensitive the data, and the greater the number of strategic applications placed on LANs, the greater the need for proven security measures such as encryption to protect it. Encryption is routinely used to protect LAN passwords that are stored on the server.

There are two basic kinds of encryption in common use, private key and public key.

Kerberos

The Kerberos technique was devised at MIT to secure and encrypt keys using DES. It is named after the mythological three-headed dog because it is a three-part system. It uses a separate computer to store and encrypt the keys so that two other computers or LANs can encrypt communications sent between them. Rumors suggest that Microsoft will use a Kerberos system to encrypt messages on Windows NT LANs.

Private Key Encryption

A *private key* (also known as secret key or single key) is used to encrypt raw data to make it undecipherable during transmission or storage. The same key is used in reverse to decrypt the data to make it usable again. This method requires the encrypter and decrypter to know the same unique key.

A popular private key encryption formula, *DES* (for *Data Encryption Standard*), has been used for years to encrypt and protect data stored in computer systems. DES is not widely used to encrypt messages on networks except in hardware-based devices (such as the LeeMah system in Chapter 4). This is because it is impractical for every user to establish a private key to secure communications taking place with every other network user. Ten unique keys would be required to send an encrypted message to ten other network users. For this reason, private key encryption systems are impracticable for securing messages transmitted on a LAN. It is even more impracticable to use DES or private key encryption to protect messages transmitted on global networks, which have millions of users.

Public Key Encryption

Public key encryption is often used as a supplement to private key encryption to make it more secure and useful for the transmission of messages. Public key encryption uses two different keys. One key is used by the sender to encrypt information and a second key is used by the recipient to decrypt the message. While either key can be calculated from the other, the public key is simple to derive but the private key is not. The public key encryption technique is highly effective for securing data on networks and is endorsed by the managers of the *Internet*.

The most widely used public key encryption system is RSA. RSA was developed by three MIT professors, Drs. Ronald Rivest, Adi Shamir, and Leonard Adelman. This public key encryption method is suitable for protecting the privacy of network messages, because it uses a pair of keys for each user, a public key and a private key. The public key is usually listed in a directory and is generally known to all network users. Only the senders have private keys. The actual keys are used by the NOS or application software and are not normally seen by LAN users.

Messages can be encrypted for a user by anyone who knows the user's public key. A message encrypted for a user can only be decrypted by using the user's matching private key. So with one public-private key pair, a sender could encrypt a message for ten users with ten different public keys, and the message could be decrypted on receipt with the recipients' ten private keys. RSA is usually used to encrypt the DES secret key that is attached to the DES encrypted message, to provide extremely secure transmission. This method is known as the RSA *digital envelope.*

RSA is said to be secure because the following make it virtually impossible to crack:

1. the encryption formula is very complex
2. the computation required to compute a private key from a long public key can take many years

The longer the keys are, the more time it takes to compute one key from the other. In fact, the use of RSA and long (64-bit minimum length) keys is believed to be unbreakable by even the National Security Agency.

Pretty Good Privacy

An example of a public key system based on the RSA algorithm is the *Pretty Good Privacy* (PGP) product. PGP, which is impenetrable, was developed by Philip Zimmermann in 1991 and was subsequently made available to users across the Internet free of charge. It is now in use by foreign governments, freedom-fighters, dissidents, human rights groups, and others world-wide to encrypt and protect the privacy of their electronic mail messages and computerized information. Mr. Zimmermann is referred to as "a folk hero on the information highway" in an article by William Bulkeley for the *Wall Street Journal.*

PGP is at the center of the controversy over individual privacy versus the need of government law enforcement and intelligence agencies to monitor communications. Monitoring communications is one way the government locates terrorists and criminal elements. This is a dilemma because fighting crime is of extreme national importance, but so is the right of the individual to privacy as guaranteed by the first amendment. It is illegal to distribute American-made secure encryption products outside the United States and Mr. Zimmermann's role in PGP's world-wide distribution via Internet is under investigation. PGP is now commercially available in the United States through *ViaCrypt.*

One cannot help but wonder whether a government mandate on the use of encryption methods to which it holds the keys—in an effort to control encryption—is pointless since the law-abiding citizens who have nothing to hide will use it; but everyone else will not.

A recent breakthrough in the improved use of computers for rapid factoring could end the controversy rather dramatically. Factoring is the mathematical operation which is required to break secure encryption keys such as RSA. Breakthroughs in factoring speed could render existing encryption methods obsolete.

Electronic Signature

Use of a public key encryption method such as RSA's dual key technique can be used effectively to establish an *electronic signature*. An electronic signature is a code that is calculated from your private key and the message itself. The electronic signature authenticates, or certifies, to the recipient that you are the person who sent the message. This is an essential feature of secure *e-mail* and other legally-binding electronic message communications, such as *Electronic Data Interchange*.

Lotus Notes—An Example

Lotus Notes provides secure e-mail and offers an interesting variety of uses of encryption within the Notes application. The encryption safeguards and security features are instrumental in delivering the following security essentials for LAN applications:

- **Integrity**—Message integrity is ensured because an encrypted message that has been altered during transmission cannot be successfully decrypted

- **Confidentiality**—Confidentiality of encrypted messages is ensured because the encryption method has not been broken. Encrypted messages are therefore unintelligible.

■ **Accuracy**—Data accuracy is ensured because errors cannot be introduced into encrypted messages.

■ **Access control**—Access control is guaranteed to positively identify each user and server through the user and server authentication process.

■ **Authentication**—Authentication requirements are met through the use of public key encryption to safeguard passwords, as well as effective management and control of user IDs.

■ **Tamper prevention**—Tamper prevention is ensured because of the inability to penetrate encrypted messages and the detection of altered messages in the decryption process (since altered encrypted messages cannot be decrypted).

■ **Source verification**—Source verification is guaranteed through the electronic signature feature.

Lotus Notes typically connects hundreds of users working in various geographic locations, even people who may be continents away from each other. It automatically replicates databases, routes e-mail, and gives different sets of users various, sometimes private, views of databases. It uses a unique combination of standards-based security techniques and safeguards to protect strategic and sensitive data against intrusion. This makes it a popular e-mail, document management, and application development platform for security-conscious organizations.

Lotus Notes uses both single-key and dual-key encryption to secure communications. In addition to certifying the identity of message originators by means of electronic signatures (using encryption), encryption is also used for:

■ User authentication

■ Single e-mail messages

■ Communication session protection (of all messages sent before stopping transmission)

■ Electronic signature source verification

- Whole document protection
- Individual field protection within documents.

Lotus Notes uses public key encryption to authenticate users as well as servers. The importance of secure installation is discussed in the chapter on software.

ENCRYPTION METHODS

Single messages are encrypted using RSA's *RC2* (single key *Rivest Cipher*) method. To encrypt all messages in a session on one communication channel, RSA's RC4 is used: RC4 with 64-bit and longer keys is thought to be unbroken and highly secure. RC2 and RC4 are replacements for DES and can only be exported with limitations imposed on the key size used. Key size is limited to 40 bits for quick export, while 56-bit keys are allowed for foreign subsidiaries and overseas offices of U.S. companies.

Electronic Signature Example

The electronic digital signature, *Sign*, option in Lotus Notes encrypts a 128-bit *fingerprint* of a message using the sender's private key. The encrypted digital signature "fingerprint" is sent along with the e-mail message. The sender's public key is used to decrypt the fingerprint on receipt, verifying the identity of the sender. If the encrypted fingerprint cannot be decrypted using the formula and key provided, the identity of the sender cannot be verified, and a security incident may have occurred.

Electronic signature works in much the same way as signing a letter ensures the recipient that you are, in fact, the person who sent the letter. The recipient of a letter would need to know you and have seen your signature to be certain that the letter was from you. The method used to *certify* an electronic signature uses a combination of your public key-private key pair, your user ID, and certificate(s) generated for the Lotus Notes servers you use. This method of *message source verification* requires your Lotus Notes ID to have been certified for the set of Lotus Notes servers you will use. Thus, any of these Notes servers, can act as a certifier for your signature. Any Lotus Notes computer can verify your signature and will inform the message recipient that you *signed* the messages you sent. However, only a Lotus Notes computer with your certified Lotus Notes ID can generate your electronic signature and attach it to a message you created and wish to sign and send.

Securing Encryption Keys and Servers

Lotus Notes servers must be physically secure or the authentication and Access Control List can easily be bypassed and databases copied to floppy diskettes. If the certificates and IDs are not kept secure, setting up the security is a waste of time.

The RSA and other public key encryption methods are worse than ineffective if they are not properly implemented. If private keys are not properly secured, encrypted messages can be unencrypted without the user's knowledge. Communicating in an insecure environment, which you believe to be totally secure, can result in disaster.

When, early in WWII—and unknown to the Germans—the Allies captured one of the devilishly clever *Enigma* machines which the Germans used to encrypt secret messages, they were able to decipher previously unbreakable German codes. The brilliant success of the British in devising computer and programming solutions to speed code breaking and message analysis is credited with much of the success of Allied intelligence and the eventual triumph of the Allied invasion on D-Day. With this intelligence, the British were able to dismantle German intelligence in Britain and embark on a war of deception and misinformation to confuse Hitler's military. The Germans were duped into believing that the Allies were already inland and about to invade Europe at Calais and Norway when in fact the Allies were landing in Normandy. It was a disaster for the German war machine and is given credit for prompting Hitler to shoot himself shortly thereafter.

Clipper Chip

Clipper is a secret encryption formula that uses 80-bit keys embedded in a computer chip that cannot be reverse engineered. It is the encryption mechanism the NSA and FBI would like to see become the industry standard. Clipper provides a *back door* in the form of *escrowed keys*. That is, keys intended to be held secure by one or more government agencies or entities. This practice permits the NSA, FBI, and other law enforcement agencies to penetrate what would otherwise be secure electronic communications. The encryption key to penetrate Clipper Chip encrypted data would be provided to the Federal agencies only after they secured appropriate legal permission (much like a telephone wire-tap).

Clipper is controversial, because U.S. software and hardware manufacturers want less restriction on the encryption methods they use, not more. In particular, they want to eliminate the existing requirement to employ less effective encryption mechanisms in products sold to foreign customers. Virtually impenetrable encryption methods, such as RSA RC4 and PGP, are being used increasingly by foreign organizations, as well as underworld entities. Such effective encryption undermines U.S. national security efforts to keep tabs on foreign and domestic criminal and subversive elements. It is not clear why we would expect Clipper to become the encryption standard world-wide when other mechanisms such as PGP are already being used both at home and abroad. Key issues remain unanswered, such as why any foreign organization (legitimate or otherwise) would choose to employ an encryption method to which the U.S. government retains access, when they have alternatives? What effect would such a requirement have on U.S. software sales overseas? Which U.S. (or international) unit would have custody of the Clipper keys? How would the keys be kept secure?

Compression

Compression is a technique used to increase the amount of data that can be stored on a disk by removing spaces and other repetitive information.

Pkzip is a shareware compression software utility that is widely used for storing large files, particularly large executable files, on disks for long-term storage or transmission. The utility has many useful options including a Pkunzip routine that decompresses previously compressed files.

Some savvy applications, like Lotus Notes and some NOSs, automatically compress stored information. Besides the obvious benefits of increasing virtual disk storage space, compression increases data security because compressed data can be difficult to interpret until it is decompressed. The most popular hard disk compression program for microcomputers is *Stacker*— currently running on a large installed base of PCs. Stacker has recently been included (along with multi-tasking and new security features) in Novell's DOS, version 7.0. Stacker also gives you the ability to check the integrity of compressed drives, then display the compression ratio and other information about the drive. In general, word processing files compress to half their original size and spreadsheet files compress even more. Once a hard drive is compressed, the compression software automatically compresses data when it is written to the drive and decompresses it for use when it is read.

Padding

The technique of *padding* is used to disguise the volume and pattern of communications messages between points on, and between, networks. A great deal can be learned about an organization and its relationships through the study of its network message traffic; thus, padding is a useful safeguard. Since padding generates meaningless messages, efforts to de-encrypt it will produce useless information for network intruders. Padding does create additional traffic on a network and this should be considered before deciding to implement it to safeguard LAN and LAN-WAN data.

Lost in a Crowd

Burying sensitive information in great volumes of non-sensitive, or useless information is another safeguard method that is sometimes used to disguise and protect private data on a network. The theory is that wrongdo-ers, looking for useful private or sensitive data, would have to wade through such vast volumes of data that they would give up before they found anything of interest. On the other hand, the chance that an inno-cent person might come across meaningful or sensitive data by accident is considered by some to be an acceptable small risk. This is the attitude that allows organizations and individuals to leave highly vulnerable com-puters, with communications software installed (with autoanswer "on"), connected to modems, and turned on, ready to receive telecommunica-tions from any source.

CHAPTER 6

NETWORK DEPENDABILITY

*L*AN dependability encompasses elements of availability, reliability, integrity, accuracy, and privacy. Dependability permits users to rely on LANs as repositories for their valuable data, for their electronic message communications, and for application processing. Dependability is determined by factors such as these:

- How often the LAN "goes down," or becomes unexpectedly unavailable.
- How disruptive downtime is to users.
- How critical the LAN is perceived to be to the business.
- How adept the staff is at resolving problems, and restoring LAN services.

When LANs were in their infancy, no one expected them to be up and running all the time. This is not the case today. As the need for networking services and LAN applications grows, and mission-critical applications are moved to LAN platforms, there are a number of interesting side effects. The greater need for network applications to be available on demand has caused more effort and resources to be given to keeping LANs running. Because of this attention, LAN downtime, which averaged between three and four hours per week in 1991, was less than half of that per LAN as reported in 1993. As you would expect, the cost of LAN downtime is increasing—to more than $4 billion a year overall—and 3 percent of companies now report downtime losses of $1 million and more per hour. Downtime is less well-tolerated by all concerned.

While downtime statistics are a partial measure of LAN dependability, subjective factors, such as individual judgment and the importance and urgency attached to LAN-enabled processes (such as e-mail), are as significant as the statistics themselves. For instance, a LAN which maintains data vital to business operations and is the communications hub of the company will likely be perceived as unreliable if it is out of service for one or two hours a week due to unanticipated problems. On the other hand, a LAN that is down twice a week for four hours at a time may still be described as dependable, if no one is greatly inconvenienced by the downtime.

When LANs become essential to carrying out the missions of organizations, they deserve to be protected as vital assets. The true value of a LAN may far exceed the actual cost of the equipment and supporting activities. Organizations are starting to recognize that fact. Prudent steps should be taken to ensure that reliable service is available to meet organizational needs and user expectations throughout all life cycle stages in the development of a LAN. Managers should be alert to constantly changing networking needs, and to advances in technology that can increase LAN dependability.

Once a critical mass of applications (or even one sensitive or essential application) is installed, the security portfolio must be upgraded to incorporate new and appropriate safeguards. Backup and recovery requirements, for example, may differ greatly at LAN startup from what is required a few development stages later. The degree of availability, reliability, integrity, accuracy, and privacy that is required initially may bear little resemblance to the requirements that exist a few months after start-up. The five elements of dependability are outlined in the following chart.

ELEMENT	DESCRIPTION
Availability	The extent to which network services (applications, printing, e-mail, etc.) and data are fully operable. Loss of availability results from hardware or software processing faults (from any and all causes) that "crash" the system, damage data, or otherwise deny LAN services to users.
Reliability	The degree to which a LAN is expected to continue to provide service without data loss or other trouble. Loss of reliability results from failures that prevent the system from continuing to operate. Each hardware component has a reliability factor, *Mean Time Between Failures* (MTBF), which can be used to determine the composite expectation of failure for the LAN. Fault tolerant hardware and software may continue to operate, despite component failures, and may even self-correct to permit full system recovery with no loss of availability.
Integrity	The extent to which data is complete, sound, and reflects correct information, as intended. Loss of integrity would result from e-mail messages being dropped during a LAN utility procedure, or incorrect payroll data introduced by multiple users making concurrent updates without the protection of file locking, or incomplete processing by an untested file conversion program.

continued

ELEMENT	DESCRIPTION
	Software applications should be designed for use on LANs with data integrity safeguard features. LAN applications should incorporate internal system controls and production controls such as sample checking, record counts, and amount totals as necessary to ensure the integrity of the data they contain.
Accuracy	The correctness of data. Untested programs, lack of reasonability testing, or careless data entry may result in loss of accuracy in processing and in inaccurate data. Without attention to data accuracy and integrity, systems can be misleading or worthless. The cost of building accuracy into applications is far less than the cost of researching problems and correcting records once a system is operational. Application design should address data accuracy requirements. Production controls (such as record and change counts) and amount totals help to verify data accuracy.
Privacy	The degree to which confidentiality of information is maintained. Sensitive data about individuals, products, plans, and company trade secrets should be kept confidential. Access to confidential information should be restricted to those with a need to know, use, or see the data. When confidential information is compromised, the loss of privacy could result in significant financial loss or liability to an organization.

FIGURE 6.1   ELEMENTS OF **LAN** DEPENDABILITY.

Network Availability

The goal of network availability is to provide the greatest possible continuous operation of network facilities and services. To achieve that goal, it is necessary to identify the threats that are most likely to result in the loss of LAN service, and then determine how best to eliminate, neutralize, or minimize them. Statistics show that LANs are more often disrupted by a failure within the system than by any threat from outside the system and human error has been proven to be, by far, the greatest threat. Human error encompasses those errors introduced by users, administrators, and operators, and is also a component of some hardware and all software failures. Some aspects of minimizing human error are addressed in the chapter on managing threats.

Hardware Faults

Reducing the errors caused by hardware faults can significantly improve LAN availability, and in turn, dependability. Preventive maintenance, greater hardware fault tolerance, and improved service can reduce hardware failures. The push of competition and a focus on quality improvement by manufacturers has resulted in hardware evolution towards faster, more reliable, more maintainable, secure, fault tolerant, self-diagnosing and self-correcting products. Despite the improvements, hardware parts do wear out and electronic components do degrade, which can result in gradual performance slowdown or even a complete breakdown. Even the best quality hardware will wear out in time. LAN hardware failures seem to be attributable to the causes shown in Figure 6.2.

Cable and network connections (called drops) should be tested *before* their first use, rather than after a problem surfaces. Why wait until users are on-line and depend on network services to identify cable problems?

Testing installed cable is a tedious job at best, particularly when there are many drops and the organization is large. Installers tend to assume that everything works until they hear otherwise. They find it more cost-effective to let the customer check out the cable themselves by trying to use it than to test each line. When a drop does not work, the irate users let the LAN administrator know. It is not a good idea to put the testing burden on the users, unless there is a significant price differential between tested and untested LAN cable installations and it is the result of a conscious purchasing decision. If you are paying for tested cable installation, be sure the appropriate tests are actually performed.

CAUSE OF **LAN** HARDWARE FAILURES	
FAILURE CAUSE	**% OF FAILURES**
Network cabling	60-80%
Repeater	10-20%
Server disk drive	10-20%

FIGURE 6.2   CAUSES OF **LAN** HARDWARE FAILURES.

While cable installation and testing are too specialized for LAN managers to do the work themselves, they need to be able to specify how a cable plant should be installed, tested, and certified. They should understand the following:

■ What can and should be tested.

■ Which devices are most appropriate for conduction tests to identify common LAN wiring faults, symptoms of problems, or contributors to network media problems.

■ Appropriate testing procedures.

Your LAN testing plan might call for several tests on the cable plant before it is used. One test would certify the cable for use before it is installed, while still on the spool. Another test would certify the cable for networking use immediately after installation, while the vendors and installers are available to correct any problems which surface. Thorough pre-testing gives the LAN manager the right to dismiss many concerns about cabling and to have more overall confidence in the network. It also allows the manager to work with a shorter implementation checklist; one that primarily targets the server, applications, and LAN users.

Cabling Flaws

LANs should be tested and certified within standards and specifications, before the network is used to process or store vital information. Since cabling faults account for about 60 to 80 percent of downtime, it is the single most significant potential point of failure in a LAN. Although most cabling errors are found during network start-up, cable pre-testing and certification can entirely eliminate these errors and the associated implementation delays. Because the wiring drops are rarely pre-tested, cable fault statistics are unnecessarily high. The potential faults that should be eliminated through testing in copper-based Unshielded Twisted Pair (UTP) and Shielded Twisted Pair (STP) network cabling include:

- Broken cable
- Cable length in excess of specifications
- Split pairs
- Transposed pairs
- Crosstalk
- Open and short circuits
- Reverse polarity
- Impedance mismatches

Software Flaws

Despite efforts to completely eliminate flaws in the software development process, errors still occur in both commercial and custom designed products. Over time, as software is used in operational systems, errors are often encountered that were not apparent during testing. These flaws can create problems and exceptions for the operating systems to deal with, which, in turn, can cause a network failure.

Network Management Tools

Network management is like managing anything else; the problems you anticipate, and have solutions for, are going to be handled more smoothly and cause less disruption than the problems you have not even considered. Network management tools permit in-depth checking on such things as the utilization of LAN resources, such as server disk capacity and communications bandwidth, transmission delay, faults, error rates, analysis of network traffic, and user utilization. Problems, and potential problems, can be identified and corrected before the LAN fails or performance is so severely degraded that service is denied to users.

The importance of tools for monitoring the performance and operation of a LAN to maximize its availability cannot be exaggerated. Basic management tools are provided with every NOS. Once LAN managers recognize the need for pro-active LAN and server management, they generally look for more sophisticated, easier to use tools from third parties. When LANs were new, few such tools existed. Brightworks and Fresh Technologies provide useful utilities at the low end, and AT&T *Accumaster Integrator* and IBM *Netview* (based on expert system technology) are at the high end. Network management tools can also provide security, configuration, performance, and accounting management services and management information. A growing number of network monitoring and analysis tools are also available and are described in the chapters on LAN hardware and software.

Reliability

Network reliability, assuming the absence of external threats, is the degree to which we can expect the LAN to continue to deliver network services to users. To achieve the greatest reliability in protecting LAN data and delivering network services to users without interruption, the most trouble-free design and hardware and software must be chosen, expertly installed, and tested thoroughly. The goal is to create a LAN that meets the requirements of the business or organization, and will experience the fewest possible errors.

LAN hardware components have associated Mean Time Between Failure (MTBF) statistics that can help determine the overall reliability of a given configuration. When a LAN is new, network reliability can only be estimated from MTBF figures, and from statistics on existing networks with similar configurations and user populations. Older LANs have downtime statistics and history.

Using the failure rates of critical components, such as server disk drives, server disk drive controllers, and other elements, you can estimate how often a given LAN configuration should fail due to hardware problems. This information can be used to design and configure and to purchase reliable LAN components.

Integrity

To be of value, data in LAN applications should be complete and sound, reflecting correct information as intended by the authorized users and "owners" of the data. Loss of integrity would result from records or messages being lost or changed without authorization, as well as from simultaneous updates by multiple users without the protection of file locking, for example. Any fault in processing (whether from hardware, software, transmission, or human interaction) can cause data integrity errors, but most are actually caused by human error. Software applications designed for LANs should support the users who will access and update the same database, at the same time, by specifically protecting the integrity of LAN data with features such as record locking.

Computer-generated and manual production controls such as sample checking, record counts, and various totals are used to verify the integrity of computerized data within applications. LAN applications do not always have production controls. This may allow data integrity problems to occur and grow that are eventually reflected in application failures, system crashes, or faulty reports. The familiar saying, "garbage in, garbage out" applies to many systems installed without production controls.

Accuracy

LAN data accuracy can be compromised by many things including untested programs, lack of reasonability testing, poor application design, careless entry of data, and errors introduced during message transmission to name a few. Without attention to data accuracy and integrity, systems can be misleading and may even be worthless. The cost of building accuracy into applications is far less than the cost of researching problems and correcting data, once a system is operational. Application design should address data accuracy requirements. Production controls such as record and change counts and amount totals help to maintain and verify data accuracy.

Privacy

Users have the right to expect their data to be protected on a network to the same degree they would ensure its privacy while the information is within their own control. Data that a user keeps under lock and key should be made at least as secure on a network. Sensitive data about individuals, plans, products, and company trade secrets should be kept strictly confidential. Access should be limited to individuals with a need to know or use the data. Unfortunately, many of the six million LANs serving 70 million workstation connections in this country are still relatively unprotected. Interconnected networks, and LANs in particular, are the target of increasing numbers of penetrations and other network security disasters.

When confidential information is stolen, mishandled, or otherwise used by unauthorized persons, the loss of privacy may result in significant loss and liability to an organization. Therefore, privacy of LAN data should be addressed by the same risk management techniques that are applied to the other significant threats to the financial health and well-being of an organization. While all organizations are responsible for safeguarding confidential information, federal employees were given a mandate to protect the privacy of data in federal computers by the Privacy Act of 1974. The Privacy Act places civil and criminal penalties on failure to comply.

General all-around attention to LAN security is the best way to safeguard the privacy of information in your LAN and to prevent misuse, including access by unauthorized individuals.

Network Design Considerations

There are also numerous design choices which can improve LAN privacy. Client-server application design, in particular, fosters data privacy by limiting the movement of sensitive information across the network. Client-server design also centralizes user authentication, access rights, and other LAN security features at the server, which improves overall security and control. FiberOptic cable minimizes the possibility of privacy loss through passive or active wiretapping. Flat panel display screens and concentrations of equipment also reduce passive wiretap opportunities. Selecting the best quality, most fault tolerant equipment will minimize network downtime and result in a more dependable LAN. The following network design practices are recommended:

■ Design the network to minimize faults and downtime. Consider fiber optics, fault tolerant NOS, workstation operating system (WOS) and applications, fault tolerant server, workstations, client-server architecture, star-wired versus linear bus topology, etc.

■ Select essential network equipment with reliability as a high priority. The LAN server, hubs, bridges, routers, and interface cards should be chosen based on the expectation of reliable performance including high MTBF statistics, the manufacturer's reputation for products of superior quality, and timely service.

■ Ensure that network cabling, hardware, and software, meet reliability standards by examining manufacturer and testing laboratory specifications, and network testing and certification.

■ Anticipate common equipment failures and reduce expected downtime with performance monitoring, preventive maintenance, redundant equipment (where possible), spare parts availability, and efficient system recovery procedures for use in the event of a failure.

■ Use a UPS that filters current to the server and provides auxiliary battery backup power during brief shortages and outages and allow the NOS to shut the server down gracefully in extended power emergencies. This prevents loss of data and the need to perform time-consuming recovery procedures before resuming network processing.

■ Consider using a simple network management protocol (SNMP) agent on the server to manage the UPS.

■ Minimize software failures with software quality assurance, system change control procedures, managed network expansions and modifications, and network testing and recertification performed annually and after major network changes.

■ A *network interface card* (NIC) failure prevents a workstation from accessing the LAN until you replace it. These NICs are essential, but not critical, because LAN service can continue to all other workstations despite the failure of one card and NICs are easily replaced with spare parts. As with all other equipment choices, the more reliable your LAN interface cards, the fewer trouble calls and general overall disruption you experience on your LAN.

Backup, Restore, and Recovery

Sometimes I think Murphy's Law was written just for LANs. A small New Jersey laser cartridge re-manufacturing company suffered a major loss recently at the result of a very common problem. One of the partners set up their LAN and the backup system. They were highly computerized from the very beginning. All went smoothly until they moved and decided to change their network server at the same time. The last thing they did before the old server went out the door was to take a final backup. When they restored the backed-up data onto the new server they found they had no customer data at all. For three years they diligently ran their backup system and believed that their data was completely protected. Only a small portion of their data was being saved because the backup was set up incorrectly. They never tested the restore and did not know that their most important files were missing. Some of the data was recreated (at great expense) and some was lost forever. This business owner now knows how important it is to test backup and restore systems. It seems that the organizations that can least afford losses experience them all too often.

Copying the information stored on the server to a backup on tape or disk is the most fundamental safeguard available. Done correctly, it offers the greatest amount of protection at the least cost. Each provider of LAN Backup, Restore, and Recovery software has a unique process and set of terms. The restore process retrieves a file, directory, or all files directly from a backup tape or disk and copies it to the server (or other storage device).

Recovery may be complex compared to a simple restore. Full file backups may be followed by further incremental backups. These may have to be retrieved and restored in the order in which they were created. To restore one file backed up on tape you have to locate the file by searching an index or a physical tape.

The ultimate in backup systems is to have a totally redundant server that contains the same data as the primary server. The redundant server acts as a "hot spare," ready to go into service at any time. The only drawback to total redundancy is the cost and the need to keep two servers current. The protection does not extend to all disasters since fire would affect both co-located servers. The more usual and least expensive means of backing up server information is to use backup and restore software to copy server data to tape or disk backup files.

The Network Archivist (TNA)

Palindrome's TNA backup and recovery system has been relied on by LAN managers to protect NetWare LAN data for years. It takes control of the backup process and leaves little room for error on the part of the administrator, as long as there are no operational problems and the system is set up correctly in the first place. Once the administrator establishes backup requirements—such as attended versus unattended backups and backup frequency—TNA controls backup scheduling, full and incremental backups, and the rotation of backup tape sets off-site for disaster protection. The backup system is menu-driven, effective, and easy to use. It requires use of the Palindrome backup tape drive unit and 8 mm tape cartridges.

TNA's backup process is based on the Tower of Hanoi algorithm which cycles backup tapes continuously. Daily rotation of backup tapes, as opposed to weekly rotation, is designed to prevent the loss of more than one full day of data. This assumes, of course, that your onsite tapes are not damaged in an emergency. If your on-site tapes are damaged, you will have to go back to the most recent backup tape set stored offsite.

Daily rotation uses seven sets of tapes, cycling the oldest sets (A and B) every 64 days; the C set every 32 days; the D set every 16 days; the E set every eight days; the F set every four days; and the G set every other day. Additional tapes are requested by the system as the tapes fill up or fail. TNA distinguishes between tapes kept onsite and those kept offsite in a tape vault and notifies the administrator when to move tapes to and from the offsite "vault." You can schedule your own movement of tapes to the backup vault if you wish to lessen your risk of losing data in the event your onsite tapes are damaged. You can also take additional backups when you feel it is necessary.

TNA is also fairly complicated, not completely documented, and not entirely intuitive. You can lose valuable backup data—not to mention the physical backup tape itself—if the backup process is interrupted or an error occurs during backup processing. An untrained administrator can lose data when trying to restore or recover files. File recovery is complicated and administrators should be knowledgeable before attempting it. Product training is offered by Palindrome.

Cheyenne ARCserve

Cheyenne ARCserve is a software-only backup system that is certified by Novell for use with NetWare LANs. It is also supported for use on Compaq-installed 5.0 GB *Digital Audio Tape* (DAT) drives on the new *ProLiant* servers. The Cheyenne system has both DOS and Windows versions, is easy to use, and does not limit your choice of backup media or hardware. Parallel streaming allows up to seven tape drives to operate at the same time for rapid backups and handles backup for DOS, Windows, OS/2, UNIX, and Macintosh LAN workstations.

Checkpoint, Recovery, and Restart

A checkpoint functions like a backup in that it is a copy of data which can be used to return to an established point of system integrity after a fatal processing error has occurred. Reestablishing integrity in distributed systems after a failure is especially difficult because multiple people may be changing databases at the same time. If no changes were made after the last checkpoint, the data can be restored to the checkpoint and the system can simply be restarted.

When data updates occur *after* a checkpoint is taken, intended changes may be in various stages of completion and it is difficult to tell which transactions were completed and which were not. Making the changes over again can result in different results than had occurred the first time. Mainframe DataBase Management Systems (DBMSs) protect data by taking checkpoints and recording subsequent transactions on a log tape. When errors occur and recovery is required, the checkpoint is used to return the system to a point before the error occurred and a utility program reapplies all transactions in the order in which they were originally applied. Some manual work may still be required to apply updates in progress when the error occurred. This will reestablish the integrity of the system and permit processing to continue. The technical staff generally handles the recovery of the data from the computer files. It is the responsibility of the production control group or knowledgeable end users to determine what changes were in the pipeline and to complete the data recovery process.

Data Recovery in LANs

LAN NOSs do not require log tapes, thus transactions in progress when a fatal error occurs must be backed out by the NOS to maintain data integrity. The *Transaction Tracking System* (TTS) performs this function in NetWare.

Trend Towards IS Control of LAN Backups

With the growing size and complexity of LANs, backups have assumed greater importance to the point where the search for better methods and tools has been given to the corporate Information Systems group in many organizations. There are a great many backup options available but some take too much administration time and give inadequate protection. One possible solution is to use mainframe computer resources to back up enterprise-wide LANs in a fast and efficient manner. The mainframe alternative offers significant benefits such as folding LAN backup into the existing secure mainframe computer operations environment. It might also make backed-up files virtually instantly retrievable. Considering the amount of time and resources spent on backing up on each separate LAN, (and worrying about backups and restoring data) this is an exciting and appealing solution for enterprise LANs and other large, interconnected LANs.

Backup Strategy

Despite variations in backup platform and product offerings, an effective backup strategy should incorporate the following points:

■ Back up servers daily, taking additional backups when extensive database changes occur (such as addition of applications).

■ Take additional precautions with vital data by making an additional copy of essential files on workstation hard drives, floppy diskettes, or another medium.

■ Do not wait for an emergency to verify that files can be recovered from backups. If you cannot recover valuable data from backups or a hard disk in an emergency, try an expert data recovery service such as Ontrack Data Recovery.

■ Choose workstation-based backup rather than server-based backup, so you can retrieve backup data even when the server is down.

■ Secure the backup workstation to prevent interruption of backup processes that can result in the loss of backup data, and protect the data (remember backup software has complete access to LAN data).

■ Administrators should be thoroughly competent with recovery procedures before vital data is stored on the LAN.

■ Schedule backups during off-hours to avoid file contention (files which are in use are open and a file backup should not be attempted at that time).

■ Supplemental backups intended to capture a particular file should be run when that file is not in use.

■ Use the NOS file recovery utility for immediate restoration of accidentally deleted files, before resorting to the time-consuming process of file recovery from backup tapes.

Unscheduled downtime always causes some inconvenience to end users. The least amount of disruption can be provided by a completely redundant system, but few applications are important enough to justify the expense.

There are several options you can consider to gain some of the benefits of redundancy, without incurring all of the costs. If a given application runs from the server, data that is exclusively in the LAN (and in backup files) is unretrievable when the LAN is down. However, if you have another server, or can run the backup software elsewhere, you can still recover files. Even then, it can take considerable time to locate the file you need and retrieve the data. (A good time estimate for retrieving files can be developed when you test your recovery procedures.) If the need for the backed-up data is too urgent to delay processing, you should consider alternatives such as making the system available on another platform. Another shortcut is backing up the file to a hard disk, floppy diskettes, CD-ROM, or Bernoulli drive, attached to LAN workstation to ensure immediate availability of the data. Regardless of the method used, you need to verify that the backups are being created as planned.

 CD-ROM is a stable, uncorruptible storage medium for data and is often used to store large quantities of important software.

However important, data is only part of the story. You need application software to process the data, and LAN applications do not always lend themselves to operation on stand-alone PCs. The application designer may have considered the urgency of your processing and used a standard file format that can be used with COTS (commercial off-the-shelf) software such as dBASE III, Lotus 1-2-3, or other software that does not require a LAN. If your application is completely proprietary, and the files cannot be processed by off-the-shelf or workstation-based software, you must rely on standard LAN recovery procedures. Ideally, you will have LAN recovery procedures from contingency planning for emergency where all concerned parties had an opportunity to express urgent application processing time constraints and other processing requirements.

Retrieving Files From Backups

Just because you backed up your server doesn't mean you have instant access to the individual directories and files on the backup tapes. Backup files are usually compressed and are useless until they are decompressed by the corresponding restore or recovery program. There are many steps involved in recovering files from LAN backups. If your backup/recovery system requires a LAN then you must have a functional LAN operating system to execute your retrieval software. Another LAN may be used retrieve your files, but your procedures must work on the system you plan to use.

Sometimes subtle differences between systems can render existing procedures useless, which is why testing your recovery procedures is so important. You may have to set up special access privileges, directories, software, and procedures on your alternate LAN to permit rapid file recovery. After getting set up on a compatible, functional LAN, you must find the version of the file you wish to retrieve in the backup file directory or index. You may need to go to the last full backup and apply any partial backups containing changes made since the full backup copy was taken.

Fault Tolerance

System failures are expensive, time-consuming, and stressful and should be avoided wherever possible. Assuming that both hardware and software contain flaws which will result in failures, manufacturers are creating essential LAN components that continue to operate, while avoiding the errors that they can anticipate. This characteristic is called fault tolerance. Fault tolerant components have the ability to accept and handle faults so that they can continue to operate, rather than hand off an error message or error code, and crash.

Fault tolerance allows systems to suffer malfunctions without the loss of data or termination of processing normally associated with such an error. There are several levels of hardware and software fault tolerance. The primary hardware method employed is redundancy (or duplication). One kind of redundancy is duplication of data on multiple storage devices. So, if one storage device fails, you may access the data from the other device. This protects the data and also allows the system to continue to function. Without fault tolerant features, the system would lose access to the data and processing could not continue, which might bring down the server.

A system crash typically requires technical experts to spend considerable time to determine the cause of the problem before hardware repair technicians can correct the problem. The data files and applications must be restored to a point before the error occurred. End users often spend more hours re-doing lost work. Too often errors in judgment or data entry occur during the data recovery process, introducing errors that will compromise data integrity and plague the system in the future.

The components that are most likely to fail should be the most highly fault tolerant. Fault tolerance is costly in terms of the engineering that goes into trapping and managing errors. As a result, the most fault tolerant products are often the highest priced. Compaq LAN servers and Novell NetWare operating systems are examples of products that have received a warm welcome in the marketplace. These products offer effective fault tolerant features that increase LAN dependability at off-the-shelf prices. They are used to illustrate desirable safeguard features. NetWare's many fault tolerant features are discussed in the chapter on LAN software. Likewise, Compaq server features are treated in the chapter covering LAN hardware.

After cabling errors in new wiring, most LAN hardware failures are in hard disks, then in the power supply that keeps electricity flowing to the components. Redundant cabling is rare because of the great expense involved. UPS devices are used on most servers but other essential components may have no power protection at all.

Some examples of fault tolerant features are:

■ **Topology**—The star-wired LAN topology is somewhat fault tolerant in that the network can continue to function even if one workstation has a cable failure.

■ **NOS**—NetWare offers disk mirroring, disk duplexing, redundant directories, and read-after-write with Hot Fix to identify and mark bad blocks on a server's hard disk, all of which allow processing to continue despite disk errors.

■ **Server**—The Compaq SystemPro server has complimentary features such as disk mirroring and disk duplexing that help to identify and manage hardware faults. The Compaq servers also offer dual processor capability that some NOSs cannot yet use.

Hardware manufacturers have made great strides in developing fault tolerant units. Just as you might choose to have an extra hard disk drive on hand as a replacement for a failed LAN workstation drive, server manufacturers incorporate redundant parts in their equipment. With redundancy, when a hard drive fails, the server doesn't always crash because of the fault. The server management software (firmware) manages the problem and keeps the server operating, although sometimes at a slower pace, while it attempts to recover. The exact sequence of events depends on the precise error and the server's design. Generally, the data is protected first by recovering it and writing it to a safe drive or area on disk, then the malfunction is addressed. If the recovery is successful, the disk drive eventually comes back online as efficiently as before. Throughout all of this, the users may be unaware that a problem has occurred.

Some of the fault tolerant features available on server hardware are:

FEATURE	DESCRIPTION
Disk Mirroring	Disk mirroring is writing data to two disk drives on the same channel simultaneously, creating "mirror image" copies that operate interchangeably in the event of a hardware failure. If the original hard disk fails, the duplicate disk takes over automatically. You can implement disk mirroring in hardware or in NOS software. Given a choice between implementing a solution in hardware or software, the hardware fix is usually the better choice, since a software solution adds to the processing burden on the server and may reduce performance. *continued*

Feature	Description
Disk Duplexing	Requires duplicating data on two disk drives (on separate communications channels) simultaneously. Disk writes made to the original disk are also made to the second disk. If the original disk or channel fails, the duplicate disk takes over automatically. This provides more protection than disk mirroring at the cost of an additional channel device.
Hot Disk Spare	Disk controller switches to the spare disk automatically when a disk drive fails.
RAID Data Guarding	Redundant Arrays of Inexpensive Disks (RAID) offer six levels of data protection and performance enhancement through *data striping* (writing data across an array of disk drives rather than to one drive), error correction, and data management.
Multiple Processors	Provide backup in case a processor fails. Redundant processors permit streamlining of many processor tasks (with NOS support).
Mirrored Redundant Servers	Servers provide the ultimate in hardware fault tolerance, since the secondary server is switched into service when the primary server fails and the failure is completely transparent to the users. This is the most fail-safe protection available for LANs. It is also costly to implement because you need to purchase, operate, and maintain two of everything.

continued

FEATURE	DESCRIPTION
NOS FAULT TOLERANT FEATURES	
Software Record Locking	Prevents two or more users from writing simultaneously to the same record. Record locking is essential to integrity in multi-user applications that are updated by more than one person at a time.
Directory Verification	A feature that protects data from failures in network hardware. Each time the server is turned on, the NOS performs a consistency check on duplicate sets of directory and file allocation tables, to verify that the two copies are identical.
Hot Fix	A small portion of hard disk storage space is designated as a Hot Fix redirection area. Hot Fix redirects the data in the bad block to the Hot Fix redirection area. Hot Fix marks the defective block as bad, so the server will not attempt to store data at that location, and swaps in spares from a reserve section of the hard disk.
Read-After-Write	A hardware verification feature that protects against loss as a result of server hard disk and network hardware failures. When the NOS writes data to a block on the hard disk, it reads back the data and compares it to the original still in memory. If the data matches, the NOS releases the data in memory. If the data does not match, Hot Fix marks that block on the disk as bad and redirects the data to another location on the drive.

continued

FEATURE	DESCRIPTION
UPS Monitoring	A NOS feature that protects data from failures in network hardware. A UPS hardware unit provides power to the server during power fluctuations and outages. A monitoring feature monitors the status of the UPS attached to the server. This is done to ensure that the UPS is operating correctly and is ready to take over if needed.
Transaction Tracking System (TTS) *(Novell Trademark)*	A Novell Netware feature that protects data from failures in network hardware. TTS protects the integrity of databases by backing out incomplete (TTS) transactions that result from a failure in a network component.
Directory Structure Duplication	A feature that protects data from failures in network hardware. A hard disk directory and file allocation table (FAT) contain the file address needed to store and retrieve data. The NOS maintains copies of both the directory table and the file allocation table on separate areas of the hard disk. If the primary copy is lost or destroyed, the secondary copy is available.

Maximizing Dependability

Downtime is the most common type of loss relative to LANs. To increase dependability, it is necessary to decrease network downtime. The most economical step in reducing downtime and protecting LANs is to implement NOS-supplied security. The Chairman of the International Computer Security Association (ICSA) has estimated that 90 percent of NetWare users have not implemented its security features.

Additional steps that will ensure the greatest possible network availability and dependability are:

- Design the network to minimize predictable network faults and resulting downtime.

- Document hours of network operation with specific off-peak hours dedicated to system maintenance and routine activities. System maintenance includes backups, system expansions, upgrades, new hardware or software testing that may affect the LAN as a whole, and utilities designed to optimize server performance. Routine activities include scheduled and ad-hoc file downloads and other high-volume data transfers.

- Manage network resources to provide service and support during specified hours.

- Ensure that network cabling, hardware and software meet reliability standards through initial testing and certification and after every significant network expansion and modification.

- Anticipate equipment failures with performance monitoring, preventative maintenance, efficient system recovery procedures, and parts availability.

- Segregate user groups into separate LANs (use bridges to connect) to localize heavy traffic between nodes. Accommodate special networking requirements such as extra security, and make the LAN more reliable and easier to troubleshoot and maintain.

- Use intelligent hubs for built-in user-friendly network management of hubs, bridges, routers, and network interface cards across interconnected LANs.

- Anticipate power problems and other disorders, to reduce downtime and probability of data loss by using a power filtering UPS with battery power for short power outages and to permit orderly shutdown.

- Minimize software failures with quality assurance, system change controls, managed network expansions and modifications, and network testing and recertification performed annually and after major network changes.

■ Routinely back up file servers and secure file backups and documentation onsite and offsite.

■ Restore data from backup files when necessary.

■ Schedule high-volume transmissions, such as file transfers, during hours of non-peak usage.

■ Employ secure dial-in to thwart network crackers.

■ Route bulletin board downloads and inward transfers through a stand-alone PC for virus control.

■ Devise contingency plans for disaster recovery and continuity of operations, including offsite storage of backup files, plans and documentation, an alternative processing site, and LAN contingency team preparedness.

The other chapters, particularly those on LAN hardware, software, and managing threats contain information on safeguard products and practical suggestions which you can use to increase the overall dependability of your LAN.

CHAPTER 7

RISK
ASSESSMENT

R isk assessment balances the losses that can be expected to occur from LAN security incidents against the cost of appropriate safeguards, defenses, and countermeasures. In risk assessment, expected loss figures are calculated and attached to given threats. Those expected losses are then compared to the cost of implementing preventative measures. As a general rule, if a preventive measure is significantly less costly than the loss it will prevent, then it should be implemented.

Who is Responsible for Risk Assessment?

The task of securing LANs is an extremely difficult one and the responsibility is not always clearly defined. Although it may not be explicitly stated in their job descriptions, the responsibility for the security of their networks—as well as any related security plan or assessment of risks—usually rests entirely with the LAN manager. Unfortunately, the issue of responsibility may not be raised at all until a major problem occurs. Security is such a troublesome and unpopular aspect of managing valuable assets that it is tempting to ignore it in the hope that trouble will never occur. Because security has been ignored for so long, many LANs are now seriously at risk.

Justifying Safeguards

In organizations that are enlightened about security issues, it is relatively easy to justify sensible LAN defenses and safeguards. The LAN manager is encouraged to be alert to the constant evolution of threats, defenses, countermeasures, and safeguard products. In this case, risk assessment can be used to ensure the greatest possible return on the total investment in LAN security, rather than as a means of justifying every safeguard expenditure.

However, the more common situation is a profound lack of appreciation of security needs beyond basic virus protection and the use of passwords to protect against unauthorized LAN users. Indeed the lack of demand for computer and communications security products, particularly in the private sector, is generally attributable to ignorance of security risks and available safeguards. Organizations which are negligent must be vigorously educated and persuaded to protect their networks and be warned about the costs and consequences if they fail to do so. LAN managers are often required to prepare a justification for the safeguards they consider essential to the protection of their LANs. Justification of appropriate safeguards is traditionally accomplished through a process of formal risk assessment and analysis.

Risk Assessment Skills

Risk assessment is probably the least exercised of all the LAN management tasks and skills. It is more complicated and demanding than the cost-justifications LAN managers routinely prepare for LAN expansions and upgrades. Conducting a risk assessment, and preparing justification packages for LAN safeguards, is quite a time consuming activity. The methods required are usually outside the range of activities the LAN manager easily performs. The subject is largely avoided by the popular PC and LAN trade publications LAN managers rely on for guidance on important network issues, as well as insight into LAN management roles and responsibilities. As a result, risk assessment methods are virtually unavailable to LAN managers, except in seminars and through the use of management consulting services.

However, let me assure you that the only security project your organization will profit from more than risk assessment is the preparation of the security plan itself.

Another benefit of a formal risk assessment process is that any attention your organization gives to the security aspects of the LAN will raise the level of security consciousness accordingly.

How Formal Should Risk Assessment Be?

There are variations on the risk assessment and safeguard selection theme. Some network security professionals are so knowledgeable about the threats, associated risks, and effective safeguards that a formal risk assessment would be redundant and would simply document ongoing risk assessment activities. Without a great depth of experience in this area, the typical LAN manager would do well to err on the side of being too formal and thorough, rather than risk drawing incorrect conclusions and making poor decisions. Imagine how much confidence you would place in a physician who based diagnosis and treatment on intuition or how you looked, rather than on thorough medical history and tests, drawing on extensive training and expertise to analyze the results.

Risk Assessment Simplified

The mechanics of risk assessment are fairly complicated. An over-simplification permits risk assessment to be viewed as a six-part process. The six essential parts are:

1. Determining system vulnerabilities and threats.

2. Determining the cost of a single loss.

3. Extending the cost of one loss by the probability of the loss occurring in a given time period.

4. Ordering the resulting expected total exposure amounts for evaluation purposes.

5. Establishing the cost of safeguards.

6. Selecting the set of safeguards that afford the greatest protection at the least cost.

Pitfalls

Any model or system is only as sound as the estimates, figures, and judgments that are fed into it. The following pitfalls can cause inaccuracies in the process that will then produce distorted results. This misinformation leads to erroneous conclusions and poor decisions. Pitfalls to avoid are:

■ Relying on safeguard vendors to assess your risks. Vendors may have a bias towards their own products. They may overemphasize the risks addressed by their safeguards downplaying other more significant risks that their products do not address.

■ Statistics on the likelihood of threats occurring can vary considerably by geographic area, business size, demographics, and other factors. Threat statistics are an essential element of the risk assessment process, but inaccuracies in probability may cause excessive protection against certain threats, at the expense of inadequate protection against others.

■ Use of rash estimates and wild guesses in place of sound threat probability and loss statistics for your area, business type, size, industry, strategic importance, sensitivity, etc. Statistics should be obtained from several different sources, such as from the reference section of a large library, and several insurance companies to provide a sound basis for analysis, comparison, related estimates, and decision-making.

■ Allowing previous choices of safeguards, defenses, and counter-measures, which may already be in place, to affect the outcome of the risk assessment process.

Selecting Resources

Many vendors, methodologies, consultants, CPAs, and software packages are available to assist you in assessing the vulnerability of your LAN. A few of these resources are described in this chapter.

The LANs in America are now seriously at risk because so many of us have ignored security for so long. The very ability of your business to continue may depend on the outcome of the risk assessment and safe-guard selection process. Regardless of the process you decide to follow, consider involving a number of security-aware individuals. For one thing, it has been amply demonstrated that better decisions are made by groups than by individuals. Thus, it is preferable to have the responsibility for security decisions and choices shared among capable decision-makers.

How This Chapter Will Help

This chapter gets at the root of the problem and addresses the processes and techniques required to complete risk assessment of a given LAN. It covers the following "how-tos."

■ Identify the risks to the organization associated with operation of the LAN.

■ Quantify the losses that will result from the disruption of LAN operations, destroyed or damaged or illegally disclosed LAN assets, including sensitive data.

■ Determine the expected number of losses from each threat (that is, the probability of a loss occurring).

■ Assess the vulnerability of assets and processes based on their sensitivity, their intrinsic value to the organization, the nature of the threats against them and the culture of the organization.

■ Establish the asset and business process replacement cost.

■ Determine the advantage and cost effectiveness of employing particular safeguards, defenses, and countermeasures.

Steps in Risk Assessment

Risk assessment involves the following eleven steps which are described in detail throughout the remainder of this chapter. They are:

1. Establish vulnerabilities.

2. Identify potential threats to the network.

3. Quantify the chance that a loss will occur from each threat.

4. Calculate the dollar amount of a typical loss for each threat.

5. Calculate the total loss risk by the formula:

   Risk = Loss potential x Probability (that a loss will occur)

6. Calculate your risk premium amount.

7. Order the risks from low (acceptable) to high (unacceptable).

8. Categorize and rate safeguards, defenses, and countermeasures.

9. Identify and select the safeguards, defenses, and countermeasures for each threat.

10. Establish the cost of implementing safeguards, defenses, and countermeasures.

11. Select the set of safeguards, defenses, and countermeasures that provide the greatest benefit to the organization for the least cost.

The risk assessment process is described in detail and spreadsheets are used to illustrate and present useful information and perform the calculations.

Establish Vulnerabilities

Vulnerability is the degree to which data, a system, or a network is at risk. Because a LAN is only as secure as its weakest link, a LAN's vulnerability is the total of all of its sensitive, critical, valuable, unsecured data, systems, applications, transmissions, and communications components. The sensitivity and value of data is the single most important aspect of determining the vulnerability of an application or network. Critical data if damaged or disclosed, would impair the company's ability to continue, conduct, and remain in business.

Sensitive data is data which must be protected and safeguarded because it is:

■ Private information about individuals which is not readily available to the public, such as their name and social security number, or their medical or financial history.

■ Proprietary or trade secret data protected by the Trade Secrets Act.

■ Data that, if disclosed, could cause loss, harm, or otherwise adversely affect an organization or individual.

■ Damage, loss or disclosure of valuable data would likely have a negative effect on the bottom line.

Application systems that contain or process financial, private, or otherwise sensitive data, such as a payroll, are considered to be sensitive applications. Data that is not sensitive in its own right may become sensitive when combined with other data in a display, report, or database. For example, a list of names in a file is not sensitive, nor is a list of social security numbers, nor a list of salaries. However, when elements of these three separate files are combined to create a report, display, or new database the result may be a sensitive view of data.

Vulnerabilities are diminished when the following characteristics apply:

■ A unit "owns" and has responsibility for specific data.

■ Data is non-sensitive.

■ Adequate controls exist.

■ No maximum tolerable downtime applies.

■ The loss potential is minimal.

■ No network interconnections exist.

 When an individual or group has a vested interest in certain data, say the way the marketing group is concerned about the marketing plan, they usually want to create, store, manage, control, report, and disseminate the data. In short, they agree to "own" the data, although it may reside on the LAN and many groups may access it. Without a good plan, the marketing department might not perform very well, thus it is in their interest to manage and protect it well.

The following definitions are guidelines for completing your Network Vulnerabilities table. A sample is given in Table 7.1.

■ Data Responsibility belongs to the organization and/or individual who created the data, or now "owns" and is responsible for its maintenance, accuracy, and integrity.

■ Data Sensitivity ranges from 0 (not sensitive) to 3 (maximum sensitivity).

■ Adequate Controls range from 0 (no controls) to 3 (adequate controls) and reflect the adequacy of specific controls in effect on the system, such as automated record counts, hash totals, batch totals for daily updates, etc. (Attach a list if necessary.).

■ Max Downtime is the maximum amount of time the users can do without the system, regardless of the cause of a system failure.

TABLE 7.1 NETWORK VULNERABILITIES.

ASSET (SYSTEM OR DATA)	DATA RESPONSIBILITY	DATA SENSITIVITY	ADEQUATE CONTROLS	MAX DOWNTIME
Time & Attendance				
E-Mail, Calendars				
Budgets				
Word Processing				
Directories/Locator				
Strategic Plans				
Training DB				
Network Server, software, hardware, and network components				

Refer to your Network Vulnerabilities chart, as necessary, throughout the risk assessment process.

Identify Potential Threats

It is essential to be clear about the dangers you are protecting your LAN against. Typical potential threats against the LAN are any acts, events, or people that have the potential to:

■ Destroy, harm, misdirect, or misuse LAN assets.

■ Compromise the security, privacy, integrity, reliability, or availability of data, equipment, or services.

■ Otherwise disrupt normal LAN operations.

You can begin by using the information in this chapter to identify and list the realistic threats against your LAN. Then carefully consider your environment, system and telecommunication architecture, requirements, business importance and strategy, culture, staff, geographic location, and other pertinent factors, adding additional threats and removing those that do not apply to your LAN.

Some typical threats to LANs are listed in Table 7.2.

TABLE 7.2   TYPICAL THREATS TO LANS.

■ Accidents	■ Hardware fault
■ Building damage or collapse	■ Power (loss, surge, spike, sag, etc.)
■ Disgruntled employee	
■ Dishonest employee	■ Sabotage
■ Earthquake	■ Smoke
■ Employee error	■ Software error
■ Espionage (industrial/ national)	■ Tap
	■ Theft
■ Extreme heat or cold	■ Virus (other rogue program)
■ Fire	■ Water (flood)
■ Fraud	■ Weather (storm, wind, ice)
■ Hacker penetration	

Indicate the Chance That a Loss Will Occur

For each threat, indicate the likelihood that the threat will result in a loss occurring within the period addressed by the risk assessment. Probabilities for organizations similar to yours in your geographic area may be available in the form of actuarial tables from your insurance company, or the reference desk of a large library. Enter the loss probabilities as a percentage, as shown in Table 7.3. For example, if every year a fire occurs in one out of ten companies which have characteristics similar to your company, then you can expect to have a fire every ten years. Although you might have a fire at any time, the risk of having a fire in any one year is one in ten, or ten percent. The probability that the loss will occur within the risk assessment period of one year should be expressed as ".1" in the spreadsheet.

The probabilities shown in Table 7.3 and the spreadsheets in this chapter are for illustration only. They have no validity and *must not be used* for actual risk assessment purposes.

TABLE 7.3   PROBABILITY OF LOSS FROM THREATS TO THE LAN.

THREAT	PROBABILITY	THREAT	PROBABILITY
Employee error	.42	Power (loss, surge, spike, sag, etc.)	.07
Software	.38	Hacking	.06
Hardware	.20	Virus	.05
Accidents	.17	Smoke	.03
Fraud	.11	Weather (storm, wind)	.01
User error	.11	Earthquake	.002
Dishonest employee	.11	Building damage or collapse	.001
Disgruntled employee/sabotage	.11	Theft	.27
Fire	.10		
Water/flood	.10		

Calculate the Dollar Amount of a Typical Loss

Calculate the dollar amount of a typical loss for each threat, including applicable costs for:

- Replacement, repair, and refurbishment.

- Lost revenues.

- Lost business opportunity costs.

- Emergency services, including additional coordination and public relations needs.

- Alternate LAN site and facilities.

- Specialists and temporary staffing.

- Restoration, recovery, re-entry or re-acquisition of data.

- Re-establishment of data integrity.

- Resumption of normal operations.

Your insurance company may be able to provide you with figures to help you estimate typical losses for each possible incident.

You can expect to have many small losses for every major loss, and that should be reflected in the probability figures you are using. To illustrate the calculation of a typical loss, take the case of a fire that starts in a faulty electrical switch and destroys the server and the server room. Assume that all significant costs of the incident, including the costs of LAN downtime and other elements of the loss, are as shown in Figure 7.3. "Lost revenue" includes lost business opportunities and "Recover data" includes reestablishing data integrity. Assume we have arranged for the use of a fully-equipped "Hot Site" for temporary LAN operations for the time it takes to completely restore LAN operations.

Calculate typical loss figures for each of the threats that you have identified. This is difficult but becomes easier as each threat is considered, since many figures—such as the cost to replace the server, or the daily expected lost revenues—need to be computed only once. The most difficult tasks are identifying all potential costs, and arriving at the expected daily loss of revenue and business opportunity cost figures. The lost revenue and opportunity costs should be obtained from your risk management, business operations, or financial executives. If your organization has a risk management function your task will be easier, because much of the information you require will already be available.

| TYPICAL LOSS COMPUTATION SPREADSHEET | | | | | |
	PER DAY	NO. DAYS	ONE-TIME EXPENDITURE	SERVICES	TOTAL LOSS AMOUNT
Lost revenue/ opportunity	80,000	4	73,000		$393,000
Hot Site expense	15,000	10		2,000	$152,000
Relocate to Hot Site	1,100	10	7,000	1,500	$19,500
Recover data			24,000	2,300	$26,300
New server			55,000	6,000	$61,000
Prepare new facility			92,000		$92,000
Return operations			5,500		$5,500
Total					$398,500

FIGURE 7.1   TYPICAL LOSS COMPUTATION SPREADSHEET.

Calculate Total Expected Loss

Calculate the total expected loss for each threat by extending the typical loss potential for one occurrence (from Step 3), times the expectation, or probability, that the loss will occur in the period.

Enter the typical total expected loss figures into your Total Risk Calculation Spreadsheet in the Typical Loss column. Your spreadsheet should automatically calculate the Total Risk amount for each threat. The Total Risk is the loss you can expect as a result of taking no action at all. Figure 7.2 illustrates the calculation of the total losses that can be expected to occur within the risk assessment period, in this case, one year.

Calculate Your "Risk Premium" Amount

This additional "risk premium" amount represents the premium an organization would pay to avoid the negative outcomes you would anticipate if your business were shutdown for a significant period of time. The negative outcomes of failure to protect valuable LAN assets resulting in a significant loss may include:

■ Adverse publicity.

■ Criticism from stockholders and the public.

■ Embarrassment.

■ Loss of reputation and goodwill.

■ Loss of revenues.

■ Loss of new business.

■ Undue trauma to employees and related stress disorders.

■ An opportunity to introduce new errors in data and processes.

■ Damages and/or lawsuits resulting from disclosure of private, proprietary, or harmful data.

THREAT	PROBABILITY LOSS	LOSS RISK	TYPICAL TOTAL
Employee error	0.42	750,000	315,000
Software	0.38	750,000	285,000
Theft	0.27	400,000	108,000
Hardware	0.2	400,000	80,000
Accidents	0.17	50,000	8,500
Fraud	0.11	100,000	11,000
Dishonest employee	0.11	100,000	11,000
Disgruntled employee/sabotage	0.11	750,000	82,500
Fire	0.11	500,000	150,000
Flood/water	0.1	1,000,000	100,000
Power loss, surge, etc.	0.07	50,000	3,500

continued

THREAT	PROBABILITY LOSS	LOSS RISK	TYPICAL TOTAL
Hacker	0.06	750,000	45,000
Virus (rogue program)	0.05	750,000	37,500
Smoke	0.03	750,000	22,500
Weather (storm, wind, ice)	0.01	1,000,000	10,000
Earthquake	0.002	1,000,000	2,000
Building damage/collapse	0.001	1,500,000	1,500

FIGURE 7.2   TOTAL RISK CALCULATION SPREADSHEET.

The risk premium percent is a multiplier for the total expected loss and is used to calculate the total expected loss amount with a risk premium amount added. The result should appear in the Lost Risk Premium Amount column.

You should use this additional factor to show your organization's desire to avoid the adverse effects of a security incident, including possible criticism from stockholders and the public for failing to take prudent action to prevent such losses. The size of the risk premium percent will depend upon parameters that include: the sensitivity of your executives, the strategic importance of your business and industry, the needs of your customers, your corporate image and culture, and the like.

Use a factor of 1.9 for extreme sensitivity to risk and reduce the factor to 1.0 for no sensitivity at all.

If there is no sensitivity (a 1.0 Risk Premium Percent) to loss from threats against your LAN, then the only consideration in avoiding or minimizing threats is the expectation of monetary loss, and a desire to avoid stressing the employees involved.

Your insurance company may add surcharges for the lack of generally accepted security and safety precautions and might give discounts if your assets are well-protected. If that is the case, you can use this risk premium percent to make adjustments for insurance incentives and surcharges.

Threat	Loss Probability	Typical Loss	Total Risk	Risk Premium %	Lost Risk Premium	Safeguard, Defense, or Countermeasure	Rating	Cost	Safeguard Advantage
Employee error	0.42	750,000	315,000	1.3	409,500	Security training	0.50	62,000	300,250
						Security plan, program	0.45	120,000	242,250
Software	0.38	750,000	285,000	1.3	370,500	Change control	0.20		
Theft	0.27	400,000	108,000	1.3	140,400	Equipment lockdown	0.99		
						Building security	0.60		
Hardware	0.20	400,000	80,000	1.3	11,050	Fault tolerant server features	0.85	20,000	136,400
Accidents	0.17	50,000	8,500	1.3	11,050	Safety and security training	0.75	10,000	4,662
Fraud	0.11	100,000	11,000	1.6	17,600	Good accounting system and management controls*	0.98		
						Controlled physical access	0.30		
						User authentication**	0.30		
Dishonest employee	0.11	100,000	11,000	1.3	14,300	Good management controls* (especially pre-employment screening, security-aware supervision)	0.75		
Disgruntled employee/sabotage	0.11	750,000	82,500	1.3	107,250	Good management controls* (especially management systems and supervision)	0.75		
Fire	0.10	1,500,000	150,000	1.3	200,000	Fire, heat, smoke alarm	0.80		
						Fire suppressant	0.60		
Flood/water	0.10	1,000,000	100,000	1.3	130,000	Safe location and building	0.75		

THREAT	LOSS PROBABILITY	TYPICAL LOSS	TOTAL RISK	RISK PREMIUM %	LOST RISK PREMIUM	SAFEGUARD, DEFENSE, OR COUNTERMEASURE	RATING	COST	SAFEGUARD ADVANTAGE
Power loss, surge, etc.	0.07	50,000	3,500	1.3	4,550	Moisture alarm	0.50		
						UPS and UPS management software	0.99	450	3,050
Hacker	0.06	750,000	45,000	1.3	58,500	User authentication**	0.85		
						Password generator	0.50		
						Secure dial-in for remote users	0.95		
						LAN monitoring and management software with break-in detection	0.25		
Virus (rogue program)	0.05	750,000	37,5000	1.3	48,750	Virus protection software	0.75		
						Security-aware management systems and security training	0.90		
Smoke	0.03	750,000	22,500	1.3	29,250	Fire, heat, smoke alarms	0.75		
Weather (storm, wind)	0.01	1,000,000	10,000	1.3	13,000	Safe location and building	0.75		
Earthquake	0.002	1,000,000	2,000	1.3	2,600	Safe location and building	0.75		
Building damage/ collapse	0.001	1,500,000	1,500	1.3	1,950	Safe location and building	0.75		

*   Management controls: security aware management systems and supervision, job design with separation of duties, cross-training, forced vacations, accountability, etc.

** User authentication at LAN logon and for especially vulnerable applications such as electronic-mail and strategic systems.

FIGURE 7.3   RISK OF LOSS VERSUS SAFEGUARD COST SPREADSHEET.

To calculate the risk premium amount, simply enter the risk premium percent factor into the Risk Premium % column in your spreadsheet. The spreadsheet should multiply the total risk (or loss exposure) by the risk premium factor giving the risk premium amount, as shown in the Risk of Loss Versus Safeguard Costs Spreadsheet in Figure 7.3.

Order the Risks

Order the risks, as shown in Figure 7.3, based on the amount of the total loss exposure—from low (acceptable) to high (unacceptable). Review the total risk figures to determine what an acceptable loss is. Sort the spreadsheet from the highest risk to the lowest, and note the items that show unacceptably high losses. Also note the items that have high risk premiums attached.

Rate Safeguard, Defense, and Countermeasure Effectiveness

List the safeguards, defenses, and countermeasures you are considering. Activities, like retrieving data from damaged hard drives, should not be listed as safeguards *per se*. Instead, they should be identified as an element in the list of corrective measures likely to be needed should a security incident occur. Categorize the list by the type of protection each safeguard affords, such as:

- Prevention
- Detection
- Correction
- Containment
- Management control

Categorizing threats helps to put the effectiveness of safeguards in perspective. While there are no fixed rules, security measures that *prevent* security incidents from occurring are usually more effective than measures that attempt to contain, control, or correct incidents that have already occurred.

Hacking, or LAN cracking, is a good example of a threat that can be prevented. Forces of nature, such as storms and earthquakes, are examples of threats that cannot be entirely prevented. However, the likelihood of events such as earthquakes may be lessened by the choice of geographical site location, and the amount of damage and overall loss may be lessened by the use of superior engineering designs and materials.

The safeguards should be listed, evaluated, culled, and ranked by the level of protection afforded and the cost. Rate each safeguard according to its expected effectiveness on a scale of 1 to 10, 10 being the most effective safeguard possible. Since few safeguards are 100 percent effective, this will be important in safeguard comparison and selection. An example of a completely effective safeguard is the RSA type 4 encryption method because it has never been broken or compromised. Encryption is useful in protecting passwords and other highly sensitive information when stored in the server or passed in messages through the network. To protect passwords for a strategic LAN application, for example, you might choose an application which uses RSA encryption for protecting passwords.

Even though a safeguard is 100 percent effective and the passwords are completely protected on the server (from intruders, etc.), the application is still vulnerable if a password can be guessed or "dictionary-dialed" by a network cracker or hacker.

Security awareness training and supervision can further decrease the chance that a weak password will be chosen and guessed. Nonetheless, it cannot *prevent* users from choosing foolish, easy-to-guess passwords. To further safeguard a LAN or strategic application, you might decide to use a password generator, or password checking program, in addition to the application that employs RSA encrypted passwords.

A Safeguards, Defenses, and Countermeasures chart is illustrated in Table 7.4. The status and other information may be noted in the chart for future reference.

TABLE 7.4   SAFEGUARDS, DEFENSES, AND COUNTERMEASURES.

CATEGORY	SAFEGUARD/DEFENSE/ COUNTERMEASURE	EFFECTIVENESS RATING	COMMENT
Prevention	Heat alarm		
Prevention	24-hour building security (guards, keys) control physical access		
Detection	Fire, smoke, heat, moisture, motion detectors and alarms		
Containment	Fire retardant systems (fire suppressing chemicals, sprinklers)		
	Escort for all visitors		
	Guard/key systems control access to network environment		
	Locked server/network wiring room Access limited to LAN Administration & Security Officer		
	Dial-back to pre-authorized off-site dial-in locations		
	Low-attenuation cabling, such as fiber and Thin Film Transistor (TFT) monitors or Tempest PCs, to eliminate emission of electromagnetic signals in physically unsecured locations		
	Encrypt, compress, or code sensitive data for storage and transmission		
	Monitor ("sweep") perimeter of network area/building with transmission signal detection equipment		
	Install tap-resistant fiber optic cabling		
	Monitor physical network and cabling for taps by visual inspection, LAN analyzer systems, and cable testing devices		
	Off-site storage of backup files, backup and recovery, disaster, and Continuation Of Operation Plans and procedures		

CATEGORY	SAFEGUARD/DEFENSE/ COUNTERMEASURE	EFFECTIVENESS RATING	COMMENT
	Disaster Recovery Plan, Continuation Of Operations Plan with alternate processing location		
	Thorough user and support staff training in LAN applications, file handling, LAN policies, standards and procedures, security awareness, and safety		
	LAN management/monitor/analysis/ troubleshooting software and hardware		
	Security breach prevention, detection, containment and correction, threat safeguards, defenses, and counter- measures, recovery methods and procedures training for staff		
	Software Quality Assurance reviews and change control procedures		
	Conscientious LAN Administration and control practices (control access, cancel IDs and passwords upon employee termination, etc.)		

Select Safeguards, Defenses and Countermeasures

Select the safeguards, defenses and countermeasures that best eliminate, or minimize, each threat. Pay particular attention to the high-dollar loss and high-risk premium items. Enter the safeguards into the *Risk of Loss versus Safeguard Costs Spreadsheet* as shown in Figure 7.3.

Establish Safeguard Costs

Establish the full cost of implementing each selected safeguard and coun-termeasure. Include staff hours, training, documentation, updates, and other costs in the total cost figure, as well as the purchase (or lease) price of the product itself. For example, one of the reasons NOS security features are not implemented is that LAN administrators do not necessarily know how beneficial they are, nor do they know how to implement them properly. So they may avoid the issue and not implement them at all. All NOS products come with documentation that may prove inadequate for gaining a thorough understanding of LAN security features. Supplemental training is available from vendors and authorized training centers for most products that require training but security may be treated as an afterthought rather than as the central theme. Training must be considered an integral part of the cost of a product, as maximum benefits are rarely realized from any LAN product without proper training. The effectiveness of any safeguard invariably depends on its proper use.

This cost will be compared to the expected loss exposure. Safeguards do not always completely protect against a threat, so many safeguards may be required for the best protection. Conversely, some safeguards protect against more than one threat. In that case, you would combine the losses for comparison to the cost of the safeguard.

Use only the portion of the safeguard cost that relates to the risk assessment period. For example, if a UPS costs $2,000, and required an additional expenditure of $2,500 for software and training, but was expected to continue to protect the LAN for ten years, the cost for one year (comparable to the risk assessment period) would be $450.

Enter the costs of the selected safeguards into the Risk of Loss Versus Safeguard Costs Spreadsheet, as shown in Figure 7.3.

Select a Set of Safeguards, Defenses and Countermeasures for the Greatest Overall Benefit

The safeguards, defenses, and countermeasures can now be matched against the threats. The threats that present the greatest overall risk of loss to the organization should be given the most attention in the matching process.

Regardless of the means used to arrive at this point, the final selection of safeguards to be implemented, and in what order, are best left to those managers who are most knowledgeable of your organization and of LAN security. In some cases, the LAN manager acts as a facilitator, putting relevant facts before a committee, then guides them through the decision-making process.

Using expert knowledge and management skills, drawn from technical as well as business ranks, select the set of safeguards, defenses, and countermeasures that will provide the greatest benefit to the organization for the least cost. Key aspects of the decision-making effort should be:

■ Expectation that loss will result from threats (based on statistics).

■ Risk-averse or risk-taking culture of your organization.

■ Type, cost, human factors, and overall effectiveness of safeguards, defenses, and countermeasures.

The safeguard cost versus risk of loss comparison is a useful way to analyze both the exposure to risk and the benefits of using the specific security measures under consideration. It can also be useful as a means of choosing among alternatives where budget is an issue. The cost of implementing safeguards and countermeasures must be balanced against the degree of risk involved if you do not protect against a particular threat.

Although there are no firm rules for selecting safeguards, in general, if the cost of installing a safeguard is low, and the risk of loss is high (without the safeguard), then the safeguard should be employed. If the cost of eliminating a risk is great, and the risk of loss is low, you may decide to implement the LAN without the safeguard in place. If the risk is unacceptably high, and the cost of the safeguard is too great to permit its use, a dilemma exists. One solution is to keep the information at risk off the network until the funds are available to implement appropriate safeguards. This approach results in delays in automating processes and is not popular with LAN users. It also generally requires considerable determination and finesse on the part of the LAN manager. Another solution is to isolate a high-risk function to a few nodes on the network or a separate LAN where strict security measures can be implemented at an affordable cost.

Some organizations cannot implement all necessary safeguards immediately because of budget constraints. If this is the case, the priorities you assigned early in the process will help determine which safeguards to install first.

If you have difficulty in making the final decision on what safeguards to employ and in what order, or wish to have the consensus of a group, consider using a group decision support system (GDSS). A GDSS, such as *Expert Choice*, greatly simplifies the group decision-making process and helps to ensure that the best possible choices are made. Participants will still have an opportunity to express their opinions and preferences to the group, but the final GDSS decision will be reflecting of all input and individual attitudes.

When Safeguard Selection is Complete

When the risk assessment process is over, and the safeguard selection process is complete, the information should be incorporated into your Security Plan. The underlying assumptions and choices must be revisited periodically to reflect changing threats and conditions, as well as recovery alternatives. For example, recent events, such as the midwest floods, the Los Angeles-area brush fires, and the California earthquake have increased the probabilities of severe weather and natural disaster occurrences. Likewise the probability of experiencing a terrorist attack increased for certain organizations after the World Trade Center bombing. And five years ago the likelihood of a virus causing a devastating loss was probably nil.

The fact that probabilities change should be a factor in how often you choose to review your risk assessment and safeguard choices, and upgrade your Security Plan.

CHAPTER 8

LAN
HARDWARE

L AN hardware security addresses the mechanical, physical, and electrical LAN components, as well as the factory installed devices and features that prevent theft, tampering, and other physical access. It also covers the failure prevention and fault tolerant hardware features that help to keep equipment operational.

Hardware and software are so interdependent that it is virtually impossible to discuss LAN hardware security without addressing software. Increasingly, software instructions required to operate, or monitor, hardware are embedded within the hardware itself (firmware) in circuit boards and chips. Firmware is more efficient in operation than software because it places no burden on the processor. Firmware is also more secure. It is difficult to tamper with, or accidentally damage, electronic circuits and Read Only Memory chips, but relatively easy to modify software.

This integration of hardware and software makes it difficult to classify devices and products. For the most part, safeguards which have hardware components are presented in this chapter. A variety of security features, concerns, and safeguards are discussed for LAN servers, workstations, and cabling. Hardware-based LAN analyzer devices that are used to analyze, secure, and troubleshoot LANs are described as well.

A number of terms we will use here are technical, rather than common American English words, and were introduced in previous chapters.

Security Devices

Factory-installed security features and safeguards are available for many LAN components. When ordering network equipment, security-aware LAN designers and managers should request built-in security features such as cover locks, disk drive locks, and other access control mechanisms. Add-on physical devices for securing hardware are described in the chapter on physical access.

Servers

Servers are normally maintained in secure areas. This may cause designers to be less demanding and ask for fewer physical safeguards. Servers are so critical to LAN operations that all available basic safeguards should be used. Safeguards for servers are easily justified because physical safeguards are relatively inexpensive and the number of servers are few compared to the great number of workstations.

Servers may be equipped with security devices such as system unit cover locks, disk array unit locks, on-off switch locks, on-off switch covers, and keyboard locks.

Failure Prevention and Fault Tolerance

Servers can have an impressive array of monitoring features, trouble alarms, and fault tolerant features, which greatly increase their dependability and the resulting utility of the LAN.

Compaq, for example, is a computer manufacturer known for designing LAN servers with an impressive level of fault tolerance and consistently high quality, at off-the-shelf prices. The Compaq SystemPro established Compaq as one of the leaders in the LAN server market several years ago.

The demand for reasonably-priced, ever more powerful and fault tolerant systems eventually increased beyond the capabilities of the SystemPro. Attempts to make LANs served by Compaq SystemPro completely fault tolerant became expensive propositions. To mirror a disk drive requires twice as much disk capacity. Duplexing a disk drive requires redundant disk controllers as well as double disk capacity, which is an expensive solution with the SystemPro. The most economical hardware approach to fault tolerance is a totally redundant SystemPro server, which is also costly, because you must double every hardware and software purchase.

Compaq's ProLiant

The *ProLiant* server has attained a new level of affordable hardware fault tolerance. It improves dependability through failure prevention, fault tolerant engineering, and an automated approach to server management. The ProLiant integrates monitoring software that identifies components which are likely to fail. Before a component such as a disk drive fails, there are warning signs that the element is not operating at peak performance. When these monitoring agents sense that a component no longer meets rigid performance specifications, it reports an "out-of-spec" failure state. Preventive maintenance can then be scheduled, and the part can be replaced before it fails altogether and causes a shutdown. Compaq replaces parts that fail to pass their specification tests free of charge within the first three years.

The ProLiant uses server management data, collected by software agents in its *INSIGHT* and *Server Manager/R* software, to provide fault prevention, fault tolerance, trouble alerts, and rapid recovery services. INSIGHT is a new software agent feature that monitors processors, controllers, and disk drives and collects the performance data used to predict trends and failures before a failure occurs in the LAN server. Remote Server/R allows the remote management of as many as 300 servers and alerts network managers to problems via modem, pager, or telephone voice message.

Four parallel *Pentium* processors, 7.35 gigabytes of disk storage, and remote LAN administration, with real-time alerts are featured in the ProLiant 4000. The starting price is in the $5,000-$20,000 range, depending on the number of processors. The Compaq *ProSignia* has fewer processors and is even more affordable.

ProLiant physical access security features include:

■ System cover lock.

■ Locking cable to secure the server to a fixed object.

■ Power-on password.

■ Keyboard password.

■ Administrator password.

■ Diskette drive enable and disable control.

■ Diskette boot control.

■ Port control.

■ Network server mode.

■ Disk configuration lock.

■ QuickLock and QuickBlank.

QuickLock disables the keyboard, without exiting server applications, then *QuickBlank* blanks-out the screen until the correct password is supplied. These features protect the server against intruders and snoops and improve network access security.

Disk data integrity protection and reliability features include:

- Disk drive status lights that indicate read/write activity, power, and service required.

- Locking front panel access to disk drives for faster servicing.

- Digital Access Tape backup drive option, with up to a 5.0 GB capacity with hardware compression.

ProLiant fault tolerant features (which are not unique to Compaq servers) are:

- Hot-swappable disk drives, which means a bad disk drive can be replaced without taking the network down and inconveniencing users.

- Controller duplexing, which uses duplicate controllers and drive arrays to permit continuous servicing of disk requests, in the event of disk controller or drive failure.

- RAID (Redundant Array of Inexpensive Disks) protection:

  - RAID level 1 mirrors data to protect it and permit faster reads.

  - RAID 4 uses one drive to guard user data on disk.

  - RAID 5 is like 4 but improves data guarding performance in distributed network operations.

- On-line disk spare automatically replaces a failed disk drive.

- Array accelerator onboard battery maintains a backup of buffered memory for up to four days to protect the integrity of LAN information in the event of power failures and parity errors.

- Advanced Error Correction Coding (ECC) memory that senses errors and self-corrects.

- Off-line backup processor to replace an out-of-service processor.

- Automatic disk recovery.

- UPS support.

NetWare Support comes in a package of utilities that is optimized for NetWare and tightly integrated with the NOS. NetWare-only features include more detailed server monitoring and reporting on server configuration, status, and performance data for tracking and predictive analysis. Some NetWare fault prevention features are:

■ Drive tracking that collects data for disk management to predict failure and permit replacement of disk drives beforehand.

■ Dynamic sector repair re-maps bad disk sectors automatically.

■ Array cache accelerator tracking monitors battery and memory status to permit replacement of suspect parts before failure.

■ Memory system tracking.

■ Environment tracking.

■ Compaq UPS tracking.

■ Server health tracking.

■ Operating system tracking.

■ Thermal tracking.

The Rapid Recovery feature automatically restarts the server after a failure, logs the reason for the failure, and optionally notifies the administrator by calling a pager. It handles automated server recovery from critical errors, disk errors, memory recovery, processor recovery, software error recovery, server failure notification, and server recovery notification.

LAN Performance Can Suffer From Flawed Installation

Many LANs were designed to deliver performance and reliability that were never realized because of flawed installations, incorrect drivers and NOS parameters, and so forth. Compaq did a test to determine what situations in server installation and set up lead to flawed overall performance. All of the test installations were flawed and took longer than expected.

Compaq's solution to the incorrect server installation problem is their automated SmartStart setup utility that allows administrators and installers to configure, optimize, and have a new server up and running in minutes. SmartStart configures the system, loads the NOS and correct drivers from a CD-ROM drive, and tunes the set-up. The NOSs which can be automatically installed are: NetWare, SCO UNIX and Open Server, Windows NT, and Windows NT Advanced Server. The automated LAN server setup ensures a correct installation, although guided instruction is provided for installers who wish to control the installation, configuration, and tuning of their networks. SmartStart is the first utility of its kind for LAN servers.

Bus Mastering

Bus mastering is a desirable feature for LAN servers because it improves performance. Data is transferred 32 bits at a time from disk to system memory, without involvement of the processor itself resulting in faster reads and better throughput in general. The bus mastering feature is offered on many servers, including Compaq's.

PowerFrame by Tricord

While many servers offer LAN security features, *Tricord's PowerFrame* is at the high-end of LAN servers and demonstrates the state-of-the-art in server technology. The PowerFrame server is known for its ability to support large numbers of users without suffering from diminished performance. In a test of six LAN super servers (including the Compaq SystemPro), the PowerFrame performed best and was praised as a reliable platform for large networks. Tricord attributes its ability to sustain performance while adding users to putting its disk input/output subsystems on the 267MB per second high-speed *PowerBus*, which frees the EISA bus for network input/output traffic. The Tricord supports up to 168 disk drives compared to 56 for the ProLiant 4000 server (which would require a total of four controllers). The PowerFrame offers redundant power supplies, hot disk drive replacement, hot sparing, supports 32 disk drives, and parity checking on main data paths. The system architecture appears in Figure 8.1.

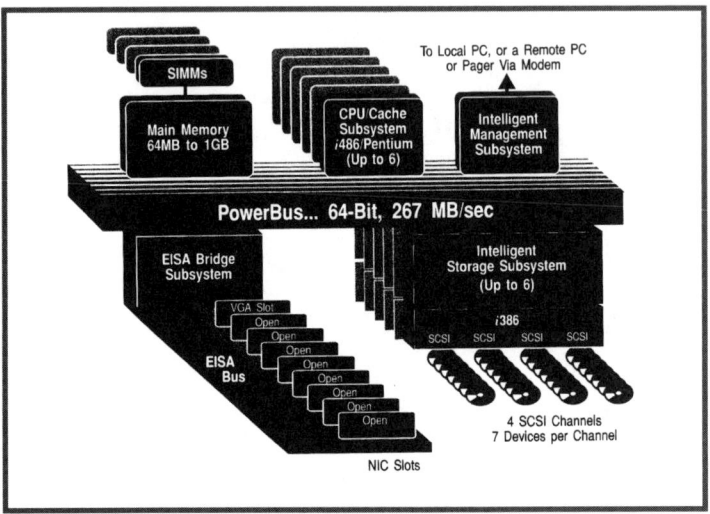

FIGURE 8.1   TRICORD'S POWERFRAME POWERBUS DESIGN.

NetFrame's *Independent Management Subsystem* is a Windows-based intelligent hardware subsystem. It connects to the PowerBus and performs pre-fault analysis to eliminate failures before they occur. It also reconfigures subsystems, upgrades FLASH EEPROMS, disables a CPU or SCSI drive, maps around bad memory, and notifies the administrator through pager alerts.

LAN Workstations

Workstations may be equipped with the same security features as are servers. Although workstations are less costly, they are also used in less secure areas like reception, open offices, and PC rooms and labs, where they are quite vulnerable. Workstations may have access control safeguards implemented in software such as screen savers, boot locks, automatic LAN logoff, and hard disk protectors that are discussed in the chapter on LAN software.

Just as engineering improvements have given us faster, more dependable servers, workstations have also been improved dramatically. Users tend to be more aware of software improvements but may not be as knowledgeable of hardware changes. The disk drive has long been the most likely point of failure in microcomputers and it has benefited from engineering improvements as a result.

In the early days of PCs, few people knew of the jeopardy that bumping a PC presented to a hard drive. Read-write heads are poised millionths of an inch over a spinning disk platter in a hard disk drive. All you needed to do to destroy your hard disk back then was to bump the PC and send the head crashing down on the disk surface. There was a fix for the problem. Running a program like SHIP or PARK before you turned your PC off each day caused the read-write heads to position themselves in a safe place. Few people knew of the threat back in 1984, let alone the simple solution. It is now ten years later, and disk drive technology has matured greatly. Disk drive read-write heads automatically go to a safe place in modern disk drives, thus no longer present problems in PCs that are turned off. Older PCs were not designed or well suited for use on LANs, thus few are used as LAN workstations. Yet well-meaning "experts" are still advising users to use SHIP and PARK-type programs to protect data on their hard drives. We need to be as aware of changes in hardware, as we are of software so we can take full advantage of the benefits and improvements in each. We have so much work to do to secure our LANs, that we must deal with real problems and threats rather than non-existent ones.

Add-in Security Boards

The most effective security safeguards for workstations have a hardware component that provides hardware-based encryption and a clock which users cannot alter.

Watchdog Armor is a popular add-in board for PCs that provides the following additional security features for PCs that already have Watchdog PC security installed:

- Disables the diskette drive until the PC is successfully booted (which requires a user password) from the hard drive to prevent unauthorized use.

- Hardware-based DES encryption for faster performance.

- A secure clock for tamper-proof time-keeping for the audit trail.

ASSURE FOR NETWORKS PROVIDES THE FOLLOWING SECURITY FEATURES:

Access control	Prevents unauthorized system access by individuals, viruses, and electronic means
Information access control	Protects against user errors and unauthorized access and modification of data
Selective encryption	Protects sensitive data on the workstation, the server, and in communications transmission (bridges, routers, interconnected LANs and WANs)
Security hardware removal lock	Locks disk access until security hardware is reinstalled
User profiles and a protected audit trail	Implements accountability for user actions and access security violations
GUI-based single security model	Centralized management

Cordant's Assure for Networks is a high-end LAN workstation security product. It is implemented in integrated hardware and software with many years of engineering behind it. Novell selected Assure to provide the workstation-server security component to complement its NetWare NOS security features in its application for a class C2 level Trusted Network rating. The Department of Defense (DoD) Trusted

Computer Security evaluation by the National Computer Security Center (NCSC) rates computer systems and networks. The NetWare-Assure security package has already been installed by organizations requiring DoD Trusted Computing Base (TCB) status, pending their C2 certification.

Assure for Networks implements security at the expense of user convenience. For example, it removes references to deleted files so they can no longer be retrieved through the DOS or NetWare undelete features.

Encryption Devices

Encryption devices can be attached to any network to secure data transmission, including LAN messages. Racal-Datacom, AT&T, and others have communications security products to meet many networking needs. Normally, two units must be used to secure a transmission between two points, one at the source and one at the destination. The unit at the source encrypts the data for transmission and the unit at the destination decrypts the encrypted data it receives for use.

AT&T's Gretacoder provides secure transmission over x.25 WANs with end-to-end data encryption. Complete implementation includes a PC-based Network Security Center that has its own rigorous security features in a multi-level system to protect against unauthorized use.

AT&T Surity protects LAN and WAN communications with units that perform authentication and encryption. A PC-based Network Security Center provides independent, secure, and controlled central administration of communication security. The system provides authentication, access control, data integrity assurance, and confidentiality for data traveling between Surity-secured nodes.

SeGaSys is a secured gateway system that channels all remote access through its centralized gateway, where callers are authenticated, routed, and controlled. It provides for secure tele-maintenance of remote workstations and network devices and security management from a single location. The system includes one security server and a communications-interface card for every incoming phone line.

Peripherals

Printing on LANs has been troublesome from a security and a reliability perspective and may be the most frustrating network service available to LAN users. When LANs were new, printers had to be attached to the server or to a LAN workstation, and NOS print services were cumbersome. LANs permit sharing of expensive peripherals. However, all this sharing can cause problems, like printing sensitive information in public areas, delayed or lost faxes and print jobs because of mis-routing, and network resources burdened by excessive print traffic. NOS and hardware improvements have streamlined network printing and today LANs are increasingly being asked to deliver mainframe-class printing performance.

The *HP LaserJet IIIsi* network-intelligent printer attaches directly to LAN wiring, rather than to the server or a LAN workstation. Print messages need not travel through the server thus print traffic across the LAN and server overhead is lessened. Inexpensive "personal lasers," can also be issued to users who print sensitive data to keep this information away from public areas.

PCMCIA Cards

IBM PCMCIA (Personal Computer Memory Card International Association) slots in portable PCs accept devices the size of a credit card to give you additional memory, fax/modem, security, or networking capabilities. A Network Interface Card can be inserted in a PCMCIA slot which permits a mobile PC to be used as a LAN workstation.

Monitors and Screens

The flicker on PC monitor screens is said by ophthalmologists to make some vision problems, such as astigmatism, worse when computer use is excessive and continues for long periods of time without appropriate rest periods. Eye strain and headaches have been known to result from prolonged continuous PC use, especially when older monitors are used.

Newer non-interlaced CRT-type screens flicker far less, thus are thought to be easier on the eyes.

Thin Film Transistor (TFT) screens are flat, have exceptional color and brightness that is controlled by a transistor for each pixel, and are expensive. TFT screens do not flicker, thus are not conducive to vision problems or eye strain. They also require very little desktop space, and produce few, if any, electromagnetic emissions. TFT screens are sought after for portable PCs as an improvement over LCD screens.

LAN Communications Components

In a discussion of LAN communication hardware, it is important to note that a suite of standards exists which permits products from various vendors to inter-network in a common communications architecture. The standards are based on the Open System Interconnection (OSI) model for network communications. OSI consists of seven layers that define the electrical characteristics, communications standards, and software application activity that takes place when systems communicate with each other.

Network communications components evolve rapidly and increase in complexity function. The following descriptions are simplistic and focus on the security aspects of the LAN.

Communications Hub

Hubs are the communications control point of a LAN. In addition to performing traditional concentrator, repeater, and control functions, hubs are becoming increasingly intelligent. They may even incorporate bridge, router, security, LAN management, WAN support, and terminal server support features. Hubs are designed to support a particular LAN protocol and may limit your choice of LAN cabling medium. Hubs are available to support the protocols for Arcnet, Ethernet, FDDI, LocalTalk (Apple), Token Ring, or Wireless LAN communications. Arcnet is on the wane due to the popularity of the faster Ethernet. Some Wireless LANs depend on a direct line of sight between devices. Unfortunately the signals from wireless LANs, especially microwaves, can be interfered with and intercepted. Interest in their flexibility and convenience is increasing, but reservations about security and interference persist and they are not yet widely used for commercial purposes. LAN hub functions are also performed by PBX equipment. The *Lap Link* Wireless LAN uses National Semiconductor's Airshare technology and is Windows-based. It broadcasts 360° on radio waves and permits file synchronization and sharing of parameters and backup tape systems.

Repeater

The repeater is a device that receives communications signals from one segment of network cable, amplifies the signals, and passes them along on another cable segment. Repeaters extend the distance a LAN cable can be run. 10Base-T LAN transceivers are usually located directly on the Network Interface Cards (NIC) in the LAN workstations (an on-board transceiver), or on the wire link between the LAN cable connector and the NIC in the workstation.

Bridge

Bridges permit LAN inter-networking by connecting LANs with like protocols and enabling message traffic to flow in both directions. A bridge is a hardware device that connects two LANs that use the same protocol. Bridges filter and pass data between LANs. Because they allow only data destined for their LAN to pass through, they can be used to isolate high traffic or high bandwidth LAN segments, as well as segments that handle especially sensitive data. Internal bridges can be installed in the file server on some LANs allowing LANs to inter-network. External bridging requires a separate communications device or PC to connect LANs. Bridges operate at Layer 2, the Media Access Communications layer of the OSI model.

| LAYER # | OSI Layer | WHAT OPERATES AT THIS LAYER | | WHAT ACTION TAKES PLACE AT THIS LAYER |
		DEVICES	PROTOCOLS	
7	Application	Applications Application gateways Network management x.400 FTAM	SMTP SNMP FTP DNS Telnet	Messages are created
6	Presentation	Middleware: RPCs, SQLs, IPCs, Windows (DOS), etc.	NCP (layer 5 & 6 only)	Messages coded (ASCII or EBCDIC)
5	Session	NOSs		Login to LAN Open communication path Make message segments
4	Transport		SPX TCP	Add error checking and correction
3	Network	x.25 Gateways Routers (connect separate networks)	IPX IP	Make packets Organize packets Make packet headers
2	Data Link	Bridges (link LANs)	Ethernet Token ring	Add checksum (for integrity) Address header for routing
1	Physical	Repeaters Network cable		Open physical communication channel Transmit packets (electronic signals) over cable media

GRAPHIC BY PETER HUNT

Legend:
FTAM - File Transfer Access Method
SQLs - Structured Query Languages
SMTP - Simple Mail Transfer Protocol
FTP - File Transfer Protocol
NCP - NetWare Core Protocol
TCP - Transmission Control Protocol
IP - Internet Protocol

RPCs - Remote Procedure Calls
IPCs - InterProcess Communications
SNMP - Simple Network Management Protocol
DNS - Domain Name Service
SPX - Sequenced Packet Exchange
IPX - Internetwork Packet Exchange

FIGURE 8.2 THE OSI MODEL.

Router

Routers enable inter-networking between LANs with different protocols. A router is a software and hardware device that connects two or more networks, and routes data dynamically between networks based on the data destination and routes available. If a router is located in a server, it is called an internal router.

Hardware-Based Network Test, Analysis, and Measurement Equipment

There are three main kinds of products in the LAN test, analysis, and measurement category with different characteristics and purposes:

1. Network management systems.

   ■ Look at your network as a whole in real-time.

   ■ Provide centralized interactive network management and control.

   ■ Often provided by the NOS or hardware manufacturer.

2. Network monitors.

   ■ Probes on network segments report activity for fault management, network planning, and tuning. Central system provides network mapping, event logging, packet capture, and transmission statistics.

3. Network protocol analyzers.

   ■ Attach to LANs by means of a tap.

   ■ Capture data for detailed analysis and protocol decoding.

   ■ Provide network analysis and statistics for problem isolation.

   ■ Typically require expertise on the part of the LAN manager.

Network Protocol Analyzers

Network protocol analyzers typically capture millions of bytes of transmitted messages and interpret protocols to locate weak signals, errors, and other transmission problems. They usually display images representing communication signals and other information vital to tuning and troubleshooting.

As these devices must "snoop" into LAN messages to be of any value, they should be used with extreme care. It is important to be aware that protocol analyzers can capture valuable data, including passwords, as information travels through the network. LAN managers should keep all test equipment under lock and key and supervise its use on the LAN.

The *Network General Sniffer* is the original "Sniffer" device and probably the best known comprehensive network analyzer product. It was originally implemented in a device consisting of both hardware and software. The term *sniffer* is now widely used to mean the network protocol, analyzer-class of product which is capable of capturing network messages, decoding and analyzing protocols, as well as developing network traffic and performance statistics for network troubleshooting and performance tuning. If the data on a LAN is encrypted, decryption equipment will be necessary.

The Sniffer from Network General provides full decoding of network protocols. It can be used as a stand-alone device, or in a client-server configuration with "pods" for monitoring remotely.

Sniffer program refers to a LAN analyzer capability that is implemented in software alone and usually runs on a server or a workstation attached to a LAN. There are several exciting products in the software category that are discussed in the LAN software chapter.

The Network Advisor from Hewlett Packard is a unique LAN troubleshooting tool that uses expert system software, as well as a screen with dashboard gauges and a trend analysis screen. When you attach the unit to your LAN, and enter the symptoms of your problem, the Fault Finder feature captures packets and learns about your particular network. It then applies Ethernet, or Token-Ring, troubleshooting expertise and searches for problems and reasons through the possible causes of the trouble. It runs its own tests to gain additional problem-solving information. A commentator feature presents the reasoning and suggested solutions for the problem devised by Fault Finder. Network statistics are monitored via the easy-to-read dashboard gauges in the colorful screen. The Network Adviser is easy to use, even for new managers, and is an excellent training tool for those who wish to know more about LAN communications.

For Ethernet LANs, the Network Advisor investigates such data as:

■ Utilization

■ Frame Check Sequence (FCS) errors (runts, jabber, etc.)

■ Bytes per frame

■ Number of nodes

■ Collisions

It can solve problems such as excessive traffic, duplicate IP (Internet Protocol) address, mis-configured IP broadcast, spanning device down, cable too long, cable resistance too high or too low, and cable noisy or broken.

On Token-Ring MAC protocol LANs, error-frames, station counts, and protocol mix are among the measurements tracked. The gauges display utilization, purges, soft errors, claim token, beacons, stations, source routing, and average frames per second for selected stations' information. This display is useful in resolving trouble such as duplicate local and remote address, transmit wire broken, receive wire broken, and station inserted at wrong speed. The HP Network Advisor comes with a 386 20MHz portable PC and the price starts at about $15,000.

There is also an HP Internet Advisor product that is useful for analysis and problem resolution on interconnected LANs.

The *RC-88 Windows-based WAN analyzer* comes with its own notebook PC. It has a special Y cable that eliminates interruptions to the line when tapping in or disconnecting from a network. There is a LAN support upgrade, where each channel can support either WAN or LAN analysis. The price starts at $4,400.

LAN Cabling

Cable faults account for between 60 and 80 percent of LAN downtime because cabling is rarely tested properly before the users attempt to use the network for the first time.

When You Have a Cable Problem

Cable testing and troubleshooting is a specialized activity that requires experience. The skills that help you to determine when to use the cable testing methods and tools, and when to look elsewhere for the source of trouble on a LAN develop with time and experience. Because of the learning curve and the fact that most LANs are only wired once, your time is better spent working on problems other than cable troubles. If you must troubleshoot cable problems yourself, here are a few hints to help you along:

1. Try to collect as much information as possible from network users, to clarify the trouble *before* starting the troubleshooting process with the network itself.

2. Have network documentation ready and use a checklist to structure the information-gathering and analysis processes.

3. Be sure you have the right tools for the task. With appropriate tools and testing devices, problems can often be identified and corrected quickly. Without them you can waste a lot of time guessing.

The traditional network troubleshooting hardware devices used by engineers attach to the LAN and provide signal analysis and other information on a small screen. Tektronix and other manufacturers offer a full line of such products.

Many *cable faults* or contributing factors in copper-based UTP and STP network cabling can be forestalled through care in installation. The following cable faults will cause LAN malfunctions and should be identified by thorough testing, and should be corrected prior to use of the network:

- Cable length exceeds specifications
- Short circuit in cable
- Open circuit in cable
- Broken cable
- Polarity reversal
- Transposed pairs (mis-wiring)
- Split pairs (causes near end crosstalk [NEXT] in Token Ring)
- Impedance mismatch

The tests that should be run to identify cable faults are:

- Distance to fault
- Resistance
- Attenuation
- Ambient noise
- Near end crosstalk (NEXT)
- Continuity
- Polarity
- Wiring order
- Split pairs (Token Ring)

Cable Tests and Equipment

Although LAN analyzers will identify cable problems, comprehensive tests of the wiring scheme (or cabling plant) require specialized network test equipment. The equipment is sometimes limited to one kind of network cable, so check the suitability of the equipment to your particular wiring before ordering. Figures 8.3 and 8.4 illustrate common cable testing devices and cable tests that should be performed on UTP cable.

TESTING DEVICE	PURPOSE
Inductive amplifier test set	Finds wire pair termination in wiring closet
Digital Volt Meter (DVM)	Measures voltage (volts), resistance (ohms), current (amps) and continuity
Oscilloscope	Graphically displays short circuits, open circuits, crimps/kinks, other impedance for LAN, mismatches on cable segments. Voltage-level data used to calculate attenuation. Measures signal voltage per unit of time.
Time Domain Reflectometer (TDR)	Finds cable length, shorts, opens, breaks. Enter adjust pulse width per wire specs, send signal down wire and length of cable is displayed
TDR + Oscilloscope + Printer	Oscilloscope displays waveform reflections from TDR
Hand-held cable analyzer and testing device (eg:StarTek)	Incorporates TDR, Oscilloscope functions and measures noise, crosstalk and attenuation, continuity, polarity, distance-to-fault measurements
Mod-TAP NA	Detects reverse polarity

FIGURE 8.3 CABLE TESTING DEVICES.

Systimax

The *Systimax Structured Cabling System* allows equipment from different manufacturers to work together on the same network. It also supports integration of a fiber backbone to accommodate future networking needs. Systimax incorporates the elements of cabling, including UTP, STP, or fiber optic cable media, connector hardware, adapters, transmission electronics, electrical protection, support hardware, and link communications devices. This is in a single integrated communication network with twisted pair and fiber-optic cable wiring. It is a computer-based system and displays the elements of the wiring plan—including connectors on the screen. Various options and configurations are available. Premises Systimax systems that support voice, data, and video are also available.

Cable Test	For Problem	Test Device	Possible Cause
Continuity	Broken cable segments Split pairs	TDR or cable analyzer	Damaged or improperly installed wiring
Attenuation	Intermittent errors caused by weak or distorted signal at receiver	Cable analyzer/tester which can generate signal and measure attenuation	Excessive segment length or otherwise out-of-specification cable
Bump/sag in baseline waveform	Improper termination or impedance resulting in intermittent or ghost problems: - many re-transmissions - network hangs - stations don't come up	TDR with waveform display	Connecting devices with different impedance as in: - tap - connector or device incompatible with others
Abrupt waveform shift: a. (-) b. (+) c. (-) less amplitude	a. Short b. Open c. Kink, damage, tap	TDR with waveform display	a. Electrical short circuit b. Cable end unconnected c. Cable damaged or tapped
Noise	Electromagnetic and impulse interference	Cable analyzer/tester	Lights, video (10-150MHz), radio, TV (10+MHz)
		Oscilloscope (when attenuation is not the problem)	Power noise (60Hz), motors, machines (large spikes)
Crosstalk	Noise from another wire pair in cable	Cable analyzer/tester	
Near End CrossTalk (NEXT)	Split pairs	Cable analyzer/tester	Cable not to specification: - too few twists per foot - incorrect wire size - poor manufacturing QC - worn coverings - improper installation
Polarity	Polarity at transmitter differs from receiver	Mod-Tap NA	(+) transmitter not connected to (+) receiver
Split pairs	High noise levels and crosstalk	Visual inspection to see if pairs are split	Wire pair separated and reconnected in wrong pair

FIGURE 8.4   Cable Tests.

The *Accu-track* component of Systimax keeps the physical cables organized and neat. This avoids the "cooked spaghetti" cable syndrome in the wiring closet, which makes it difficult to quickly locate a particular wire.

Resources invested in cable management systems are far more effective and productive than investments in developing cable troubleshooting skills.

Threats in Hardware

Tempest

This is a standard devised by the Department of Defense to protect against loss of privacy. *Tempest* equipment is designed or modified to prevent it from emitting electromagnetic signals which can be captured, decoded, and used. Tempest equipment is rarely cutting edge technology, because new products must undergo further engineering to block signal emissions and testing to ensure success. It also tends to be much higher in price than non-Tempest equipment because of the value added.

Some computer and network components, such as thin film transistor (TFT) screens and fiber optic cabling, have low electromagnetic signal emission properties. Low electromagnetic signal emissions are often a fortunate accident of electronic component design rather than an intentional engineering feat. Security-aware LAN managers are usually ready to take advantage of low emission products, no matter why they are produced.

If emanations are a concern and you cannot invest in Tempest equipment, there are other ways of reducing the possibility of compromising electronic signal emissions from your LAN. They are:

1. Maintain a secure emanations control zone around your facility.
2. Use electronic computing equipment in a centralized place so the signals will intermingle, making it difficult to isolate messages and interpret captured information.

3. Use paint and wallcoverings designed to absorb emanations and block electronic eavesdropping. Aluminum foil also blocks electronic eavesdropping.

4. Use network components with low electromagnetic emission properties.

Flectron absorbing wallcoverings is a metallized fabric that when used as a wallcovering material blocks eavesdropping equipment from picking up electromagnetic emanations from computers and networks. Flectron was developed by Monsanto in response to growing concerns about protecting sensitive information and industrial secrets from covert snoopers, including industrial spies.

Remanence

Electromagnetic impulses that remain imprinted on storage devices after data has been deleted are a source of concern for extremely security-conscious organizations. Government agencies require that great care is taken to thoroughly write over areas where classified data was stored prior to being deleted. Programs and services are available that will ensure that no trace of deleted information remains on disks, tapes, and even in computer memory. Images can also be left on laser printer drums and should be cleared after classified data has been printed on the device.

Heat versus Electrical Surges: Which is Worse for PCs?

A question that has been debated as long as PCs have been around is "Is it better to turn PCs off overnight, or leave them on even when they are not in use for extended periods of time?"

Electronics engineers agree that heat and power surges are the culprits that age the sensitive electronic circuitry in microcomputers. However, those same engineers do not agree on whether or not power surges, like the one you get when you turn on your PC, are worse for computer electronics than the heat generated from leaving the device on continuously.

It seems to me that if the processor is kept sufficiently well cooled while it is running, that there should be no negative effect from keeping it on. On the other hand, there is no way of eliminating the effect of the initial surge of power through a PC when it is turned on. So, my solution is to leave the computers on and keep them as cool as possible.

Grounding

Computer equipment is often grounded to protect users from the threat of electric shock. Grounding of LAN hardware components that require electric power for their operation can create electromagnetic interference on LANs. A hard to detect noise problem is created when components of networks are connected to different sources of power because copper wire LAN cabling, such as the extremely popular UTP and STP, conducts electricity. There are two good solutions to this double-edged threat:

1. Use of a power conditioner for each component or device. (UPSs may provide power conditioning, but not all UPSs are designed to protect against power loss and condition power.)

2. Use of fiber optic cable to reduce interference and line noise from the flow of electrical current. Fiber optic cable does not conduct electricity thus does not allow electrical current to flow between fiber-connected LAN components.

Miscellaneous Hardware Solutions and Concerns

Fancards Keep PCs and Servers Cool

If you cannot keep your environment cool enough, installing a Fancard is one way to keep a PC or server running cooler than it would otherwise. The Fancard needs no additional power and has two small fans that are effective in keeping the system unit and its circuits cool. The Fancard proved its effectiveness during Operation Desert Storm when the heat in the desert was causing the PCs and networks used by American troops to malfunction. When the Fancards were installed, the computers stayed cool enough to work flawlessly.

Green LAN Technology

IBM (and other manufacturers) are offering energy-saving features on their LAN equipment. IBM offers a feature that uses energy-saving technology to permit computers to lapse into a standby mode when not in use. When computers are powered off, information in the computer's memory is usually lost. However, when the IBM *Smart Energy Standby*™ feature is activated, only a partial shutdown takes place. The screen blanks, but a low level of power keeps the information in memory intact until the *Rapid Resume*™ feature is used. Thus, the Standby feature eliminates the need to turn PCs off when they are not in use.

Millions of PCs are routinely left on overnight to avoid the wear and tear of start up boot power surges on their sensitive electronic parts. Use of the Standby-Rapid Resume™ power-saving mode eliminates the problems of:

■ Damage to PCs from boot up power surges.

■ Wasted electric power from leaving PCs on 24 hours a day.

■ Productivity loss during lengthy boot processes.

■ Screen snooping at unattended workstations.

This power-saving feature was originally designed to conserve battery power on notebooks and other portable PCs. I have it on the IBM PS/Note notebook computer I bought to write this book. I touch a switch to enter standby mode, without exiting WordPerfect when I finish working. With a touch of the Rapid Resume™ switch, I can pick up exactly where I stopped. It is a marvelous productivity (and energy-saving) feature that is found on other computers as well.

Increasingly Powerful Processors

The capacity and processing speed of servers and PCs depends on factors such as the microprocessor chip, ROM BIOS (Read Only Memory Basic

Input/Output System) chip, as well as supporting sub-systems and operating systems. All of these devices can limit the speed at which the computer is able to complete its processing tasks.

The original IBM PC was introduced on August 14, 1981, when many microcomputers were already in existence. It quickly became the standard by which all microcomputers were judged because of its superior engineering and the confidence PC users placed in the quality of IBM products and support. When LAN technology was introduced in the early '80s, both minicomputers and PCs were used as servers. In time, it became evident that the PC needed qualities such as fault tolerance, with faster processing speeds and greater throughput, before the networks could be relied on for any degree of serious processing. In the thirteen years since the IBM PC appeared on the scene, PCs have matured. The evolution of microcomputers in terms of their bit capacity (how much data they process at one time), their memory in megabytes, and their processing speed in megahertz is shown below.

MICRO-COMPUTER	MICRO CHIP	BIT CAPACITY	MEMORY (M_BYTES)	SPEED MHZ
Non-IBM	8088	8/16	.64	4–10
PC	8088	8/16	.256	4.77
XT	8088	8/16	.64	4.77
AT PS2/30-60	80286	16	16	6–12
PS2/70,80	i386	32	16+	16
Non-IBM	i386	32	16+	33
	i486	32	4096	50
	i860	64	4096	25
Pentium	Pentium	64	60	100
PowerPC	PowerPC 601	64	264	80

Pentium Systems

Intel's new Pentium microprocessor chip offers a clock speed up to 100MHz with a true 64-bit data path, superscalar design, and a 16K cache. One of the strong selling points of 486 PCs has been that many are Pentium compatible, implying that Pentium chips can simply replace the older 486 chips. In fact, Pentium chips can replace many 486 chips, but will still have only a 32-bit access path. The additional heat generated by Pentium processors requires more ventilation than many "Pentium-upgradable" systems presently have. The more powerful Pentium units also require more power than the 486 systems do; thus, a larger power unit and greater cooling capacity may be required.

PowerPCs

The newest chip making news is the PowerPC, the product of a high-tech consortium including Motorola, IBM, and Apple Computer. Apple has the first PowerPC computer out and IBM's PowerPC is due in September of 1994. It runs IBM or Mac software in emulation mode as fast as a 486 does and is extremely fast in native PowerPC mode. I like to use it for graphics work because of its tremendous speed.

Backup Media for Small LANs and PCs

Some popular backup media for data on small LANs and critical data that must be instantly available for retrieval are tape, Bernoulli disk, and floppy disks. Tape drive suppliers offer units that can mount inside a PC system unit for single system protection. External units can be used to back up multiple hard drives. Many tape hardware devices are available including DAT, 4MM, 8MM, etc. To retrieve files from a tape you must search for the file in the index then read through the tape until you locate the file itself. It can be a slow process.

Bernoulli drives have long been used to provide additional on-line storage, as well as backup capability for PCs. Data can be backed up to removable 150 million byte Bernoulli disks (300 MB when compression is used), which can then be secured and rotated off-site. The Bernoulli drive offers up to 300MB of compressed storage on the dual drive (600MB if compression software is used). They offer rugged, shock-resistant removable and expandable mass storage and fast (18 ms) on-line access, as well as the ability to function as an easy-to-use and reliable backup device.

During the terrifying San Fernando earthquake (which measured 6.6 on the Richter scale) there were reports of Bernoulli drives hitting the floor and working perfectly afterward. When the computers were crushed by a flying desk in the offices of the Expedition Group, even the SIMM memory chips in the PCs were cracked, but the Bernoulli backup disks and all the data survived.

A computer animation producer had his Bernoulli drive "tossed into the air by the quake, but it worked perfectly when [the] power was restored four days later." Rugged as the Bernoulli drives are, it is still advisable to take regular backups and ship them offsite to make recovery from an earthquake or other natural disaster a trouble-free event.

If you back up to floppy disks and the process takes too long, consider using a Floptical disk drive that can read and write 21 million-byte floppies as well as standard 3.5-inch floppy disks. A comparison of backup media for small LANs follows.

	TAPE	BERNOULLI	FLOPPY	FLOPTICAL
Capacity (Uncompressed 300 MB dual drive)	150 MB	150 MB	1.44 MB	21MB
Speed in minutes (To back up 145 MB)	40	10	90+	30
Drive Cost	$175-$385.	$500.	$85.	$399.
Media Cost (Per MB)	$18	$110.	$100.	$135.

Incompatibility

Although PCs and LAN components are more interoperable and scalable than ever before, with more than 74 million PCs in use, there are still possible compatibility problems. Horror stories about hardware incompatibilities are commonplace and sometimes even the hardware manufacturers themselves do not know what works and what does not. Incompatible equipment accounts for much downtime in LANs and should be avoided wherever possible.

LAN
Software

There are a number of threats that can result in loss arising from the use of software on your LAN. The threats, and some solutions, are discussed in this chapter, as are software products in the categories of:

- Workstation Operating Systems (WOS)
- Network Operating Systems (NOS)
- Graphical User Interfaces (GUI)
- Groupware
- LAN Utilities

Since the information and examples in this book are based on my own experience, some products naturally receive more attention than others. There are undoubtedly many fine safeguards and software products that are, unfortunately, not discussed here at all.

Threats from Software

While software is essential to the use of computers and LANs, you should guard against the following threats from software:

1. Loss of productivity because software fails to perform as expected.

2. Flawed (possibly insufficiently tested) software that can damage or destroy valuable data.

3. Failure of software programs to handle error conditions such as insufficient memory for processing that results in abrupt application system termination and loss of data and/or productivity.

4. Software that fails to protect against:

    ◼ Unauthorized access and modification of data

    ◼ Accidental user errors

    ◼ Erroneous data entry

    ◼ Masquerading as another user

    ◼ Loss of data integrity through simultaneous updates.

5. Liability from violation of software copyright law, which is known as software piracy.

Software Piracy

Piracy is the copying and use of software in violation of copyright laws. The illegal use of software is said to cost offending firms about $50,000 in penalties, when they are caught. Regardless of the exact amount of the penalty, it is poor risk management policy to permit software piracy in your organization. Piracy of American-made software is a common practice in some parts of the world. It is less common in the United States because the cost of software is so low that it is worth the purchase price to be able to call the manufacturer for technical assistance when you need to, and to have the product documentation on hand.

Are Software Glitches Intentional?

It is frustrating to encounter a glitch that prevents you from using a software package you have purchased. It is even worse when you are under a tight deadline, and you realize that the flaw was probably known to the manufacturer when it was released for sale to the public. Sometimes there is an essential piece of information missing, which forces you to communicate with the manufacturer before you can use your software effectively.

For example, the TSR program I used to capture printed WordPerfect tables as graphics files for this book "hung" my system after it created a certain number of .TMP files, which forced me to reboot. In desperation, I had to call the manufacturer to pinpoint the cause. Manually deleting the .TMP files cleared up the trouble quickly. The files could easily have been cleared by the program itself, which would have saved me hours of wasted time investigating possible TSR and memory conflicts. When I encounter application software glitches such as this one, I always wonder whether it is an oversight in design or an intentional device used by software companies to discourage illegal use of their products. Whatever the reason, these problems should not be tolerated. Software purchasers have the right to enjoy the use and utility of the software they purchase without suffering what amounts to abuse at the whim of manufacturers.

Flawed Software

A more irksome problem is COTS (commercial off-the-shelf) software that either does not work, or damages data. Developing functional software holds no mystery for me since I started programming 26 years ago. I have designed, specified, written, tested, installed, quality assured, and supported enough software which functioned as expected, to know that software manufacturers are shirking their responsibility when they habitually distribute systems that seriously malfunction. Some manufacturers compound the insult by failing to support users who encounter serious bugs. The prevailing *caveat emptor* attitude should be tolerated no longer by those who are victimized by inadequate testing practices and lack of vendor support for flawed products. MS-DOS 6.0, for example, lacked protection for users of the DoubleSpace data compression feature against corruption or loss of data on hard disk drives under certain conditions. Rather than a wholesale recall which would have been forced on manufacturers of some other kinds of products, the manufacturer solved the problem by selling a temporary upgrade version to consumers.

Compare that level of user support to Novell's handling of a serious encryption algorithm problem that was discovered in versions 2.15c and 3.10 of NetWare in 1990. Novell devised a fix for the trouble and made it available for users (at no charge) within two days.

Users Test the Software

The common practice of distributing minimally tested software is a form of theft of service which costs unsuspecting organizations dearly. Imagine the days and weeks employees spend testing buggy code and reporting the flaws back to the software developers. Users are in effect doing the testing the manufacturers should have done. Releasing a COTS software product for sale before it is tested properly, amounts to consumer abuse and in extreme cases, consumer fraud. A careful reading of the computer and communications trade literature will help LAN managers to avoid buggy, unsupported software.

Some customer-site testing is a necessary part of the software development cycle, since developers benefit from the feedback they get directly from software users in the field. Software vendors often schedule beta tests in which users review products as part of a comprehensive testing process for software which is still in development. The end products are far better as a result, which is a boon to both the manufacturer and the user community. Companies can determine whether a software product will meet their specific needs from involvement in beta testing, and can actually influence product design by participating in this worthwhile process.

Time for a Change

The software reliability problem has reached monumental proportions because of the degree to which we rely on PCs to help us run our businesses, not to mention the country itself. The roughly six million networks in this country make it even easier for flawed software to cause havoc. Software companies establish their lack of responsibility for damage caused by their products by requiring users to agree to their terms as a condition of opening the seal on the software envelope. When was the last time you took the time to read one of those disclaimers? The practice was necessary to permit fledgling software companies to get off the ground in the mid-80s, but it is ridiculous to allow it to continue without taking the needs of users into consideration. Times have changed. Our PCs are no longer toys that we can put aside if buggy software causes trouble. We depend on them for too many things.

Operating Systems Require Special Care

Operating systems are the underpinnings of computer applications and network services. Because we rely heavily them, manufacturers of operating systems should be held to a higher performance standard, which includes reasonably well tested and correct programs and systems, as well as responsible user support.

Seasoned LAN managers would never willingly install a new operating system or NOS in a production environment without waiting to see what operational problems are identified by the early users. After the viability of the product has been established, they test the new release to see how it will perform in their own unique environment, and to be certain there are no surprises or conflicts. Test LANs are often used to verify that new COTS products work as well as to support in-house software development activities. Only when LAN managers are quite sure the new system will present no difficulty to their users do they install it on the production LAN that users rely on for network services. Even then, they are careful to take extra backups and provide a bridge back to the old system, just in case a serious problem does arise.

Is Government Intervention Necessary?

The software industry has matured to the point where manufacturers should take responsibility for protecting consumers from loss as a result of using their products. This does not mean that manufacturers should be liable for misuse or incidental difficulty. But they should be required to demonstrate that their product works before unleashing it on the public. At the least, they should quickly recall or replace defective software with a product that works and does not damage data in the process.

Automobile manufacturers have also made great profits from selling their products to consumers. Some were slow to realize that they also had an obligation to support their products and take responsibility (as well as corrective action) when they were seriously flawed. It took government action to force some manufacturers to recall products with design and manufacturing defects, and otherwise meet their responsibility to consumers.

Safety: When Lives Hang in the Balance

When software is relied on to manage critical processes, the concept of software quality assurance takes on new meaning. Nuclear reactors and other energy sources can be controlled by software process control systems. Sophisticated medical equipment may also be controlled by software and can cause injury if the software is even slightly flawed.

It must be in the nature of humans to believe that "the system works" and that if your conclusions differ from those of a computer, that you are wrong. A study of physicians in the late '70s and early '80s showed that they were willing to rely on the diagnostic capabilities of an expert computer system, even though they knew it had not been fully tested and certified as 100 percent accurate. It is frightening to think of the effect poorly tested software can have when it is presented as error-free and lives are at stake.

Software used in process control, particularly in medicine and energy, requires the most stringent control possible. Radiation is routinely used to destroy tumors as therapy for some cancers. The delivery of radiation must be precisely controlled to avoid damaging healthy tissue. In one highly publicized instance, a computer-controlled accelerator designed to deliver radiation therapy to medical patients apparently malfunctioned due to faulty software. Excessive radiation caused six accidents resulting in serious radiation burns, debilitating injuries, and death to unsuspecting patients from 1985 to 1987. The machine was said to have so many safety features that accidents were supposed to be impossible. Even after accidents were reported the errors and flaws were difficult to locate because software specifications and documentation were lacking.

Some lessons about the use of software in hazardous processes and life threatening situations from this series of dreadful accidents included:

- ■ The importance of fail-safe design which must stress safety, even at the expense of user-friendliness.

- ■ The risk of placing too much confidence in software, when the addition of hardware safety features would increase safety.

- ■ Wherever safety is an issue, you cannot over-emphasize the importance of basic software engineering, documentation, testing, independent software program code inspection and analysis, as well as other comprehensive software quality assurance practices.

- ■ Controls should be used on the operation of equipment with the power to injure or kill wherever possible, so that errors, flaws, and malfunctions are reported and acted on immediately to prevent subsequent or additional injury.

Safeguards and Solutions

U.S. Air Force Accident Risk Assessment Report (AFAR)

The United States Air Force requires that users and operators be informed of the hazards associated with the use of any given system through an Accident Risk Assessment Report (AFAR). The AFAR also contains safety-related test failure and impact data as well as descriptions of corrective actions taken to prevent future accidents.

Disclosure of the dangers and risks of using potentially hazardous devices should be made to all users of such equipment, whether they are patients or astronauts. The AFAR might provide a useful model for non-military equipment that poses a safety hazard to users or patients.

Test and Error Data Standards for Software

Once a satisfactory model has been established for disclosing safety hazard data to the using community, we can take the "disclosure thing" to another level. We can provide testing, resource requirements, and error data to consumers of COTS software so they can make better informed purchase and installation decisions.

Generally Accepted Application Development Standards

Considerable effort has gone into the development of user requirements analysis and application software design and development techniques since computers were invented. These generally accepted system development standards and practices can minimize errors and streamline system design and development processes. Some of the benefits of software systems engineering are lost in PC and LAN applications because standards are not used. Applying standards to your LAN applications is essential if you are to have a smooth and efficient operation which gives your users the support that they need.

Record Locking

Record locking prevents loss of data integrity by locking data that is already in use by another person who has update rights. This is an essential feature for LAN applications in which update capabilities are distributed among multiple users. If two or more people update the same data at the same time, a loss of data integrity can result. When an employee is terminated, for example, several employees may need to make related changes to payroll data. Without record locking, everyone could read and process the same record at the same time. Let's assume they do. The benefits person changes benefit data, payroll changes employee status to former employee and personnel updates the employment dates, in that order. Without record locking to prevent simultaneous updates, each changed record would replace the previously changed record. The last change would have restored the terminated employee's original benefits data and full employee status as it made the intended employment date change. The employee's payroll/benefit records would then be inaccurate and without integrity.

Unauthorized Access

Protection against unauthorized access and modification of data may be employed in LAN applications such as off-the-shelf e-mail, e-forms, and custom designed applications such as business planning. The level of security employed may not meet your requirements in terms of protecting sensitive data. So do not assume that just because a password is required the application is secure. Many horrified users realize too late that a system has stored their userIDs and passwords (or their data itself) in a file where they are accessible, unprotected, and vulnerable to misuse. Likewise, if your e-mail system does not have user authentication at the least, and preferably digital signature, you cannot be sure a message really came from the person who seems to have sent it. Some e-mail applications have adequate security for their purpose, but others do not. The LAN manager must be sure their security requirements match the capabilities of the application software on the LAN.

Accidental User Errors

Accidental user errors can often be avoided by making data entry straightforward and by using simple tests for reasonability on forms, database fields, and spreadsheets. For example, if you have ten salespeople, you should only permit the use of ten codes. If the data *must* be keyed in instead of being selected from a list, be sure the code entered is a valid salesperson code. Cross checking between keyed fields, such as salesperson number and sales territory number, or displaying the salesperson name that matches the keyed-in code for visual verification by the user, are simple examples of how applications can be programmed to catch errors before they get into the system. It is always easier to prevent an error than to correct one, just as it is easier to correct an error immediately than to find it and correct it later, after it has caused other, subsequent errors.

What Causes Workstation Crashes?

Did you ever wonder why some software hangs up and forces you to re-boot almost every time you use it, while other software never suffers from those sudden stops? When an error situation occurs, it is usually because the application has asked DOS to take some action which it cannot complete properly, such as read or write a disk or pull some information into memory. The operating system sends the application program an error interrupt code which identifies the particular error, say, "insufficient memory". If the error code is anticipated and handled by the software, the program can continue to process and can display a message telling the user, "Insufficient memory, remove TSRs or increase memory for printing". If the program does not anticipate and handle the error, it may "hang" or "crash" the workstation. Some programs do a better job of looking for errors and finding a way to continue processing than others.

Nothing User-friendly About It!

We are on the wrong track with respect to software user-friendliness. User-friendly software is easy-to-use, reliable, fault tolerant, and has a pleasing, intuitive man-machine interface. It does not crash, lose or damage your data, hang up your workstation, or ever give you no option but to re-boot. Software that has a pretty screen and lots of features, but forces you to reboot and lose your work from time to time, is not user-friendly. It is hard to imagine a less user-friendly act than a software application failing to handle error conditions such as "insufficient memory" so that the users are forced to reboot their workstations without saving their work. LAN users with Windows 3.1 clients are particularly subject to crashes, which are usually attributed to insufficient memory. Workstations with 8 or 12 MB of memory rarely crash, but those with the specified minimum of 4 MB crash or hang up routinely.

Applications which require more resources than advertised will result in frustration for those users who try to use it with minimal resources. Suppose your software says it can run in 4 MB of RAM. In fact, any one of its processes probably will run with 4 MB of memory, but the software allows you to run two processes—say, printing and data entry—at the same time. To run them at the same time, however, you would need to have at least 6 MB of RAM on your workstation. That represents a frustrating situation for users who will probably have to reboot every time they try to process and print at the same time. A few precise specifications on the shrink-wrapped box about specific simultaneous operations, and the memory and other resources needed to meet standard performance criteria in a given typical configuration of hardware and software, would be "user-friendly." If a software product cannot continue to process under some circumstance unless it has a total of 6 MB of memory (including the memory required for normal operation and overhead), then that 6 MB should be the specified minimum memory requirement. If standard benchmarks were used, it would be a revelation to users in terms of the amount of memory that is actually required to run some popular software in common LAN and PC software configurations.

With so many users relying heavily on their PC and LAN software, the time has come for standards to apply to COTS products for PCs, and especially for LANs.

Software Metering to Manage Usage

I know of one large company that had a problem purchasing all of the software their people needed. So, the employees copied what they felt they needed to do their jobs. A consultant called attention to the liability, believing it was an anomaly and would be corrected once management realized the seriousness of the situation. Instead, they ignored the situation and, after the consultant mentioned it again, abruptly called her unprofessional and canceled her contract.

A short time later, a letter of apology from that company to a training vendor, who caught the same company copying their video tapes, was made public. The out-of-court settlement featured a full-page public apology and an undisclosed amount of money. The amount of the settlement would probably have bought them the videos and software they needed...and then some.

LANs are particularly vulnerable to violation of copyright laws, because you may have more LAN users with access to the network than you have software licenses. Some software products (such as cc:Mail) must be purchased for each individual user, because an application userID is required for security. Other software has no tie to particular individuals. For instance, you might have 105 people who decide to use your LAN spreadsheet program all at the same time. If your software license only covers 100 of the 105 users, your organization is actively breaking the law. This poses a security threat that exposes your company to penalties for copyright law violation.

Software metering tracks the number of users of each software package on the LAN, and can be compared to the number of licenses you have purchased. If a legal license threshold is exceeded, the metering program generally takes some action. The actions vary from noting the situation and triggering an exception report, to preventing user access once the number of current licenses has been exhausted. An exception report is nice to have so that you can determine when you may need more licenses, but it does nothing to protect your organization from liability. The LT-Auditor 4.0+ NetWare LAN monitoring product has an enforcement option switch in its software metering feature. When turned on, the enforcement option holds user requests for software in a queue when all licenses are in use, and automatically notifies users when a license becomes available.

Users who forget to quit applications and logoff the LAN can tie up licenses needed by others. Automatic logoff safeguards release licenses no longer in use and ensure LAN workstations are not left logged-on and vulnerable.

Network Operators Have Responsibilities, Too

Network operators, including the growing number of Internet gateways which provide user access to the Internet for a fee, should be required to protect the data they keep for their users, to the same degree the user would protect it, if it were in their own control.

Workstation Operating System Software

DOS

DOS, the Disk Operating System, is the leading PC and LAN workstation operating system. Three major software vendors currently offer DOS software: Microsoft, IBM, and Novell. Novell became a strong entrant in the field when they acquired DR-DOS and offered the newest version as Novell DOS 7.0.

Microsoft's MS-DOS is the operating system used on most PCs and pre-installed on most new systems. When conflicts between the DoubleSpace compression feature in MS-DOS 6.0 and the Windows disk caching feature (as well as other TSRs) resulted in corruption of files and even entire hard disks, some users switched to IBM's PC-DOS version 6.3 which corrected the problem. IBM pre-loads their own PC-DOS product on new IBM PCs, rather than MS-DOS. Difficulties such as cross-linked chains have also been reported by users running other operating systems with data compression features, complex configurations, and many TSRs.

One client had classic MS-DOS 6.0 DoubleSpace data integrity problems on her laptop including many cross-linked files. She will have to locate and eliminate the source of the problem and then re-establish data integrity on her notebook PC. She has several alternatives to choose from:

1. Download DOS 6.0a from Compuserve.
2. Spend $9.95 to upgrade to MS-DOS version 6.21 which eliminates the problem by eliminating the compression feature alto-

gether. (Microsoft has been required to recall MS-DOS and other software containing the DoubleSpace compression software as the result of a copyright dispute).

3. Spend $9.95 to upgrade to MS-DOS 6.22, which fixes the DoubleSpace-TSR data integrity problem by replacing both the compression and memory management code.

4. Switch to another DOS product with disk compression, such as Novell DOS 7.0 or PC-DOS 6.3, or another operating system altogether.

5. Purchase *Stacker* 4.0 for hard disk compression.

6. Stay tuned. The Microsoft-Stac dispute was settled as this book was in the final edit. We can expect a new version of MS-DOS featuring DoubleSpace compression in a Windows/TSR-compatible form, to be released quickly.

Windows users are reluctant to switch from MS-DOS to another operating system. They fear that other software manufacturers do not have sufficient knowledge of Windows internals to enable efficient OS-GUI integration. The next version of Windows (called Chicago) will integrate the WOS (workstation operating system) itself which could have many performance advantages.

The client with DoubleSpace problems decided to switch nonetheless, when she found that Novell DOS 7.0 will automatically convert her DoubleSpace compressed hard drive to a Novell DOS Stacker-compressed drive. (She expected to have to uninstall MS-DOS 6.0, decompress her disk drive and do a low level format at the very least before converting to Novell DOS 7.0 with Stacker compression.) (Note that the professionals often resist the urge to purchase software until a "point" release, meaning the current version is no longer an "x.0" number).

Novell DOS 7.0

Novell DOS 7.0 is the first release of the DR-DOS product upgrade under the Novell label, and it has some attractive performance and security features, beyond multitasking. Personal NetWare is also included with the product.

Personal NetWare allows you to run a peer-to-peer or server-based network under DOS or Windows, or connect to a NetWare server as a NetWare client.

Novell DOS 7.0 contains the following security features:

- Secure mode hard disk security using *MASTER KEY* password and floppy boot protection for the hard drive
- Screen saver keyboard LOCK (started either by TSR time out or hot key command) with a password required for reentry
- File and directory passwords
- Disable security
- Deleted file tracking and recovery
- Damaged disk data recovery
- Save deleted files on disk
- Full or partial express backup and file recovery
- *Search and Destroy* anti-virus scan and TSR

In addition to Stacker, Novell DOS 7.0 contains a disk optimizer and memory manager/ optimizer for improving the performance of your PC without the purchase of add-on products.

OS/2

OS/2 is an IBM PC operating system with a windows-like GUI. OS/2 supports Windows 3.1 applications and even has a version that runs under Windows. OS/2 is a stable base for LAN clients and servers. It is often used for LAN applications that exchange data with IBM mainframe database management systems such as DB2.

UNIX

UNIX is a robust multi-tasking operating system which is well known for its strength in communications, as well as its complexity. There are many trap doors and back doors for the convenience of UNIX developers, that cause havoc every time a network hacker or cracker takes advantage of one to penetrate other networks. UNIX was developed by AT&T Bell Labs in the '50s for internal use, because a computer scientist found existing operating systems to be inadequate for his purposes. UNIX was not then intended to be a commercial product, let alone the operating system of choice for telecommunications gateways, it just evolved that way.

Firewalls protect UNIX host computers from intrusion through electronic networks. UNIX host computers usually manage Internet gateways and are often the targets of intrusion attacks. Some attacks have been appallingly successful, as in the example of the Morris Internet worm. For years the Internet networking community has plugged trap and back doors in UNIX as they were detected. The UNIX gateway community was once reasonably small and self-contained and was able to take care of these security incidents as they occurred. Capable programmers constructed "Firewalls" using software which was available through the Internet, to protect their UNIX systems. With the explosion of interest in the Internet—there are 15–20 million current users—and growing awareness of security problems, more formal solutions have developed to secure UNIX gateways. Several UNIX firewall products exist, or are currently in development.

The *InterLock for Internet* safeguard product consists of software and hardware that prevents intrusion of TCP/IP (UNIX-Internet) networks and restricts the flow of private information to the public Internet. InterLock accomplishes this by controlling access to network services, providing password protection, and data encryption. Administrators are able to apply their local security rules to the system. InterLock supports the following over the public Internet or between private network segments:

- Secure remote terminal access
- Secure file transfer
- Secure mail exchange between hosts for authenticated users
- DES encrypted (or unencrypted) data transfers between two or more InterLocks

Network Operating Systems Software

The security, fault tolerant, and other relevant features of the key NOSs are shown in Table 9.1. Although NetWare 2.x is no longer being shipped, it is included because of the large installed user base. Windows NT has a relatively small share of the NOS market at present, which is expected to increase.

TABLE 9.1.   COMPARISON OF NOS SECURITY FEATURES.

	NetWare v2.2	NetWare v3.12	NetWare v4.0	Windows NTAS	Sun Solaris (UNIX)
Capacity					
Server/Peer	Server	Server	Server	Peer	Either
# Users	100	250	1,000	>1,000	unlimited
# Open files	1,000	100,000	100,000	8,000	11,000
# LANs	4	16	32	2	unlimited
# Vols. per server	32	64	64	24	n/a
Storage limit	2GB	32TB	32TB	4GB	2GB
32-bit NOS	No	Y	Y	Y	Y
486-aware	No	Y	Y	No	Y
Security					
Access control	Y	Y	Y	Y	Y
Auditing	No	+	Y	Y	Y
Backup service client and server	N	Y	Y		Y
Data Recovery					
Directory rights	Y	Y	Y	Y	Y
Disk duplexing	Y	Y	Y	Y	Y
Disk mirroring	Y	Y	Y	+	Y
Duplicate FATs	Y	Y	Y	No	n/a

continued

	NETWARE v2.2	NETWARE v3.12	NETWARE v4.0	WINDOWS NTAS	SUN SOLARIS (UNIX)
Duplicate directory verification		Y	Y		N
Fault Tolerance					
File attributes	Y	Y	Y	Y	n/a
Hot Fix	Y	Y	Y	Y	Y
Inherited rights (IRM)	No	Y	Y	No	n/a
Intruder detection	Y	Y	Y	No	No
Intruder alert	No	No	No	Y	No
Keyboard lock with reentry password	N		Y		Y
Object/property rights	No	No	Y	No	No
Record locking	Y	Y	Y	Y	Y
Resource mgmt.	No	Y	Y	Some	Y
Salvage files	Y	Y	Y	No	No
Security check	Y	Y	Y	No	Y
SFT III	No	No	Y	No	No
Shared security	No	No	No	Y	No
Supervisor restriction	No	Y	Y	No	No
TTS	Y	Y	Y	No	Add on
UPS monitoring	Y	Y	Y	+	No
User rights	Y	Y	Y	Y	Y
WOS flush	No	No	No	Y	No
Write verification	Y	Y	Y	No	No
Administration/ LAN Analysis					
Auto WS update	No	No	No	No	No
Cache statistics	Y	Y	Y	Y	No
Centralized rights	Y	Y	Y	Y	Y

continued

	NETWARE v2.2	NETWARE v3.12	NETWARE v4.0	WINDOWS NTAS	SUN SOLARIS (UNIX)
CPU usage	Y	Y	Y	Y	Y
CPU stats	No	Y	Y	Y	Y
Disk usage	No	No	No	No	Y
Files open	Y	Y	Y	+	Y
Global directory	No	No	Y		No
Multiserver admin	Y	Y	Y	Y	Y
Packet analysis	No	Y	Y	No	No
Performance Features					
Directory caching	Y	Y	Y	Y	Y
Directory hashing	Y	Y	Y	No	No
Disk migration	No	No	Y	Y	No
Elevator seeking	Y	Y	Y	Y	No
FAT Index	Y	Y	Y	No	n/a
File caching	Y	Y	Y	Y	Y
Optimization	No	Y	Y	Y	Y

Legend:

GB	Gigabyte
TB	Terabyte
+	Optional (at additional cost)
TTS	Transaction Tracking System
SFT III	System Fault Tolerance Level 3

Client-Server versus Peer-to-Peer LANs

Client-server is a LAN computing architecture in which a front-end (client portion) interacts with the user, and performs much of the information processing, and peripheral input and output operations. The back-end (server portion) acts as a database engine and communications controller. Security is usually centralized and managed at the server, so that as long as your server is secure, your LAN is protected. The result of distributing tasks between the server and the client workstations according to computing resource requirements for processing speed, memory, disk speed, disk capacity, and input/output equipment optimizes overall network throughput.

Peer-to-peer LAN workstations share the NOS and also the burden of network services, network communications, and security. Since there is no single point of control these LANs are more flexible but also more vulnerable to faults and intrusion. Peer clients cannot be properly authenticated without a secure storage location and processor for IDs, passwords, and encryption keys. WFW, Personal NetWare, and LANtastic are examples of popular peer-to-peer LANs.

In an effort to realize productivity gains and some degree of security from networks, organizations are increasingly turning to client-server applications supported by server-based LANs. They employ sound security features, like centralized control of application software and server data, while they minimize the processing burden on the server by off-loading tasks to client workstations. NetWare, NTS, Vines, and LAN Manager are examples of server-based LANs.

NetWare LANs

Novell, Inc. offers a variety of NetWare NOSs including Personal NetWare, a peer-to-peer or server based LAN for workgroups. The client-server NOSs are NetWare 3.x (for up to 250 users) and the enterprise 4.x LAN which supports up to 1,000 users and includes NDS (NetWare Directory Services). NDS is a global, distributed replicated database of network resources. The NetWare installed base is estimated to be about 64 percent of all LANs and accounts for approximately 70 percent of new LANs sold. There are 6 million LANs in the United States alone, encompassing more than 70 million LAN workstations. Novell LAN users enjoy reliable and enthusiastic support from the manufacturer as well as from a vast community of Novell CNEs (Certified NetWare Engineers). Novell has supported users online with the NetWire service on Compuserve since 1986. NetWire is now staffed by some 600 volunteer NetWire system operators (SYSOPS) who will get answers to your questions, usually within 24 hours. Every NetWare LAN manager should have access to this resource because the latest files and driver updates can be downloaded immediately, and the discussion forums are informative. You can get your specific issues addressed in the forums, although many users are unwilling to pay the price of "going public" with their internal technical problems.

PERSONAL NETWARE

Personal NetWare essentially replaces NetWare Lite and is available both as a separate product and bundled with Novell's DOS 7.0. Personal NetWare security features include:

- Access control through passwords and access rights.
- Single Logon with password protection.
- Lock keyboard with password required for reentry (for client and server).
- Master key password.
- Disable security.
- Disable user accounts.
- Deleted file tracking and recovery .
- Full or partial express backup and recovery.
- Search and Destroy anti-virus scan and TSR.
- Secure mode hard disk protection after floppy boot (client and server).

Novell's NetWare 3.x is a widely-used NOS with solid security and performance features. It serves up to 250 concurrent users, meeting needs where there are too few interconnected LANs to justify a full enterprise networking solution. Even before version 4.x appeared, NetWare was usually rated the fastest and most reliable NOS overall by the PC and network magazines. LAN administration was tedious, however, and had to be performed separately on every LAN server. Banyan Vines, by contrast, had long offered global naming and administration services through its highly regarded Street Smart feature.

NetWare 3.x performance features include:

■ **Disk mirroring** writes data to two disk drives on the same channel simultaneously to give "mirror image" copies of data. If the original hard disk fails, the duplicate disk takes over automatically.

■ **Disk duplexing** duplicates data on a second hard disk on a separate channel. Disk writes made to the original disk are also made to the second disk. If the original disk or channel fails, the duplicate disk takes over automatically. This provides more protection than disk mirroring, at the cost of an additional hard disk controller.

■ **Software record locking** prevents two or more users from writing simultaneously to the same record.

■ **Write verification** checks data written to the hard disk. It reads back the data and compares it to the original data still in memory. If there is a match, the data in memory is erased. If the data does not match, Hot Fix marks that block on the disk as bad and redirects the data to another location on the hard disk.

■ **Hot Fix** is used when write verification determines that there is a bad data block on the disk. Hot Fix redirects data to be stored to the Hot Fix redirection area. It marks the defective block as bad so the server will not attempt to store data at that location.

■ **UPS monitoring** is a NOS feature that protects data from failures in network hardware by monitoring the status of the UPS hardware unit attached to the server. When a problem occurs, such as the UPS battery failing, the monitor triggers an alert.

■ **Transaction Tracking System** (TTS) protects against loss of data integrity by backing out incomplete transactions when a failure in a network component prevents the transaction from being processed completely.

■ **Directory structure duplication** is a feature that protects data from hardware failures. A hard disk directory and FAT (file allocation table) contain the file addresses used to store and retrieve data. The NOS maintains duplicate copies of both the directory table and the file allocation table in separate areas of the hard disk. If the primary tables are lost or destroyed, the copy is used.

■ **Directory verification** protects data from failures in network hardware by a consistency check on the duplicate directory and file allocation tables to verify that they are identical.

Note that many of these are hardware not software features, but cannot actually be used until the NOS provides the necessary program instructions. For instance, a multiple processor feature offers at least two processors, one of which can be made available for use in case a primary processor fails, if so designed by the hardware and NOS providers. This capability has been available in Tricord and Compaq servers for some time, but NOS software support has been lacking thus far. Novell is expected to provide support for multiple processors by the end of 1994.

ACCESS RIGHTS TO DIRECTORIES AND FILES

Users can view and use only directories and files to which they have access Rights. NetWare Rights either permit or prevent users from accessing and processing files. File and directory attributes can also be assigned to limit user access activity. The combination of Rights and attributes may be hard to grasp but is so important to the security of NetWare LANs that it is worth spending the time to understand and implement them properly. Setting Rights and attributes correctly accomplishes the following desirable ends:

1. It prevents users of the LAN and intruders from accidentally (or otherwise) accessing, using, changing, replacing, or destroying any data except the data to which they have been given access.

2. It can prevent piracy of LAN software.

3. It prevents viruses from infecting .EXE and .COM programs which are marked with marked with RO, X (Read Only, Execute only) attributes.

The Rights in NetWare 3.x are:

S	Supervisory	**M**	Modify attributes (not file contents)
R	Read	**F**	File Scan to view file and directory structure
W	Write	**A**	Access Control to grant rights
C	Create	**E**	Erase directories and files

User Rights are set in a hierarchical pattern in the directory with the Root level being the highest level. Rights set at the Root cascade down to lower level directories, unless blocked by specific Rights assignments at a lower level, or by an Inherited Rights Mask (IRM).

NetWare attributes apply to files and directories and override user access rights. Attributes may further limit your ability to use applications and files. NetWare attributes are:

RW	(read and write)	**RO**	(read only)
S	(sharable)	**T**	(transactional)
SY	(system)	**A**	(mark as archive needed)
H	(hidden)	**P**	(purge on delete)
RA	(read audit)	**WA**	(write audit)
CI	(no copy [inhibit])	**DI**	(no delete)
RI	(no rename)	**I**	(Indexed)
X	(execute only for .EXE and .COM files)		

Note that:

■ **Program file attributes** are usually RO (read-only) and S (sharable). Use the X (execute-only) attribute with caution because you cannot change the attribute once set and programs marked X cannot be backed up or updated.

- **Data file attributes** are usually RW (read/write), S (sharable), and possibly: A (archive needed) or T (transactional).

- **Directory attributes** also override access Rights and limit a user's ability to access and process in a directory. Directory attributes are: DI, H, P, RI, and Sy.

Utility programs are used to set up, administer, and monitor the LAN to gain early warning of problems that could pose a threat to the security of the LAN. Use of third-party software is essential for administering, monitoring, troubleshooting, and managing large LANs. There are also utilities that LAN administrators can use to penetrate the NetWare Bindery when they get locked out of their own systems. LAN administrators can obtain such tools from the COM-SEC bulletin board. Be aware that in the wrong hands these programs are hacker's tools and can be used to compromise the security of NetWare 2.x and 3.x LANs. Do not download them unless you need them, and do not share them with anyone. If you must use them, keep them under lock and key.

Novell's NetWare version 4.0 was quickly replaced by version 4.01 to correct a slow synchronization of directory replicas under certain circumstances, such as directory updates and when WAN links were not immediately available.

NetWare 4.x is distinguished by an enterprise network approach that supports the movement from isolated departmental LANs to an integrated enterprise LAN environment. LAN administration is simpler because of new management tools and NDS, the new NetWare Directory Services feature. NDS maintains information on every user, group, server, volume, directory, computer, printer, etc. through a system of objects, properties, and values and is the main advantage of the new product. Because there is only one enterprise directory with NDS, users now have just one logon across all servers. NetWare 4.0 was LAN Magazine's selection for best enterprise NOS of 1993. It supports up to 1,000 concurrent users with multiple operating systems and servers. Data management is improved, and disk compression saves as much as 50% of file server disk space. A backup service (with a compression option) is provided for DOS, Windows, and OS/2 clients, as well as the network servers.

Security has changed significantly in five areas with NetWare 4.x:

1. The Bindery has been eliminated in favor of NDS, which greatly reduces the risk of network compromise.

2. Public key cryptography has been added with a single private key assigned to users on login that determines what rights the user has to network resources.

3. Rights security, which previously existed for users, directories, and files has been added for objects and properties. This enables security to be established directly for entities used in object oriented applications without translating requirements from the command environment to the new OOP (object oriented programming) environment.

4. An audit monitor has been added which tracks events and usage and maintains secure records.

5. Intruder lockout applies to the interconnected enterprise LAN, not just the LAN where the failed logon took place.

Minor changes include:

■ The Inherited Rights Mask is now the Inherited Rights Filter (and it has not changed)

■ NWADMIN is used in place of SYSCON to perform administration tasks

■ The new "fire phasor" emits a loud noise from a workstation to call attention to security violations, error situations, and even important messages on the screen.

Even with the exciting new features there are still third party opportunities because more utilities and management tools are required than are provided. There are little problems such as the need to sort the global directory and not being able to do so in NetWare.

UNIX

UNIX is essentially a mature, robust operating system that incorporates sufficient communications features to permit it to be classified as a NOS. UNIX is run on platforms from mainframes to PCs. Unfortunately, there are already so many versions of UNIX (Santa Cruz Operation [SCO], Sun, HP, and Novell), that it is difficult to establish standards or a firm base for independent application software development, let alone a meaningful comparison with other NOSs.

WINDOWS FOR WORKGROUPS

Windows For Workgroups (WFW) is a popular peer-to-peer LAN configuration which enables Windows users (clients) to share clipboards. It is otherwise similar to the peer-to-peer Personal NetWare and LANtastic DOS LANs. Newer versions of Windows software are expected to be replaced by WFW client workstation software.

WINDOWS NT

Windows NT provides general purpose support for power users and single workgroup application servers. Microsoft has applied for a C2 level security classification for Windows NT server from the NCSC per Trusted Computing Base standards. Windows NT provides a secure logon which avoids the possibility of intrusion at that point.

WINDOWS NT SERVER (NTS)

Windows NTS meets the need for dedicated servers and multi-server network administration in a small user base. It offers good performance features and ease of use, multitasking and symmetric multi processing, RISC processing, network login for users, unlimited users, file locks, open files, and long file names. Its security features include encrypted passwords, secure authentication, good audit features, and is designed to meet C2 level security (B2 with third party add on). Users are reluctant to use the NTS file system. They tend to prefer DOS FAT file system which eliminates many NTS potential benefits.

ARTISOFT'S LANTASTIC

Artisoft's LANtastic peer-to-peer network provides support for Windows, DOS, voice mail, and live voice chat over network lines. It supports connections to NetWare and OS/2 hosts.

Trusted Computing Base (TCB) Security Evaluation

If you had to choose a NOS for a secure LAN today, you would have to choose NetWare 4.x according to a communications security expert and well-known Communications Week columnist, Wayne Rash. In terms of formal certification, formal evaluations and opinions are rendered according to Trusted Computing Base (TCB) criteria performed by the NCSC (National Computer Security Center), which was originally a part of the Department of Defense. NetWare 4.x and Windows NTAS are being evaluated at present for a C2 level of security by the NCSC against criteria in the Trusted Computer Security Evaluation Criteria (known as the "Orange Book"). TCB criteria were used to classify products according to the degree of security they require to give some structure to the task of purchasing government systems and networks that have security requirements. NetWare 4.x is presently in use by several government organizations that require a NOS with a C2 classification, meaning that network access is controlled. At a C2 level, users are made accountable through login, security events (logins, file creation, opening, and deletions) are logged for audit, and LAN resources are isolated (workstations, servers, users, etc. are uniquely identified). The private sector also uses TCB certification levels and Orange Book guidelines to evaluate or describe security in computers and networks because there is no commercial equivalent.

Graphical User Interfaces

Graphical User Interfaces (GUIs) isolate users from the operating system and are intended to make computers easier to use. Casual PC users are able to use software applications with little training with a well-designed GUI. The most notable GUI is Microsoft Windows.

Windows

Windows 3.1 presents an attractive, intuitive GUI which is rapidly becoming the interface of choice for client workstations on LANs. Most new PC systems are bundled with pre-installed Windows 3.1 software. Many applications have been developed to use Windows 3.1. It allows non-technical people to use a wide variety of software without steep learning curves and special training. So much software works only with Windows that even if you prefer another interface, you often must use it to run the latest software. Windows 3.1 requires 4 million bytes of memory to deliver decent response time, and works better with 8 or 12 million bytes. Because it is a graphically oriented user interface, it is difficult to use without using a pointing device, such as a mouse, to select menu items. Since keyboarding can be faster than pointing and clicking, use of a mouse can slow a user down in some applications. Prolific users of a few basic DOS applications (such as WordPerfect and Lotus 1-2-3) may enjoy greater personal productivity in their work without using Windows. Windows continues to evolve as a workstation and server platform for application development, and newer versions are expected to virtually replace the installed base of Windows 3.1 as well as DOS LAN client workstations. Chicago, the code name for the new 32-bit version of Windows, includes the WOS code, thus is designed to eliminate the need for any other operating system. Chicago is in Beta test at some 20,000 customer sites.

In terms of security, there is a screen saver with a password option in Windows 3.1 designed to prevent unauthorized individuals from gaining access to the system and the hard drive. Intruders with minimal PC skills might simply boot the PC with a system disk in the floppy drive and proceed to use the workstation. They could enter the Windows directory on the hard drive and edit the WIN.INI file to remove the password option. The next time the PC is booted, no password would be required. Worse still, the password could then be reset, preventing users from using their own PCs. Boot protection safeguards can prevent this situation.

Groupware

A special type of LAN software called groupware has become extremely popular because it enables groups of people to share information across a network. Groupware products dramatically simplify administrative tasks such as scheduling group meetings or streamlining paperwork-intensive systems. They generally permit fast development of applications that support business process redesign and workflow improvement. When your users are remote, however, you cannot rely on the NOS to protect your applications.

WordPerfect Office

WordPerfect Office provides office automation groupware benefits through e-mail, e-forms (InForms), file sharing, calendaring, and task management features. It presently lacks fundamental user and server authentication security features that are essential in a secure platform for workgroup computing.

Lotus Notes

The market leader in groupware is Lotus Notes. Notes sales began doubling every year, once the user community understood the groupware concept and its potential benefits. It has an easy-to-use GUI, and permits integration and sharing of many kinds of data in a document-based framework. Notes is a client-server application development tool for Windows, OS/2, and UNIX servers with Windows, OS/2, UNIX and Macintosh clients. The ease of access and controlled sharing of information throughout an organization encourages efficient communication, which leads to streamlining of processes and vastly improved management controls. There is no circumstance where groups of people must work together where improved communications would not provide benefits. After several years of use, Return On Investment (ROI) figures average 400 percent for Notes projects. It seems that the "promise of automated MIS", which managers have been hoping for since the '50s, may finally be upon us.

 I viewed the writing of this book as a workgroup project, which I managed with Notes. It simplified the process greatly and I was the sole Notes user. I can only imagine how much easier it would have been if my editors, reviewers, and production staff had access to the entire manuscript throughout the process. Graphics support, document sharing, voice annotation, phone message integration, and e-mail communication could have reduced errors and saved days of revision.

Lotus Notes safeguards and security features complement each other to deliver the following security essentials for LAN applications:

- Integrity
- Confidentiality
- Accuracy
- Access control
- Authentication
- Tamper prevention
- Source verification

Lotus Notes provides secure e-mail and a unique combination of standards-based security techniques and safeguards to protect strategic and sensitive data against intrusion. Lotus Notes typically connects hundreds of users working in various geographic locations who may even be continents away from each other. It automatically replicates databases, routes e-mail and gives different sets of users various, sometimes private, views of databases. In addition to certifying the identity of message originators by means of electronic signatures (using encryption), it protects information by permitting encryption of:

- E-mail messages
- Whole documents
- Communication sessions

■ Fields within documents

Lotus Notes uses public key encryption to authenticate users, as well as servers. This gives users the assurance they must have, that their information is secure. Installing the product, administering, and designing Notes security and applications are not trivial. Expertise is required to ensure the full protection of your data and applications and to realize the maximum benefit of the groupware capabilities.

Highly competent experts have expressed concern about "faulty record locking" and the ability to access Notes databases from remote locations. This lack of understanding of a solid product is disconcerting. The problem lies in the lack of understanding of the product concept (replication and database design techniques) and the importance of correct security implementation rather than weakness on the part of Lotus Notes security.

A kind of groupware that is intended to simplify and automate the flow of work, and streamline paperwork, is known as Workflow software. Most of the popular Workflow software products require and work with Lotus Notes, thus have the same security strengths.

Application Software

LAN application software usually relies on the NOS to provide all essential security, and that is a mistake if you have remote users. Note the discussion of securing LANs with remote access in the electronic access control chapter.) Most LAN application development tools, such as the CASE products, are disappointing from a security perspective because they lack the features that would permit application developers to easily incorporate security features into new applications. Some popular LAN application system development products are:

- **IEF**—a CASE software tool.

- **Lotus Notes**—an off-the-shelf groupware product and rapid application development tool.

- **Montage ORDBMS**—an Object-oriented Relational DBMS.

- **ORACLE**—a scalable DBMS and forms-based application development tool for platforms from LANs to mainframes.

- **Powerbuilder**—an important tool for rapid application development.

- **Sybase**—an application system development and database development tool

- **WordPerfect Office**—an off-the shelf groupware tool which supports InForms, a popular e-forms product.

Two products designed to meet the growing need for security in Internet (TCP/IP) applications are the SecureWeb Viewer Developer's Toolkit and the SecureWeb Server Developer's Toolkit. They will enable application developers to incorporate "certificates" or public key encryption authentication into secure applications designed to run on the *World Wide Web*. The World Wide Web provides multimedia access to information on the Internet through a common user interface and offers a wealth of opportunity for application developers.

A few applications have security features or problems that are worth noting.

WordPerfect 5.1 and 6.0 for DOS

I have used WordPerfect for most of my word processing since version 5.0 and find it an extremely powerful personal productivity tool. I used WordPerfect macros to import Lotus 1-2-3 spreadsheets into applications that featured impressive looking custom printed reports almost before version 5.1 was out of the box. With version 6.0 for DOS, WordPerfect just keeps getting better. It offers many desktop publishing features including outlining, hypertext, good graphics support, faxing from the application, document compare, text floating, cell references to tables or formulas, more than two document windows, cross references, printing in colors, sound clips, and watermarks, to name a few.

WordPerfect permits you to password protect your files, over and above the security provided by your NOS. However, if you forget your password there is no way to recover your file. It is lost forever. Password protecting the whole workstation instead of protecting individual files is safer overall. If you choose to password protect individual files try using the same good password every time, so you can easily remember it. If you wish to protect a file from being accessed and your workstation is not secure, you can keep the file on a floppy disk and lock the disk away.

On the LAN, WordPerfect locks document files which are already in use to prevent multiple updates and resulting loss of information integrity. Setting WordPerfect up on a network takes some extra work and the documentation, which is generally excellent, is quite helpful in this respect. WordPerfect works particularly well on NetWare LANs.

ORACLE

ORACLE is a scalable forms-based database and Rapid Application Development tool. It has been used on mainframes and mini computers for many years and has a broad user base.

SYBASE

SYBASE is a popular development tool for groupware LAN applications. SYBASE offers error handling mechanisms that prevent a client workstation from crashing if a severe error is detected. After a client has lost its connection to the server a new connection is established automatically when the error condition is corrected. It also records every update operation on a log that is very useful in recovery. It includes updates in temporary databases used as scratch space in the server by database users. You can avoid the overhead associated with disk logging by specifying a UNIX file as a logging device to force disk access to be controlled by file system buffering.

Utilities

There is an extensive array of COTS utility software available for managing and protecting your LAN assets. The utilities that affect security include:

- Access control software
- Menu systems
- Data protection and recovery
- Fault tolerant features and add-ons
- LAN monitoring, management, and analysis tools

Access control safeguards and LAN monitoring, management, and analysis tools are discussed in the chapters on physical and electronic access and LAN hardware.

Workstations and servers may be protected by access control safeguards such as screen savers, "boot" locks, automatic LAN logoff features, and hard disk protectors, which may be installed on each PC or on the server itself.

Menu Systems

In addition to making it easier to use a LAN, menus also control user access to LAN resources such as files, directories, and applications. When you wish to keep tighter control of your LAN than the NOS permits, custom-designed menus can help. Some menuing systems provide another level of control on user access to LAN resources such as printers, faxes, access to other networks and gateways to mainframe applications. One such custom NetWare 3.x menu system limited user access to selected menu applications on a need to know basis, eliminated printing setup hassles through a simple menu-level process, and made the entire system easier to administer, manage, and use.

Sabre

Sabre is a popular menuing system used as a replacement for NetWare menus. NetWare 4.x incorporates a slimmed down version of Saber; however, the full menus are still considered highly desirable to many NetWare users.

Access Control Software

Boot locks protect PC LAN workstations from being booted from either the floppy drive or the hard drive without entering the correct password. This is a no-cost feature in Novell DOS version 7. It is interesting to note that boot passwords are frequently stored in the PC's battery-backed CMOS memory, which is primarily used to store system setup data and the date and time. When the CMOS memory is intentionally damaged, corrupted by a system error, or lost when the battery fails, the boot password is also lost. Some PCs will store a "resume" password in CMOS along with the boot password. When the CMOS information is lost, the PC "forgets" that it needs a password at boot or resume time. And, whoever resets the CMOS can also reset the password. Portables with standby and resume features can also lose their CMOS (and password[s]) if left in standby mode until the CMOS battery runs out.

Screen savers blank the screen so unauthorized persons may not view LAN information. Screen savers may be set to appear automatically when the PC has not been used for a specified number of minutes, or when the user strikes a specific-screen blanking hot key. A password can be used to prevent intruders from gaining access when the user is away from the workstation. Be sure the screen saver you use prevents an intruder from rebooting the workstation from the A: drive, removing or resetting password information (as in Windows 3.1), and gaining full access to your system.

Lock offers an impressive array of security features, including authentication, boot lock, access control and rights, anti-virus protection, hot key logoff, screen blanking, keyboard lock, encryption, audit trail and centralized administration. The system, source code, site licenses, and reseller licenses are available for this product, which is downloadable from a bulletin board for a 30-day evaluation.

LAN Monitoring, Management, and Analysis Tools

Tools are available that can assist administrators and managers in monitoring, managing, and analyzing the security and well-being of their LAN. The tools include the LT-Auditor 4.0+, the Network Advisor, LT-Stat, and the new server management tools. Their purpose is to provide information about the functioning of the server itself and issue alerts when out-of-tolerance conditions arise. Additional products in this category are discussed in chapters throughout the book. Products are listed in Appendix C.

Server Management Software

Server management tools are a relatively recent addition to the array of LAN management software products on the market. They enable LAN managers to quickly identify potential security incidents and other trouble on the LAN.

INSIGHT Manager from Compaq Computer (do not confuse with HP's discontinued LANsight monitor for LAN Manager) is a valuable aid in managing Compaq LAN servers. INSIGHT requires Windows 3.1 and provides server information as well as onscreen and pager event notification. Insight is covered in more detail in the chapter on LAN hardware.

Performance Console from Computer Communication is a NetWare 3.x NLM that monitors key file server functions and displays them in a dashboard-like screen. It reports on CPU utilization, connection usage, dirty cache, available file cache, LAN adapter usage, disk drives, percentage of valid packet and volume usage, and has visual and audible alerts that are set by the server administrator. It costs about $99.

Ontrack Data Recovery for NetWare (3.x and 4.x) provides excellent utility programs for file system analysis and repair, record erase, data edit, etc. for the knowledgeable LAN manager.

Data Protection and Recovery

Integrity Master, which is on the diskette attached to this book, detects corrupted files and viruses, repairs what it can and informs you about the situation. This is a powerful shareware system by Wolfgang Stiller and is not intended for beginning LAN managers. Using it on a LAN requires tuning as you will see. If you decide to use and register the software you will also get an informative little book on *Defeating Viruses and Other Threats to Data Integrity* and a clear description of methods for correcting DoubleSpace problems. More detail is provided in the chapter on network dependability.

Norton Utilities 8.0 has helpful Windows tuning and more diagnostic, recovery and repair features for DOS 6.x compressed drives.

Fault Tolerant Addons

Vinca's Standby Server consists of software, boards, and cables, and provides server redundancy at a cost in the $1,695–$1,995 range. The servers do not have to be an exact match nor dedicated; and only 1 copy of NetWare is required. Mirroring of data to hard disk drives in a second machine allows the second LAN to share data on the hard drive of the failed server.

Novell's SFT III, System Fault Tolerance level 3, starts at about $100,000. It is fault-tolerant software that provides protection from downtime for LANs running mission-critical applications by providing immediate redundancy and full disaster recovery protection as long as the server is still operating. This is accomplished by mirroring two servers in synchronization as a precaution against failure in either one. The feature is available for LANs with up to 250 users.

CHAPTER 10

CONTINGENCY PLANNING FOR EMERGENCIES

ontingency planning is the process of devising plans and strategies for coping with emergency situations that cause disruption of normal LAN operations. The idea is to be thoroughly prepared for various kinds of disasters by having tested plans and procedures to follow that keep loss of data, processing time, and network service to the absolute minimum. Because so many essential business processes are computerized, businesses that cannot get their computer operations up and running soon after a disaster usually suffer serious losses and many go out of business. A 1978 University of Minnesota study showed that after ten days of computer downtime, the work which could be accomplished without computers dropped to a mere nine percent. Today's organizations are computerized to a much greater extent than they were in 1978. As a result, the work we can accomplish without computers is significantly less.

The newness of LANs means we have few examples of businesses that have successfully worked through prepared contingency plans in the face of an emergency. A quick survey of recent major disasters indicates that LANs and microcomputer systems do not fare as well in disaster recovery situations as do mainframe systems. They are less likely to have contingency plans, despite the value of the service they provide and the data they contain. The core of the problem appears to be a stunning overall lack of formal contingency planning in organizations that rely heavily on their computers and networks. After Hurricane Hugo, 61 percent of surveyed firms were unable to process their accounting data. Fifty-six percent had no contingency plan, and all of these companies experienced significant downtime (up to four months) as a result. Surprisingly enough, internal auditors had failed to recommend contingency planning in *every one* of these cases, and outside auditors had failed to recommend that contingency plans be prepared in 91 percent of the cases.

When the Chicago River flooded Chicago's central business district in 1992, it wrought havoc on 200,000 people. Two hundred buildings were evacuated, and of the 30 data centers affected, 18 had to be relocated to "hot site" recovery locations.

The disruption of computer and network operations when terrorists bombed the World Trade Center was a catastrophe for the businesses without Disaster Recovery (DR) and Continuation Of Operations Plans (COOPs). The New York City Mayor's Task Force study of 200 of the 900 companies affected showed that 90 percent had no disaster contingency plans and no idea where to get backup facilities.

We have come to expect a certain lack of security awareness on the part of PC and network users. The inattention to contingency planning on the part of LAN managers, however, may not be due solely to a lack of awareness of threats or their consequences. It seems that many who are expecting a major disaster still fail to take the necessary steps to protect their network resources. According to a 1992 IntelliQuest survey, more than half the respondents were expecting serious data losses, yet 63 percent of those had not taken steps to deal with the problem. The reasons for the disconnect between awareness and action are not quite clear. The oversight may be rooted in any or all of the following:

■ The great complexity of threats and available safeguards.

■ A willingness to go along with the crowd (ignoring the possibility of not being able to recover from a disaster).

■ A lack of publicity regarding the effect of disasters on organizations that do not protect highly computerized and networked business operations.

■ A lack of skill in presenting a strong case for security planning and LAN risk management to senior executives.

■ A lack of interest on the part of senior management.

Whatever the reason for the omission, an opportunity for significant improvement in risk management exists in organizations across the U.S. Although they are generally more security-conscious, and their financial institutions are required by law to have contingency plans, a survey of British firms showed only 62 percent had DRPs, of which a third were never tested. Of those with disaster plans, 86 percent had no plans for continuation of operations at an alternate location according to the October '92 issue of Computer Weekly.

The importance of contingency planning for emergencies in the management of LANs cannot be stressed enough. No matter how well-controlled and efficient your LAN operation, a disaster can destroy the entire facility within seconds—data, server, workstations, communications hardware, physical cabling plant, plans, designs, documentation and procedures, original software diskettes, and backup copies—all of it.

Imagine what it would feel like to stand outside your company headquarters and watch the building burn to the ground. In times of great stress, as in the middle of a disaster, people do not think clearly. In such a state of shock and bewilderment, it might take some time to re-orient yourself and to question, "How soon will the LAN be needed?" and "What can I do to get it back on track?" If you had previously prepared and tested contingency plans, and had stored them offsite with backup files, procedures, and other essentials, you would have only to retrieve and follow them. This is not to say that preparing the contingency plan is a trivial matter. Far from it. It is, however, easier to address contingency as part of a comprehensive security plan than in isolation. Much of what you must do in disaster recovery is dictated by choices regarding backup method, level of data and hardware redundancy, and so on. Contingency planning is best tackled as a unique project by your best team because of its importance to the business and because of its complexity. Top management support for contingency operations must be won or the resources allocated will likely be inadequate to the task.

This chapter gives a methodology for creating these plans and includes some simple examples. *Your* contingency plans should be more detailed and specific. PCs 'R' Us, a Lotus Notes Business Partner, offers low cost DRP and COOP template applications which can be customized for your precise environment. The plans are implemented in Lotus Notes which enables group participation in the planning process, facilitates rapid development, and simplifies contingency plan execution. The Notes groupware platform provides a vehicle for involving and training emergency response teams. It also offers security for highly sensitive information as well as the communications mechanism and workflow structure to support an emergency response team in action. The plans in this chapter will be referred to in the sample LAN Security Plan addressed in the case study in Chapter 11. The mechanics of planning for disaster recovery and continuation of operations at an alternate location follow.

Methodology for Contingency Planning

Developing disaster recovery and continuation of operations contingency plans consists of analyses of business and organizational needs, evaluation of alternatives, decision-making, design of contingency systems and operations, development of the plan, testing, and implementation (should it ever become necessary). Typical contingency planning activities are summarized in the following chart.

PHASE	ACTIVITIES
Analysis	Analyze essential business and organizational needs for LAN services (e-mail, file storage, etc.) and application processing following an emergency.
	Establish relative importance, urgency, and priority of essential LAN services and applications.
	Identify reasonable contingency alternatives:
	▪ Manual processing
	▪ Hot site
	▪ Cold site
Evaluation of alternatives	Evaluate alternatives based on expected loss avoidance, cost of solution, difficulty of implementation, constraints, insurance coverage for replacement of equipment and continuation of operations, and other considerations.
	1. How to construct the contingency plan:
	▪ Self-prepared
	▪ Recovery service provider
	▪ Consultant
	2. Required level of security
	3. Backup strategy, methods, and systems:
	▪ Backup to off site mainframe
	▪ In-company secure backup storage
	▪ Outside secure backup storage/service provider
	▪ LAN-based backup
	▪ Backups stored on site, off site, or both
	▪ User controlled backup

continued

PHASE	ACTIVITIES
	■ No backup
	4. Logistics (off site offices, LANs, servers, resources)
	5. Resources to allocate
	6. Alternate site possibilities:
	■ In-company off site facility
	■ Recovery service provider
	■ Emergency facility provider:
	1. Hot site versus cold site
	2. Portable site versus fixed
	■ No alternate LAN or processing site required
Decision-making	Decide about the following:
	■ Selection of DRP and COOP teams
	■ Choice of backup strategy (if not a constraint)
	■ Are asset inventories and other documentation adequate?
	■ Choice of on site or off site secure storage site for plans, backups, documentation
	■ When must applications be operational? Are any critical to survival of the business? What is the cost of downtime?
	■ Selection of alternate site for emergency use, equipment suppliers.
	■ Does sensitive LAN data require special provisions?

continued

PHASE	ACTIVITIES
	■ How specific should the plan be regarding private and sensitive LAN operations information?
	■ Who must see the plan, and given the distribution, how can it be secured?
	■ How will emergency operations be financed?
Design of Contingency Plan Details	Given requirements and constraints, construct solutions that work for partial vs. total destruction and temporary vs. permanent disaster scenarios for events identified in Risk Assessment including:
	■ Data destruction (due to human error and other causes)
	■ LAN penetration attack
	■ Virus/rogue program attack
	■ Equipment failure
	■ Software error
	■ Fire, flood, weather
	■ Sabotage
Development of the Plan	Identify DRP team, COOP team, LAN user support team, responsible users.
	Establish constraints and assumptions for your unique environment.
	Involve users, executives, and technical staff in decision-making.
	Write it down, obtain approvals.
Testing	Test several disaster scenarios.

continued

PHASE	**ACTIVITIES**
	Certify, gain approval for, and secure the plan.
	Re-test periodically.
	Continuously improve the plan in subsequent tests.

FIGURE 10.1   CONSTRUCTING CONTINGENCY PLANS FOR EMERGENCIES.

Remember that even if you have one absolutely essential LAN application which must be supported during the recovery period after a disaster, all applications do not necessarily have to be supported while the LAN is out of service. Some LAN applications may be handled manually or as stand-alone PC tasks during disaster recovery. Let the needs of the business and the cost of downtime determine which applications are to be supported off site, and whether LAN operations are continued off site at all. Every resource dedicated to COOP efforts reduces the support available for the primary disaster recovery effort and ongoing business activities. Working with the business units to categorize applications by relative importance, urgency, priority, and cost of delay in processing simplifies the task of analyzing LAN contingency requirements.

The selection of a standby site where LAN operations can be continued should consider business operations as well as technical requirements. Hot sites are fully equipped and ready for operation as soon as your backup files are restored, whereas cold sites are essentially low-cost empty space for which you must supply the equipment, software, staff, supplies, etc. Hot or cold portable sites can be delivered to the disaster location itself which may be desirable in some cases. Commercial disaster recovery services are available and will manage an entire emergency operation for you, or you can choose other options.

Many facilities can either be shared at a lower cost, or used exclusively. Beware of the arrangement in which a facility is shared on a first-come first-served or similar basis where you have no guarantee that your needs will be met in the event of a widespread disaster. If emergency facilities are needed for operations of many other organizations that share your emergency sites, you may not get either the support or the facilities you are counting on. No one plan works for every organization, so be flexible and creative in considering the alternatives available. Your plan may call for hot site or total emergency facility operation for a short time which could be followed by a move to less expensive cold site facilities for the remainder of the emergency period. This might be advantageous in terms of the overall cost, immediate processing requirements, insurance provisions, space needs, staff convenience, and other factors.

Decision-making

If the LAN will be out of service so long that it becomes necessary to initiate the COOP, then disaster recovery should be started while the COOP efforts are underway. DRP and COOP teams should be drawn from the same body of skilled individuals who are knowledgeable of LAN operations and sensitive to business requirements. The teams should consist of different individuals so that the teams can operate concurrently, if that becomes necessary. The size and number of your teams will depend on the applications and number of users you must support.

Contingency plans contain extremely sensitive technical and confidential employee information, thus the plans themselves must be kept secure. The common practice of having employees and consultants keep copies of contingency plans at home creates a security threat. A safety deposit box near the primary workplace or the secure off site storage location is a safer repository for copies of the plans.

Design

Construct several disaster scenarios to ensure that your design meets a variety of recovery needs. LAN disaster scenarios can vary from a momentary loss of power, to a virus that destroys data, to a devastating event such as a fire that consumes servers, data, workstations, and facilities. The range of threats that can result in disaster are enumerated in the process of Risk Assessment covered in Chapter 7. In contingency planning, it is essential to consider all possible threats. A plan constructed to recover from a single threat, like a fire, may be completely inadequate in other situations, such as a virus attack or power failure.

Development

In development, the contingency plans come together into a workable whole. The more business units and other participants have contributed to the process, the more comfortable they will be with the plans, and the more willing they will be to adopt, support, and follow them. The stronger and cost-effective the plans, the better the chance of gaining financial support for the project from senior management.

Testing

The planning effort will be virtually worthless if the plans are not tested. They should be tested several times before they are made final. They should also be reviewed, improved, updated, and tested periodically after that, not less than once a year. Independent testing (by a group other than the one that prepared the plans) yields excellent results since there is a natural tendency to overlook flaws and omissions in one's own work.

Disaster Recovery Plan

The DRP, or contingency plan for disaster recovery, is intended to minimize the effects of a disaster on the network and its users. The plan consists of the methods and procedures disaster recovery team members will follow to restore LAN services as needed. Typically the DRP is used to recover from catastrophic events that disrupt network operations and require extensive corrective action to re-instate data, applications, and network services.

The steps in the DRP will vary for every LAN, because each LAN is unique. A typical Contingency Plan for Disaster Recovery follows.

Contents of DRP

1. Restrictions placed on distribution and use of the Plan, in keeping with the highly confidential and private information it contains.

2. LAN Disaster Recovery team information including: names, home phone numbers, and roles and responsibilities in the recovery process.

3. Decision criteria for implementing the DRP and/or COOP.

4. List of assumptions and constraints.

5. List of critical applications, databases, responsible users, and LAN support persons (or a staff) in each work group.

6. Processing requirements for each essential application.

7. Log of DRP reviews, participants, and test results.

8. Step-by step instructions for disaster recovery for various types and/or severities of disasters.

A sample DRP follows.

Sample Disaster Recovery Plan

1. **Markings showing restrictions** should be printed clearly on each page so there is no doubt that the Plan is strictly confidential and for internal use by authorized personnel only. (Document classification markings to protect trade secrets, confidential and private information are addressed in Chapter 11, *Managing Threats Against the LAN.*)

2. **LAN Disaster Recovery team information** should include the names of team members, home and work telephone numbers, anticipated activities during recovery, roles and responsibilities performed by the various teams (DR team, LAN user support team), and the user representatives who are expected to participate in the recovery process. Refer to Figure 10.2.

3. **Decision criteria for implementing** the Disaster Recovery and Continuation Of Operations plans are concerned with maintaining availability of essential LAN applications and services. The sample decision criteria presented in Figure 10.3 apply only to the current disaster incident.

Name, Business and Home Phones	Role	Responsibility	Activities	Decisions
{DR team leader}	LAN DR Team Leader	Coordinate and implement Plan	Notify team	When to invoke DRP
		Lead recovery effort	Review plan	
			Modify plan if situation warrants	Which applications require recovery and in what order?
{Alternate DR leader}	LAN DR Team Leader backup	Work with Team Leader in coordination, control and recovery activities	Participate in disaster identification, control, and recovery	Choice of alternate processing site Changes necessary to develop more effective DRP
{DR team members}	LAN DR Team members			
List at least 1 for every user group: 1.	LAN User Support Team members	Assist users in identifying priorities and participate in recovery if needed	Inform users Gather files, information, and documentation to restore/recover data and applications	Importance, urgency and priority of group needs
		Represent application users in DRP activities		Changes necessary to develop more effective DRP
List at least 1 user per application: 1.	Users	Express priorities and constraints on data, applications, and support as input to DRP	Coordinate with associates, gather records and controls on data	How best to express needs, priorities, and constraints as requirements
			Identify individual responsible for recovery process outcome and processing control	When must applications be operational?
		Work with LAN User Support Team in preparing to recover from disaster		Importance, urgency, and priority of applications to be recovered

FIGURE 10.2   DISASTER RECOVERY TEAM INFORMATION.

Once your contingency plans are prepared and tested, be conservative in their use. Do not be in a rush to implement them whenever the LAN goes down. Determine the scope of the problem and what action must be taken to reinstate the applications and ensure the integrity of the data. If the tasks can be completed by the LAN Administrator, within tolerable time limits using normal LAN administrative procedures, then that is the preferred course of action. Invoking the plans causes considerable disruption because staff efforts are channeled in directions outside of "business as usual." Very often damage is limited to one application or database that can be repaired, restored, or recovered, while the LAN is actively serving the rest of the user population. Another typical emergency is the temporary power failure, during which the UPS initiates an orderly LAN shutdown rather than a crash. Emergencies such as these can usually be handled by your LAN Administrator, and do not generally require employment of a contingency plan.

EMERGENCY CONDITION	RECOVERY IS A NORMAL LAN ADMINISTRATION TASK	LAN RESTART EXPECTED WITHIN TOLERABLE TIME LIMIT	LAN RESTART OUTSIDE TOLERABLE TIME LIMIT
Essential LAN applications or services are unavailable due to an emergency halt in LAN operations	LAN Administrator Handles Emergency	Execute DRP	Execute COOP
LAN data is lost, damaged, or compromised with respect to integrity, accuracy, or privacy causing a halt to LAN operations			

FIGURE 10.3   DECISION CRITERIA FOR IMPLEMENTING DRP OR COOP.

Before invoking the COOP, be sure that the critical time frame for processing can be met through its execution. Consider the following case. Your Controller's quarterly results are in the LAN server and must be presented to the Board of Directors in four hours. Time is of the essence because the reports must be filed with the SEC tomorrow. Suddenly, the LAN shuts down with no warning because of a virus attack. It took six hours before the LAN was available after the last virus attack. This one, you believe, is worse. You are convinced that the LAN will not be available in time to retrieve the data for the Board. In your contingency plan testing, it took 4 hours and 20 minutes to get the LAN up at the alternate processing site. (And that was under ideal test conditions—everyone working at top speed and no unforeseen events—not at all like the real world.) There are no other critical requirements. In this case, the COOP is not a viable solution. The data was all entered between 8:00 and 10:00 that morning and the backups have not run yet (backups are scheduled for 2:00 a.m. each day). It appears that retrieving the data from a backup file is not a possibility (although, if the data could be retrieved, the required reports could easily be run on a stand-alone PC).

A knowledgeable LAN support team and involved users should have identified this critical application in contingency planning. The teams would have realized the DRP and COOP recovery windows could prove inadequate in meeting time-critical processing needs, and would have recommended that the files for this special application be backed up to a secure hard drive at 15 minute intervals. Or the CFO could have explained the risk in setting such a small time window for report generation and review. Or, you could tell the Board to wait (after you've found another job, of course).

At first this seems like a great deal of planning, strategy, and setting up of procedures; however, once you begin to plan for and protect your organization against losses that can result from disasters, it becomes second nature. The challenge is in doing it thoroughly. It is an extremely rewarding aspect of LAN management and you will have satisfaction in knowing your LAN is secure and your organization is protected.

4. **List of assumptions and constraints** which describe your unique networking environment and provide the framework for your DRP and COOP. Sample assumptions and constraints follow.

   ■ *Contingency plans and materials* are stored with server backup tapes at another branch office in the secure server room in a locked cabinet.

   ■ *Our alternate processing site* is the branch office that also provides LAN services in an emergency. The arrangement is reciprocal, which means that we store their files and materials in our server room, and provide them with a hot site in the event of an emergency on their LAN. (Both facilities can accommodate the additional work, staff, and supplies and priorities have been established.)

- *E-mail is the communication link* of choice for the recovery process. Communications must be updated daily using pre-arranged mailing lists and a general information bulletin board.

- *The rendezvous point* for employees, if the building is inaccessible, is the cafeteria in the branch office.

5. **List of essential applications and databases,** responsible users and LAN support staff in each workgroup, as shown in Figure 10.4.

ESSENTIAL APPLICATIONS	ESSENTIAL DATABASES	RESPONSIBLE USER	LAN USER SUPPORT PERSON
Financial Reports (WP5.1, Freelance, Lotus 1-2-3)	Fin94xxx series (.WKn, .dbx, .doc, .xfr, .fax), etc.	Ass't. Controller	M. Smith R. Black (Alternate)
Time Reporting (for Payroll)	Tim94xxx series (.wkn, .xfr, .fax), etc.	Ass't. Dir. Administrative Services	C. Jose M. Warren (Alternate)

FIGURE 10.4   ESSENTIAL APPLICATIONS AND DATABASES.

6. **Processing requirements for essential applications** are summarized briefly in Figure 10.5. Details of application processing requirements are found in the copy of LAN operations and application documentation stored with these contingency plans. Only essential LAN applications are to be summarized in this chart. Many applications, while not essential, are considered by users to be of extreme importance and may be identified in secondary charts.

7. **Log of DRP reviews, participants, and test results** is useful for tracking progress in establishing a viable DRP for the organization. Refer to Figure 10.6.

8. **Step-by-step instructions for disaster recovery** are designed to guide the DR team through the process of recovering LAN applications, data, and services, and restoring LAN availability to users.

ESSENTIAL APPLICATIONS	PROCESSING REQUIREMENTS	LAN USER SUPPORT
Financial Reports (WP5.1, Freelance, Lotus 1-2-3)	Fin94xxx series is processed at each month end with results due about the 2nd. Quarterly results are due about the 3rd. Financial Reports can be processed after Fin94FLx.wk1 is downloaded (after production control releases Financial Ledger closing results). Quarterly adjustments must be applied (Fin94QAx.wk1) before quarterly reports (see schedule attached). If these reports are not processed on schedule the world stops!	M. Smith R. Black (alt)
	DRP Team Note: Due to their extreme importance these applications are now backed up on a secure workstation and stand-alone applications have been provided to ensure deadlines are not missed despite possible LAN trouble.	
	Since the data is reviewed at three other LAN sites prior to final printing, LAN downtime is a major inconvenience but can be tolerated, except at the end of the Quarter.	
Time Reporting (for Payroll)	Tim94xxx series is processed every Friday at 2:00 p.m. If time records are not received by 3:30 p.m. on Friday we will not get paid the following week. No missed deadlines can be tolerated.	C. Jose M. Warren (alt)
	DRP Team Note: In the event of a LAN problem, LAN user support will carry time records on diskette across town to the branch office for transmission. If all else fails, the records can be e-mailed, transferred electronically, or faxed to the home office, but the fax must be received by 3:30 p.m. So, if a problem occurs, notify LAN support *as soon as possible*.	
	COOP offers little advantage if the outage lasts less than a month.	

FIGURE 10.5   PROCESSING REQUIREMENTS FOR ESSENTIAL APPLICATIONS.

REVIEW OR TEST	DATE	PARTICIPANTS	RESULTS AND NOTES FOR IMPROVEMENT
DRP Review			
DRP Test			
DRP Execution			

FIGURE 10.6   LOG OF DRP REVIEWS AND TEST RESULTS.

The instructions are primarily for the manager in charge (or the Disaster Recovery Team leader) who is expected to coordinate the activities of other DR participants as necessary. The steps are as follows.

1. Establish that a qualified disaster recovery (DR) team leader is in charge of decision-making for the LAN before proceeding. The ideal person, is the official disaster recovery team leader who actively participated in creation of the DRP. The team leader initiates and coordinates LAN recovery efforts and operations with one goal in mind, to reinstate full LAN services and operations within the shortest possible time. The disaster recovery leader should be present, in possession of relevant plans and documentation, and in charge of the situation.

2. Using contact information in the DRP, the team leader notifies missing DR team members of the disaster. If the server is

down, the team leader establishes the communication method (such as e-mail through an alternate server) and sets up a meeting time and place, if necessary.

3. Visit the backup file and documentation storage location and inventory the materials on hand. Note any discrepancies.

4. Determine the nature and scope of the disaster and approximate the magnitude of the loss and the time required to reinstate LAN operations. The size of the problem must be determined before any action is taken. Previously prepared forms, estimates, replacement and rental cost schedules, and other worksheets should be used to streamline the process. Factors that must be considered are:

- The nature and full extent of the current loss (permanent loss versus temporary unavailability) in data, privacy, equipment, services, processing, and dependability.

- The ultimate potential loss.

- Can the loss be minimized by containment (by means of a server shutdown or other action)?

- Has data been lost, destroyed, or compromised?

- Are the premises accessible and safe?

- Is the equipment usable?

- Is the damage reversible?

5. Establish contact with facilities planners, risk management, insurance contact, purchasing, etc., to ensure LAN requirements are fully understood. Determine where operations will resume when the recovery is complete.

6. Poll the user support team to identify any new or special requirements that are not already documented in the Plan. Verify that the Plan reflects the status quo.

7. Determine whether network service requirements, or processing time constraints, require LAN operations to continue off site. If the normal site is accessible and the equipment is operable, recovery of data and applications will usually take place there. If the normal server and network control site is inaccessible, recovery must take place off site. Backup files, disaster recovery plans, and procedures are stored off site (at the alternate processing location, if possible) to simplify this process.

8. If the COOP is needed, notify the COOP team and put the plan into effect. Work closely with the COOP team leader. Go to the off site backup storage location and gather necessary backup files, backup/restore and recovery procedures, operations documentation, LAN Administration schedules, documentation, inventories and procedures, and user application documentation. Meet the COOP team at the alternate processing location, review the facilities, note any problems, and turn over the files and documentation to the COOP team as needed to reinstate essential LAN operations. (The DR team leader may have to work with the COOP team to recover data and start up interim LAN operations at the alternate site. This would depend on the number of available qualified COOP team members.)

9. If any file must be obtained from the backup files and the COOP is not in effect, go to the off site backup storage location and gather necessary backup files, backup/restore and recovery procedures, operations documentation, LAN Administration schedules, documentation and procedures, and user application documentation. Go to a prearranged location where you can access and retrieve the files from the backup.

10. Impress upon users that they must secure and back up their own data until normal LAN operations are resumed.

11. Using previously created, tested and updated inventories, estimates, spreadsheets, project management tools, systems, and forms, plan the recovery process down to the task level. Every repair, purchase, cleaning, data recovery, restoration, duplication, replacement, test, etc. should be noted with the person responsible, contact, estimated times and completion dates. Provide informative summaries with reasonable details for the

various teams and contacts who need to be kept informed throughout the recovery.

12. Monitor the progress of the recovery, and communicate the changes and progress on a daily basis.

13. When normal operations are about to resume, alert the various teams, users, and other concerned parties.

14. If the COOP is in effect, schedule test runs to transport backup files from the alternate processing site to the primary LAN facility. This should be done in preparation for the return to normal LAN operations. When the LAN is operable, several tests should be run to ensure that a smooth transition can be made from interim LAN operations at the COOP site, to full LAN operations at the primary LAN facility.

15. If no COOP is in effect, restore the files as needed and test them to verify the integrity of data and application systems.

Continuation of Operations Plan

The Continuation Of Operations Plan (COOP) is the means by which applications can continue to be processed at an alternate location, when the LAN is unavailable for an extended period of time. The COOP should be put into effect when the network is expected to be unavailable beyond a tolerable downtime for any critical application. When this occurs, the DR team leader apprises the LAN COOP team members and the contact person at the alternate processing location and other affected parties of the need to put the COOP into effect.

Applications are scheduled for recovery and operation at the COOP site, based on their priority, the urgency of the information, and the period of downtime considered tolerable by the application users. The elements of the COOP Plan are:

1. Restrictions placed on the distribution and use of the Plan in keeping with the highly confidential and private information it contains.

2. LAN COOP team information including: team member names, home and business phone numbers, member roles and responsibilities, and other participants.

3. Decision and action criteria for implementing the plan, and the applications' scheduling assignments at the alternate location.

4. List of assumptions and constraints about your unique networking environment that establish a framework for the COOP.

5. List of essential applications and databases with responsible users and LAN support people in each workgroup (refer to Figure 10.3).

6. Processing requirements for essential applications, summarized briefly in Figure 10.5.

7. Log of COOP reviews, tests, participants, and results of reviews, as well as the tests performed to establish the viability of the plan.

8. Steps required to implement the COOP.

9. A sample COOP follows.

Sample Continuation of Operations Plan

1. **Plan Restrictions** should be clearly marked on each page so there is no doubt that it is confidential and for use by authorized personnel only. (See document classification guidelines in Chapter 11, *Managing Threats Against the LAN.*)

2. **LAN COOP team information** should include: team member names, home and business phone numbers, roles and responsibilities performed by the COOP, user support teams and other participants, anticipated activities during off site operations, and decisions required. See Figure 10.7.

3. **Decision and action criteria for implementing the plan** and the applications' scheduling assignments at the alternate location are presented in the chart in Figure 10.3. (Note the earlier discussion of implementing the contingency plans in the sample DRP.)

Name, Business and Home Phones	COOP Role	Responsibility	Activities	Decisions
{COOP leader name}	LAN COOP Team Leader	Coordinates and implements COOP at alternate location	Notify team. Review plan; modify for current circumstances as needed	1. Which applications require COOP 2. When to invoke COOP 3. How much lead time required to set up alternate location
{Alternate Site LAN Administrator}	COOP LAN Administrator (and Backup LAN COOP Team Leader)	Performs LAN Administration at alternate site	Routine LAN Administration tasks: server backup, change requests	Which change requests to carry out at COOP site and which to implement when LAN recovery is complete
{COOP team members}	COOP Team Member	Supports COOP activities as required	Prepare COOP site Set up user workstations Assist with LAN, troubleshooting, QA	Recommendations for ongoing improvements in interim LAN operation and COOP
List at least 1 support person for every user group: 1.	LAN User Support Team	Assist users in preparing and processing at alternate location	Gather files, documentation for restoration, recovery, and processing QA LAN operations	Changes which affect user needs and COOP
List at least 1 user for every key application: 1.	Users	Prepare and process LAN applications at alternate location	Gather records, schedules, controls, etc. Control production as required Verify integrity of data	Usual business decisions

FIGURE 10. 7   CONTINUATION OF OPERATIONS PLAN TEAM INFORMATION.

4. **List of assumptions and constraints** about your unique networking environment to establish a framework for the COOP. Some sample assumptions and constraints follow.

   ■ *The rendezvous point for the COOP team* (and other employees) will be the cafeteria of a branch office, if our building is inaccessible.

   ■ *Contingency plans and materials are stored* with the server backup tapes, site contact(s), documentation, procedures, and recovery procedures for LAN applications and databases at a branch office in the secure server room in a locked cabinet.

   ■ *Our alternate processing site* is a branch office, which will also provide us with LAN services, should an emergency arise. The arrangement is reciprocal. This means that we store their files and materials in our server room, and provide them with a "hot site," in the event of an emergency on their LAN.

- *E-mail will be the communication link* of choice throughout the recovery process. Availability will be on a need basis only and can be arranged through the LAN Administrator. Communications must be updated daily using prearranged mailing lists and a general information bulletin board.

5. **List of essential applications and databases** with responsible users and LAN support people in each workgroup (refer to Figure 10.4).

6. **Processing requirements for essential applications** are summarized in a chart similar to that shown in Figure 10.5. Details of application processing requirements are found in the copy of LAN operations and application documentation that is stored with these contingency plans. Only essential LAN applications should be summarized in this chart. Many applications, while not absolutely essential, are considered by users to be of extreme importance and may be identified in other, secondary charts.

7. **Log of COOP reviews, participants, and test results** is useful for tracking progress in establishing a viable COOP for the organization. Refer to Figure 10.8.

8. **Steps required to implement the COOP** are provided to guide the COOP team through the process of establishing LAN operations at the alternate processing location. Essential applications, data, and LAN services will be made available to users on a needs basis. Needs were established when the COOP was developed during contingency planning.

   Note that the instructions are primarily for the COOP team leader, who is expected to work closely with the DR team leader to coordinate the activities of other COOP participants. The steps are as follows.

   1. Establish that a qualified COOP team leader is in charge of establishing LAN operations at the alternate site before proceeding. The ideal person is the official COOP team leader, or qualified alternate, who actively participated in the creation of the plan during contingency planning. The team leader initiates and coordinates LAN setup and operations to provide

essential LAN services and operations to appropriate business units and people within tolerable downtime limits. The COOP team leader should be present, in possession of plans and documentation, and ready to assume LAN responsibility at the alternate location immediately. The DR team leader is the COOP team leader's primary contact. The DR team leader is in charge of the overall effort, and coordinates all participants working to quickly restore normal LAN operations.

REVIEW OR TEST	DATE	PARTICIPANTS	RESULTS AND NOTES FOR IMPROVEMENT
COOP Review			
COOP Test			
COOP Execution			

FIGURE 10.8   LOG OF COOP REVIEWS.

2. The team leader notifies missing COOP team members of the emergency and of the decision to implement the COOP. The team leader also arranges the first meeting of the team.

3. In the first meeting, the COOP team leader presents the situation, including the nature and scope of the disaster, the size of the loss, the estimated time required to restore normal LAN operations, and the game plan for recovery. The status of

data, facilities, equipment, and personnel at the primary and alternate sites is also given. Tasks are assigned and preliminary target completion dates set.

4. Maintain regular contact with the DR team leader and facilities managers in the alternate location to ensure ongoing LAN requirements are fully understood.

5. Poll the user support team to identify any new or special requirements that are not already documented in the COOP. Verify that the Plan is complete and workable.

6. Determine whether network service requirements and processing time constraints that require LAN operations can be met. Identify any problem areas to the DR team leader.

7. With the DR team leader, go to the off site backup storage location and gather necessary backup files, backup/restore and recovery procedures, operations documentation, LAN administration schedules, documentation and procedures, and user application documentation. (The DR team leader may have to work with the COOP team to recover data and start up interim LAN operations at the alternate site, depending on the allocation and availability of qualified staff.) Using backup files, disaster recovery plans, and procedures, restore or recover databases and applications as required by the schedule of essential applications to be supported in the COOP.

8. Work with the COOP site LAN Administrator to monitor progress in establishing interim LAN operations, communicate problems, changes, and progress to the teams, DR team leader and others on a daily basis.

9. When normal operations are about to resume, alert COOP teams, interim LAN users, and other affected parties.

10. Cooperate with the DR team leader in scheduling test runs and transporting backup files from the alternate processing site to the primary LAN facility in preparation for the return to normal LAN operations. When the LAN is operable, several tests should be run to ensure a smooth transition from

interim LAN operations at the COOP site, to full normal LAN operations at the primary LAN facility.

Disaster Recovery and Contingency Planning Services

Firms such as AT&T, Comdisco, IBM, Simpact, and SunGard as well as a growing number of consulting firms also offer disaster recovery and business continuation products and services. These assist organizations in planning to recover from disaster and resume business operations with minimal loss and as little disruption as possible. If the tasks of contingency planning and disaster recovery are beyond the capabilities of your staff, you can benefit greatly from seeking expert assistance and using existing commercial services.

The City of Hartford's essential business services were up and running at a SunGard Recovery Services hot site in Philadelphia within 24 hours after Hartford's computer and communications rooms flooded. Fortunately, their contingency plans had been tested only 10 weeks before the flood and the quick response kept the problems from becoming apparent to the public. Disaster recovery took place in Hartford while business operations continued at SunGard's facilities. Within a week, production and test systems were restored and the disaster was officially over.

One of the largest providers of end-to-end business recovery services is Comdisco, Inc. Comdisco offers a wide range of alternate facilities and recovery services including the largest network dedicated to business continuation and the ultimate protection, *standby processing*. Standby processing requires the continuous real-time capture of your data as it is processed so your LAN operations can be resumed at the alternate site as soon as your staff arrives.

All of the Comdisco clients who were affected by the World Trade Center bombing recovered successfully. One client wanted to keep their entire staff working following a disaster, if possible. All 55 of their displaced employees were back at work at their alternate work site in nearby New Jersey the very next day.

CHAPTER 11

MANAGING THREATS
AGAINST THE LAN

*I*n this, the final chapter, the threats and solutions come together as we consider the actions the LAN manager needs to take to establish appropriate management controls in order to adequately protect the LAN and support its users.

Given the following three simple (and often repeated) truths about networks, a LAN Manager's responsibility is awesome:

1. No network is completely secure.

2. A network is only as reliable as its weakest link.

3. The only thing certain about a network is that it will change.

LAN managers must, therefore, expend great energy trying to maintain secure and dependable LANs. Believing that the best defense is a good offense, when managing a LAN I like to have a comprehensive LAN Security Plan as well as carefully thought out LAN policies, plans, standards, and procedures. These topics are covered in this chapter along with a Case Study and a few final notes on threats and safeguards. You should refer to earlier chapters for information about the components of the Security Plan that were covered previously, such as risk assessment and contingency plans for emergencies.

Security-Aware Management Systems and Controls

Society, our institutions, and organizations are changing rapidly and the management systems we use to control things strain to keep pace. Since most losses and threats come from within an organization, security-aware management systems are essential in preventing loss from threats, particularly threats posed by irate, inept, or untrained employees. Hardly a day goes by without a news story breaking about an employee striking out because of some real or imagined grievance. Downsizing has reduced the number of employees required to conduct business and middle management jobs are quickly disappearing. Jobs that are being created are either in the professional or clerical or service worker ranks. Many companies still have employees they don't know what to do with and it is easy for people to feel they are working harder with less job security than ever before. The general atmosphere of uncertainty places additional stress on already tense employees and work situations. If policy makers are out of touch with the needs of employees, your job of securing your network is going to be more difficult. Since most, if not all, employees have access to the LAN it can be an attractive target for venting anger and hostility through sabotage.

Pitfalls of Lax Management Systems and Controls

Some years ago, a clever operations manager was the only person who understood the back office systems and computer operations in a large bank. He felt he had the ultimate job security because he would share his knowledge with no one. He was difficult to work with and gave direction on a need to know basis only. For years he had hired people whose loyalty was to him, not the bank. He had more power than most of the senior executives until they realized how vulnerable they were. They were unable to run their back office computer operations (in other words, the bank) without him. He was eventually put on a special project with a priority on documenting the operations systems. Competent managers were transferred in to get the computer operations situation under control. It makes you wonder how that could happen in the first place. What ever happened to succession planning, crosstraining, and good old common sense?

In the course of a review to determine the causes of systemic delays in the implementation of computer systems in an insurance company, I discovered that premium checks were being left in unlocked drawers for days on end because the clerks didn't have time to process them. And that was just the tip of that management controls iceberg.

Prepare for the Worst

When a disgruntled former employee destroyed a server's hard drive with a hammer all of the company's vital data was lost. The typical DRP and COOP contingency plans were useless because he had also stolen all of the backup files. Without their essential data the business might well have had to close its doors. The damaged hard drive was rushed to Ontrack Data Recovery and the data was indeed recovered. But the problems in the management systems of this company remain.

Why was the former employee allowed to be on the premises without supervision? How did an unauthorized person gain physical access to the server? Why were there no backup files stored securely offsite as part of a fall-back contingency plan? How did this person gain access to backup tapes and how was he able to remove them from the building? They say that to be successful in business it helps to be a little paranoid. When it comes to keeping your network and your company up and running this extra sense and awareness of danger can be a big asset indeed.

LAN Cracking on the Rise

We have little hard evidence of the number of network penetration incidents which occur, or their success rates. One indication is the number of security incidents on the Internet, which have increased steadily for several years. A common trait among hackers is that they like to leave their mark behind to show that they were clever enough to penetrate a network. Professional network crackers do not crack networks for an ego boost. On the contrary, professionals aim to penetrate a network, get what they came for, and get out without leaving a trace. The professionals are the people who know how to find your most valuable data and how to benefit from stealing it.

Theft of Company Secrets

Conventional wisdom in the security and intelligence community says that the probability of loss from passive or active wiretapping is far less than the threat of loss from a disloyal, careless, or unthinking employee because it costs less to bribe an employee than to set up an electronic interception. I see it as a matter of relative risk. If professionals can crack a network and search for useful information with virtually no risk of exposure, why would they risk prosecution and infamy by trying to purchase the same information from an employee? Just because we know more about the instances where employees give or sell employer's secrets than we do about network cracking incidents, it does not mean that networks are not penetrated regularly. Many LANs are penetrated without anyone ever suspecting that it happened. We know about many cases of attempted bribery only because loyal employees have reported them, and have even helped to apprehend industrial spies. By contrast, few LAN administrators are astute enough to recognize an attempted LAN penetration. The increased use of LAN monitoring and audit tools can report data accesses and security violations and help to identify security incidents; but the most vulnerable LANs and least knowledgeable administrators may not have these tools.

It is true that a company that wants to know something about a rival firm has only to run attractive job advertisements in that area and then sit back and listen to what their rival's employees have been working on. We tend to be so open and take so much pride in our accomplishments that we often talk too much about an employer's products, problems, plans, and so forth. The practice of baiting employees in search of jobs in the hopes of getting secrets may be unethical, but it is not illegal.

Employee Ethics

Since employees are the greatest single threat to LAN security, appropriate attention must be given to the management systems that govern their selection, hiring, management, supervision, training and development, and separation when their employment is terminated.

Employees are often given the message that if they are "too ethical" and lack flexibility and the ability to see shades of gray in business and political dealings, they may not be management material. If they are encouraged to see the shades of gray when acting in the interest of their employers, why should employees have compunction about seeing shades of gray in their own self interest? If traditional relationships of trust between employers and employees no longer exist, then traditional management methods should not be expected to work either.

A Case of Organized Insider Theft

Organized insider theft does occur, but it is rare. One large company was losing from four to six Macintosh computers a week. Because they were self-insured no one took action until their insurance reserves were depleted. When the President was informed he called *B-SAFE Industries, Inc.*, a firm with a reputation for supplying solutions for security problems (they even supply anti-terrorist equipment to law enforcement agencies). B-

SAFE installed 20 Spider theft alarm units. No computers were stolen until the next weekend when another (still unprotected) machine disappeared. More than one thousand security devices were installed after that. The next time a theft was attempted, a motion sensor alarm turned a closed circuit television camera on, which filmed the theft and assisted in identifying the thieves. Three employees—an office worker, a cleaning person, and an internal security guard—are now serving time in jail.

Why Some Employees Steal

Most thefts by employees are thefts of opportunity rather than planned and well-coordinated events. An employee who notices a mobile unprotected PC or other item of value and is able to rationalize that, since the company "owes them," they are justified in adopting the item, may do so! Ignoring this problem, as so many companies choose to do, does not make it go away. Calling it what it is, employee theft, and eliminating the more blatant opportunities for theft, will help to eliminate this problem.

A related mistake, caused by poor management systems, is the creation of an atmosphere of "compromise" in the workplace. When employees must break rules to survive they learn rationalization techniques for cheating rather than how good it feels to follow the rules so their whole team can benefit. Using company resources for playing computer games is not very different from using LAN resources for personal profit. And using the LAN for personal profit is not very different from selling company information stored on the LAN for profit. The point is that one "compromise" leads to another and it is best to avoid the problem altogether. The little things, such as using the LAN for computer games and making personal phone calls against the rules, make employees feel like hypocrites or cheats—until they stop feeling anything at all—and can easily be avoided. By considering employee needs for communication with the outside world during business hours, managers with a "no personal phone calls" rule might establish a policy allocating a certain number of messages units to each employee for personal calls. This would tell employees that their needs are being considered despite the business need to keep phone bills in check. Just raise the subject of rules that are flaunted or ignored in your organization in a TQM meeting and see what suggestions are made to eliminate the problem of forced ethical compromise.

A Security Officer is Not Enough

It is not enough to give responsibility for security to a security officer who is likely to be isolated and unpopular because of the duties of the job. Incorporation of fundamental security into everyday management and the culture of the organization through well-designed plans, procedures, objectives, quality improvement and performance measures, is essential.

Quality Improvement as a Management System

Gaining the willing and enthusiastic cooperation of employees should be the main goal of every management team, since the company ultimately succeeds or fails on the strength of its employees. If managers were evaluated on their performance in this respect more companies would have success stories to tell.

IN A RECENT WALL STREET SCANDAL

An employee allegedly took advantage of inadequacies in the system of management, accounting, and computer system controls at Kidder, Peabody & Co. to generate phony profits for the firm and whopping commissions for himself. An accounting loophole apparently permitted the trader to show fictitious profits in the government strips market amounting to $350 million in 1993, for which he received commissions and a $9 million bonus. Government strips—securities created by splitting the interest payments and principal owed from bonds and trading each separately—are an example of derivative products. The $10 trillion derivatives market trades on anticipated changes in the prices of traditional securities instruments such as stocks, bonds, currencies, and commodities and changes in interest rates. Derivatives are often used to hedge business risks or for speculation. Creating derivatives has progressed beyond basic options, futures, and indexes to the point where the risks involved may be incomprehensible to ordinary investors who do not possess both quantitative analysis skills and sophisticated computer systems.

The complexity of derivatives and related accounting may well have played a role in the alleged fraud. Nonetheless, a firm's management systems and management, accounting, and computer system controls must keep pace with their business activities, regardless of their complexity. And financial institutions must continue to be held to a higher standard because the public must trust them with enormous assets, thus they have greater opportunity for abuse. Had this flaw in the system been discovered and reported by an ethical employee or astute auditor, there would have been no story to tell.

Document Classification and Marking

Seemingly open and shut cases of industrial espionage have been lost because employees were able to convince a jury that they did not know they were doing anything wrong when they sold company information to outsiders. Document classification and marking, employee training, and establishment of accountability are essential in protecting valuable business information.

Security-aware organizations categorize written and computerized information by an information classification to assist employees in protecting valuable information assets including trade secrets, plans, other proprietary data, and sensitive and private information. Government agencies classify data as to its secrecy or sensitivity and have iron-clad rules about handling classified data. Many private companies do not have such precautions and are extremely vulnerable as a result.

Document classification notices are prepared to identify each information classification used in the organization and may include guidance for handling the information. The appropriate notice is then printed on every written page and is attached to every computerized file. Some possible classifications are:

■ Confidential
■ Company confidential

■   Proprietary

■   Private

■   Sensitive

■   Unclassified

Employees must be trained to recognize each classification they will encounter in their work and to observe any special requirements for handling each kind of information. Many companies do have protective intellectual property polices. They may require employees to sign statements acknowledging their intention to comply with restrictions on disclosure of company information and trade secrets.

Employee Security Training

Your security policy should require users to attend appropriate LAN security and administration training prior to their first use of the network. Security awareness training informs employees of their responsibility to safeguard and protect LAN assets. It should alert employees to threats against the network (and other computer assets), vulnerabilities, safeguards, and the administrative policies, standards and procedures which are in effect for the purpose of protecting these critical assets.

The necessary information can be easily incorporated into user training for LAN applications. It should stress the key role played by employees in securing the LAN and enumerate their specific responsibilities. A password game or exercise should be used to establish or reinforce good password setting habits. Role playing can help employees to become security-aware and to develop protective skills for dealing with threats.

After training, employees should be asked to attest to their understanding of their responsibilities. They should indicate their intention to comply with computer security laws and regulations as well as the policies and procedures of the organization by signing a *Responsible LAN User Agreement*. On completion of the agreement, users should be given their userID and password(s) which enable them to use the network and the appropriate LAN services and applications.

The Company Security Plan

There should be one comprehensive, overall Security Plan for an organization regardless of how many supplemental plans and procedures exist for the computer facilities, network operations, individual units, and identifiable LANs which may be part of the organization. The Security Plan addresses the management controls, accounting controls, and computer controls necessary to protect the assets of the organization. It also specifies the methods—such as internal and external financial, systems, and management audits that are used by Computer Information Systems Auditors (CISAs), auditors, and consultants—employed to test the Plan and ensure compliance.

At a minimum, the company-wide Security Plan should cover the following elements of LAN security:

- Risk Analysis should identify threats, vulnerabilities, and existing safeguards for the organization as a whole. It should address the potential for disaster and network failure from all causes including natural forces, fire, theft, accident, equipment malfunction, hardware, software, and so on
- Backup and recovery strategy
- Contingency plans for emergencies including DRP and COOP plans
- Data security review to ensure protection is adequate for the sensitivity of data stored, processed and communicated
- Asset protection and risk management
- Privacy of information
- Document classification and marking
- Records storage, retention, and distribution
- Physical security
- Safety

Be vigilant in maintaining the security safeguards your organization chooses to adopt. When security practices are allowed to differ from the policies specified in the Security Plan, it is an indication of underlying management control problems.

The Need for a LAN Security Plan

There should also be a LAN Security Plan which may address the overall enterprise network and specify action to be followed for each LAN. The expansion and interconnection of individual LANs into an enterprise network changes the LAN Security Plan picture. Whatever the size of your LAN you should have a Plan to cover all your associated risks. How can you tell how many plans you should have? There is no firm and hard rule. In general, every large network has a manager. Workgroup LANs and small LANs may only have administrators. If you are managing a network you need to have a formal Security Plan. If your organization is so large that there are many managers, the Enterprise LAN manager is usually the responsible person. If there are several managers, you might collaborate on a common Security Plan and adapt it for your individual LAN needs if necessary. Administrators play a vital role in administering their LANs but are rarely responsible for creating the LAN Security Plan.

LAN Plans, Policies, Standards, and Procedures

LAN plans, policies, standards, and procedures are essential to protect and administer LAN resources. They should reinforce, augment, and further document the company-wide Security Plan in effect for your organization and your LAN. They are the written statement of your LAN management systems and controls. The plans, policies, standards, and procedures which should exist for a typical LAN include:

■ Strategic Business and Information Systems Plan (this addresses the needs of the organization as a whole and is not addressed in this book)

■ LAN Staffing Plan

    Management Roles and Responsibilities

    LAN Administration Roles and Responsibilities

■ LAN Security Plan

  1. Policies

  2. Risk Analysis

  3. LAN Asset protection strategy

  4. Backup and recovery strategy

  5. Privacy of information

  6. Records retention

  7. Safety

  8. Disaster Recovery Plan

  9. Continuity Of Operations Plan

  10. General security review and oversight of threats and safe-guards employed

■ LAN Implementation Plan:

    Prepare for the LAN

    Configure the LAN

    Implement the LAN

■ LAN User Responsibilities

■ Standards and Procedures for LAN Users (sample in Appendix D):

  1. LAN and Application Userids

  2. Directories and Files

  3. LAN Printing

  4. Virus Prevention

  5. Trouble Identification

  6. Trouble Reporting

  7. Storing Files on the LAN Server

  8. File Transfers

   9. Requesting Changes Such As New LAN Applications

   10. Records Retention on the Server

■ Standards and Procedures for LAN Administration (sample in Appendix E):

   1. Facilitate LAN Printing

   2. Add New Users

   3. Delete former employees

   4. Reset Passwords

   5. Troubleshoot Problems

   6. Report Problems

   7. Back Up Network Servers

   8. Perform Routine Server Maintenance

   9. Monitor LAN Usage

   10. Document and Analyze Problems

   11. Recover LAN Applications and Data

   12. Continue LAN Operations Offsite

■ Guidelines for Application System Development (not addressed in this book)

■ Standards for Application System Implementation on the LAN (not addressed in this book)

LAN requirements are typically stated in written Strategic Information Systems Plans, network documentation and business system requirements documents. Relevant documents should be listed in the References section of your LAN Security Plan. LANs often receive little in the way of formal requirements definition because although the benefits of investing in LAN hardware and software are widely accepted, they may be difficult to quantify because they are distributed across the organization. When new and emerging LAN technology is desired, it is generally tested and proven in small inexpensive pilot studies prior to being rolled out throughout an organization. LAN needs analysis is generally an ongoing effort with users continuously requesting changes and expressing new requirements.

Several brief samples of policies, plans, standards, and procedures follow in this chapter and the appendix. They are intended only to illustrate LAN security principles and management controls of interest to LAN managers. These samples can be useful to you in establishing management controls around your own LAN operations. The information should not be used verbatim but may be used as a starting point to devise workable solutions which fit your own particular needs and unique environment. What may be an appropriate safeguard for one LAN may be inadequate, too costly, or even detrimental to another.

The network referred to in the samples is a fairly typical LAN installation, configured with a NetWare 3.x NOS and a Compaq SystemPro server.

LAN Security Plan

A common mistake in preparing LAN Security Plans is repeating information already written down in the company-wide Security Plan. It is not necessary to repeat information because the plans should be used together. It would be a waste of your time and will not address your LAN needs. The following elements of LAN security should be addressed in your Plan:

1. LAN Security Policies.
2. Risk Analysis to identify threats, vulnerabilities, and existing safeguards with respect to the potential for disaster and network failure from all causes including natural forces, the environment, penetration attack, malfunction in wiring, hardware, or software.
3. LAN Asset protection strategy: address threats and safeguards.
4. Backup and recovery strategy (if different from company Plan).
5. Privacy of information (if different from company Plan).
6. Records retention (if different from company Plan).
7. Safety (if different from company Plan).

8. Disaster Recovery Plan for the recovery of LAN-based systems as needed in an emergency.

9. Continuity Of Operations Plan for the operation of the LAN in an alternate location in the event of a disaster such as a fire or major network failure.

10. General security review and oversight of threats and safeguards employed.

Fully implementing all possible safeguards would be prohibitively expensive and could seriously degrade performance and usefulness out of all proportion to the risks involved in most LANs. The intent of your Plan should not be to implement all possible precautions, but rather, to balance responsible management of network assets against the need for user-friendly network efficiency.

Sample LAN Security Policies Statement

LAN Security Policies are intended to safeguard network assets from loss or harm, destruction, disclosure, or alteration. This includes unauthorized and accidental access of information and the introduction of viruses, worms and other "rogue programs" into the LAN. The policies are as follows:

■ **Access control policies**

1. Users will be permitted to access only data which they have a need to see, use, or modify.

2. Individual access rights will be approved by area managers and put in effect by the LAN Administrator.

3. Area managers will notify the LAN Administrator immediately of changes in employee status. User IDs and LAN access rights should be cancelled immediately on termination of employment.

4. Passwords will be required to access the LAN. Passwords should be difficult to guess, kept confidential, safeguarded

(eg: memorized rather than written down), and changed every 30 days.

5. Using software or files from a PC outside the office, Bulletin Board System (BBS), or other risky source is prohibited because they may be infected with a virus, worm, or other "rogue program." Caution must always be exercised with LAN-connected PCs since new and unknown viruses may be unleashed at any time and *no* anti-virus software has been proven to be 100% effective. A stand-alone PC is available for BBS connection, software virus scanning, and new software testing.

6. Diskettes which contain software or files from PCs outside your organization must be "scanned" for viruses at designated stand-alone PCs before the diskette is used on a network workstation.

7. Virus protection software on the file server is an aid in identifying and removing viruses. Prevention of virus attacks rests with LAN users.

8. Audit software will be used to identify unauthorized access attempts and other security violations and unusual occurrences. Users will be held accountable for security breaches.

■ **The LAN is available** for use around the clock except when daily backups are being performed between 6:00 and 8:00 PM each weekday. Files that are in use are skipped by most backup systems. To prevent this, LAN users are prevented from logging in during backup operations.

■ **Backup file copies** of the LAN server are completed daily. Backup files, plans and procedures are stored onsite and offsite to provide the most comprehensive protection against loss of data and loss of network service which could otherwise result from a disaster or network failure.

■ **DRPs and COOPs** are provided to ensure availability of critical LAN resources and access to essential LAN data in the event of a network failure or major disaster.

■ **Network dependability** is improved by considering the typical failure rates of LAN components in the design and configuration. The emphasis on dependability has resulted in the following safeguards being implemented:

  1. Fault tolerant and reliable hardware and software chosen to increase dependability and provide greater utility to users. An example of a fault tolerant feature is disk mirroring, or writing data to two disk drives simultaneously to give "mirror image" copies which can be used interchangeably in the event of a hardware failure.

  2. Uninterruptible Power Supply (UPS) devices are attached to the servers and other vital components to protect against power outages as well as power shortages, spikes, and surges.

  3. LAN equipment was chosen for exceptionally reliable performance as well as the manufacturer's reputation for high-quality product manufacturing and timely service.

■ **Privacy of information** is maintained for data stored on the network including e-mail. The LAN is to be used for authorized business purposes only and employees shall be held accountable for violations of this rule. Every attempt is made to maintain the privacy of data on the network. This includes protection from unauthorized physical and electronic access, even by the LAN administration staff. In situations where a LAN administration staff member *must* access mailboxes or private directories or files, the Security Officer will be present. Audit tools are used to record administrative as well as user access and modification of LAN data. This audit log is reviewed by the LAN Manager and Security Officer periodically to deter irregularities which could compromise the privacy of the LAN.

■ **Retention of records** in the LAN environment is the responsibility of the owner (e.g.: originator or primary user) of the data.

Files are retained on the server until they are deleted and purged. After files are deleted they are available for "Salvage" until a Purge removes them from the server. The server will be purged of deleted files every 6 months, although more frequent purging may be necessary as time goes on. Users will be given 30 days notice prior to a Purge so files can be salvaged. Note, however, that *NetWare automatically purges* deleted files when more disk space is required during normal processing. When you accidentally delete a file you should report the problem as soon as possible so the file can be salvaged.

■ **Electrical shock** is a danger for employees who work on the PCs and other electronic components which are connected to LANs. This equipment poses a threat to the safety of the staff because it is equipped with power supply units and usually conducts electricity. Network users are not trained to recognize or cope with electrical hazards. Thus, network users should not be permitted to connect, disconnect or modify network connections, wiring, or PCs which are connected to the network without approval. If users need to modify or move LAN equipment they should contact their LAN administrative staff for assistance.

Static-free carpeting is routinely used in offices because the shock potential can injure human beings and because static electricity can damage electronic computer and communications equipment.

Employee Safety

Employee safety is an important security and management responsibility. Awareness and concern in identifying and minimizing potential safety problems can result in reinforcement of employee trust as well as loss prevention.

Employee stress is an increasingly important safety-related workplace issue, which you may address in your security policies and plans. Stressed, unhappy employees have more accidents and make more errors than do well employees. Managers should take more than a passing interest in employee physical and mental health. LANs have made it so easy to be highly personally productive in the use of computers that we tend to overdue it. Long periods of time spent at the workstation keyboard can result in a number of ailments including Carpel Tunnel syndrome, eye diseases, eye strain and headache, neck strain, and back strain. Frequent breaks from desktop computers and overall good physical fitness help to prevent a number of computer user's stress-related disorders. Some such disorders are:

- Carpel Tunnel syndrome is caused by repetitive wrist and hand movements and is best prevented by taking breaks away from the computer and by using wrist supports at the keyboard. When the pain of Carpel Tunnel does strike it can sometimes be alleviated by wrist bandages which provide support.

- Back strain may be caused by carrying PCs, printers, and other heavy office equipment around. LAN and microcomputer support staff are highly susceptible to this problem since they often move equipment. A person with good muscle tone may be able to move a PC or two with no adverse physical effect whereas a person with poor muscle tone may bend over slightly and wind up in traction for a month. Use your common sense and, unless you are in excellent, well-exercised physical condition, do not even consider moving heavy equipment around.

- Eye problems caused by the absence of natural light can be alleviated by taking work breaks and looking out of doors, into the distance if possible. This lets natural light into the eyes and exercises the eyes at the same time.

- Neck and back strain may be caused in part by long hours at the keyboard, uncomfortable chairs, or poorly designed office layouts. If employees have to strain to see a screen, they should discuss the problem with a responsible person. Sometimes a small adjustment can prevent a major health problem. In general, desktop computers seem well-placed for tall people because they are able to maintain a natural head position while viewing the screen. Short people can have difficulty finding a comfortable working position in traditional office settings. Alternatives for short workstation users are an under the desktop position for the monitor (it is comfortably viewed through a glass desktop) or placement of the monitor directly on the desk rather than on top of the system unit.

Sample LAN Implementation Plan

The LAN Implementation plan consists of three parts:

1. Prepare for the LAN
2. Configure the LAN
3. Implement the LAN

Prepare for the LAN

The following steps are necessary to prepare an organization for the implementation of a LAN (or the major expansion of an existing LAN).

1. **Inventory existing PC and communications equipment:** system units, modems, special purpose PC boards, phones, printers, CD ROMs, scanners, plotters, other peripheral equipment, hubs, bridges, routers, servers, NICs, and software.

2. Establish LAN requirements in relation to strategic business and IS plans for your organization including administrative, management, technical, and security needs. Survey users as required.

3. **Determine constraints** on the LAN implementation and network application system development:

   ■ Budgets

   ■ Hardware and software availability

   ■ Politics working against a flawless network implementation

   ■ Demands of internetworking on your unit and organizations to be connected

- Special problems such as lack of standards, lack of security and insufficient protection of organization resources (may be evidenced by existence of viruses, loss of data, missing assets, and network penetrations)

4. **Identify applicable policies, standards, regulations, guidelines, and procedures** and determine which additional requirements may apply to the LAN.

5. **Determine the responsible** organizations and individuals for implementing aspects of the network and related tasks.

6. **Determine an appropriate architecture** and network configuration for each network phase considering the number of users, applications to be supported, and peripherals to be supported, NOS, server hardware, network topology, communications protocol and access method, communications hardware (hubs, repeaters or transceivers, server and PC-network interface cards (NICs), cable connectors, network links (bridges, routers, gateways), LAN software, cable media and wiring (or wire-*less* scheme).

7. **Configure the LAN.** If you have not yet configured your own LAN, you have an opportunity to address security needs and include security. Use the information in the other chapters, especially those on risk assessment, hardware, and software to act in a prudent and security-aware manner and make wise, educated choices.

Configure the LAN

To configure the LAN you must choose the cabling media, topology, network access method, communications protocol, hardware, the NOS, and other software. Selecting specific equipment is extremely important because although two products may have similar technical specifications, one may have security features and safeguards that another does not. Cable plant, topology, network access method, and communications protocol are interrelated in terms of LAN configuration so that a choice of one component may limit, or dictate, choices in the other categories. A choice of one component, such as cabling may:

- Limit potential bandwidth utilization and network transmission speeds

- Determine network communications equipment, PC-network interface card and connector requirements

- Affect network topology and protocols which can be supported

- Require additional security safeguards

The standard for the majority of new LAN installations, 10Base-T, is a variation on the Ethernet protocol IEEE 802.3 Local Area Network communications standard. The 10Base-T standard supports 10 million bits per second baseband communications over unshielded twisted pair wiring. Characteristics of 10Base-T are:

- "Star" network topology, in which each station is wired to the communications "Hub" for centralized network control. This topology allows the network the flexibility of operating with one or more inoperable workstations or lines. On the downside, it forces all communications to go through the server and LAN communications Hub which slows LAN printing and adds to network congestion.

- Supports data communication over unshielded twisted pair (UTP) wiring media.

- Requires network communications equipment, such as a Hub and NICs with transceivers (repeaters) for attaching workstations to the LAN.

- Transmission at speeds up to 10—and vendors claim, even 100—million bits per second (Mbps) are theoretically possible. In reality, speeds are limited to the capacity of the slowest communications component encountered between the sending unit and the destination unit. Transmission speeds on twisted pair wire may be substantially slowed by hubs, servers, bridges, routers, and other components. Throughput is a better indicator of LAN operating speed than media capabilities.

■ Carrier Sense Multiple Access/Collision Detection (CSMA/CD) network access method wherein the workstations listen to signals on the network; if no transmission is sensed the workstation transmits. If a collision of transmitted messages occurs, the transmitting workstations wait a random period of time and retransmit. This network access method is suitable for low traffic networks and most office automation LANs are in this category. Heavy network communications traffic may result in excessive numbers of collisions and, in the worst case, a "broadcast storm" of message retransmissions is possible in which no message is able to get through the network.

■ Utilizes a 3 MHz (per second) frequency bandwidth suitable for data transmission and limited graphics and even video, but not suitable for heavy graphics or video traffic.

LAN capacity is limited by its configuration, or choice of network components. LAN performance is limited by its capacity, the number of users and the traffic load. To illustrate the point, the performance limitations of a 10Base-T Ethernet LAN are contrasted with a Fiber Distributed Data Interface (FDDI) LAN in Table 11.1.

If you do not have the appropriate networking expertise in-house, your best resource for configuring your LAN is a highly experienced network design team which has designed networks to meet requirements such as yours. The designers may also provide the equipment. Beware the possibility, however, that your LAN may be designed more to the specifications of equipment the vendor happens to have on hand than to meet your business, technical, and security needs. You should review your configuration thoroughly to be sure your needs are being met before the LAN is installed. Outsourcing is a means of having your LAN configured, installed, and maintained by an outside firm (and administered too, if you wish). It is another way to get the ongoing support and technical expertise you require but may not have on staff. As networks become more complex, the trend towards outsourcing has become more pronounced.

Table 11.1   Performance limitations of LAN components.

LAN Performance Attribute	Primary Limiting Component	Secondary Limiting Component or Factor	10Base-T Ethernet Specs or Example	FDDI Specs or Example
Bandwidth	LAN Cabling	Hub, NICs	3 MHz	1 THz
Transmission Speed	Topology, hub or concentrator	Cable speed; repeater transceiver, bridge/router # and speed; network load; overhead (eg:encryption); PC/server NIC limitations	10-10 Mb/sec	100 Mb/sec
Throughput	All as affect transmission speed and	Protocol (network access/contention method, treatment of errors), network load (packets in transmission)	500 Kb/sec-5 Mb/sec range	As much as 1 Bb/sec
Hardware Inter-connectivity	NOS	Availability of physical connection equipment	Good. Many products available at a reasonable price	Fair due to newness, expense, & connector availability
Office Automation Capability; E-Mail, E-Fax, E-forms; Groupware	NOS	LAN-ready add on software	Transmission speed and bandwidth limitation	Little transmission speed and bandwidth limitation
LAN Applications	LAN-ready Application Software	LAN application development tools	Supports data, sound, graphics, and some video	Supports multimedia: data, sound, graphics, video
LAN Utilities, Diagnostics & Administrative Tools	NOS	Interoperability of network components	Novell LANalyzer for Windows, Compaq INSIGHT, NetWare Monitor	HP Network Advisor, Compaq INSIGHT, NetWare Monitor

If you are on shaky ground technically, but are required to configure and support your own LAN, you can acquire tools which will assist you in making critical decisions and in LAN management and administration. An appropriate suite of LAN planning, analysis, administration, and management tools will pay for themselves by saving you enormous amounts of time and frustration.

The COMNET III network capacity planning and performance prediction tool can be useful in anticipating the needs of large LANs.

Implement the LAN

The following tasks are required of the LAN management and administration staff to implement or complete a major expansion of an existing LAN:

1. **Work with technical experts** to choose, schedule, install, maintain, and expand the network and its components.

2. **Develop a training plan** (or provide expert guidance for your training specialist in its development) to assist staff members in preparing themselves to use the LAN and its facilities.

3. **Establish polices, standards, and procedures** for LAN operations.

4. **Review the Security Plan** to ensure it adequately addresses risk analysis, the protection of network assets against threats, security training, and safety issues relative to the LAN.

5. **Write a LAN Implementation Plan** which will document LAN planning, development, implementation, and operations activities.

6. **Create a User Guide** which should be made available through the network. Procedures should be provided to assist users when they need to accomplish such tasks as:

   ▪ Apply for and cancel userids

   ▪ Change personal passwords

   ▪ Create and name directories, files, applications, and workgroups

   ▪ Store files on the LAN server

   ▪ Gain or cancel access to LAN applications, directories, databases, and files

- Upload data to a host computer or download data from a host computer
- Schedule regular uploads and downloads
- Request that new software be installed on the server

7. **Develop a network** of LAN User Support groups to ensure appropriate support for end users during network expansions and problems. With Division management, identify a backup for the LAN Administrator.

8. **Implement the network:**
    - Monitor network cabling, hardware installation, and testing
    - Set up server(s), network software, LAN utilities, and workstations, coordinating with technical support and the vendor
    - Configure the NOS setup (establish drives, workgroups, workstations, directories, files, Userids, access rights, etc.)
    - Test the network
    - Resolve problems with network wiring, hardware, software, and installation with technical support, vendors, and equipment manufacturers

9. **Complete and test** network administration and operating procedures including backup and recovery and other LAN utilities.

10. **Arrange for a security review** and LAN certification (and accreditation for Federal government LANs).

11. **Convert LAN** to operational status.

12. **Purge test files, reset passwords,** give LAN Policies, Standards, and Procedures to users.

13. **Ensure users complete LAN security awareness training** in use of security policies, standards, and procedures and turn in their completed Responsible LAN User Agreements.

14. **Continuously improve** the quality of network operations and services through day to day quality improvement practices.

LAN Staffing Plans

As LANs mature and increase in importance to organizations, their staffing is becoming a more formal process. The following sample plans address LAN staffing needs.

Sample Management and Administration Responsibilities

The responsibilities of organization-wide Enterprise Network System (ENS) management includes strategic planning, network security oversight, integration of departmental and workgroup LANs with the fiber optic backbone network through use of bridges, routers, and gateways, oversight of the LAN environment including network architecture; configuration, installation and technical support, procurement assistance for hardware, software and services.

LAN management responsibilities are:

- Plan and coordinate with technical experts to configure, implement, manage, or expand a LAN which will serve the intended user population
- Manage network implementation, startup, day-to-day operation, and future expansion
- Identify applicable policies and procedures
- Devise a workable implementation plan addressing hardware, software, training, testing, security, performance, and applications
- Plan and coordinate with training suppliers to prepare users for LAN implementation
- Establish administrative procedures, user procedures and related documentation
- Develop a LAN support network in the user community
- Establish new communication links as needed
- Install new software on the network

■ Monitor network performance, working with technical experts to correct problems

LAN administration responsibilities are met by the LAN Administrator who has primary full-time formal responsibility for administering the LAN, and the User Support group. The User Support group consists of users who are able to support their work group in emergency situations. The LAN Administrator and User Support group members have formal roles in the DRP and COOP teams. LAN administration responsibilities include:

■ Accept, log, investigate, analyze, and resolve trouble reports about the network

■ Take regular backups and rotate backup files to offsite storage so as to minimize exposure to loss of data or data integrity

■ Recover and restore deleted and damaged files as needed

■ Provide on-the-spot assistance, troubleshooting, and training for LAN users as needed

The LAN Help Desk is a centralized support system for LAN Administrators and users. Many questions and problems are handled quickly by technicians who have access to state-of-the-art troubleshooting tools and information. The Help Desk filters initial trouble reports and passes urgent problems and situations which require in-person assistance on to local LAN Administrators.

Sample LAN User Responsibilities

It is the responsibility of network users to review the LAN policies, standards and procedures and the Security Plan they are intended to implement and reinforce. LAN users should:

1. Understand the potential threats against the security of the LAN and the safeguards in effect.

2. Comply with these policies, standards and procedures.

3. Safeguard their individual LAN password.

4. Communicate any breach of LAN security or malfunction to their LAN User Support group, LAN Administrator, or Security Officer immediately.

5. Agree to be a responsible LAN user. Demonstrate your commitment by completing the *Responsible LAN User Agreement* which is displayed in Figure 11.1.

RESPONSIBLE LAN USER AGREEMENT

I understand the potential threats to network security and my role as LAN user in safeguarding network assets. I agree to be a responsible user and to abide by the policies, standards, and procedures in effect to safeguard the LAN.

LAN User: _____

Date: _____

FIGURE 11.1 RESPONSIBLE LAN USER AGREEMENT.

LAN Security Case Study: Terrific Consultants, Inc.

There are a great many threats and safeguards and it is not always obvious which ones you should address when designing your LAN. You can gain insights into the solutions, safeguards, methods, and procedures which might be appropriate for your LAN by reviewing one security-aware LAN manager's choices and plans. To illustrate the principles of LAN security we can take the example of a mid-sized division of a Fortune 1000 company (or a small company) expanding their LAN as the result of a Business

Process Reengineering (BPR) exercise. The new organization is designed to take strategic advantage of networking and groupware technology.

Terrific Consultants, Inc. is a consulting company and Value Added Reseller of software and services, groupware applications, and computer hardware. The managers have considerable expertise in software, hardware, networks, and security, which enables them to make enlightened decisions about their LAN. Management is security-aware and committed to protecting their assets with appropriate safeguards.

The division is moving into larger quarters and will upgrade their network concurrent with the move. This will give them an opportunity to rework their old Security Plan and thoroughly test several new technologies they are evaluating for the new environment. They have the luxury of choosing their LAN safeguards while planning their new architecture, environment, and applications.

REQUIREMENTS FOR THE NEW LAN

The requirements for the new LAN in this case study are summarized at a high level in the chart which follows. The network is intended to enable employees to dramatically change the way they work. A paper-intensive Export Management System will be replaced with an electronic information-based one. Business Planning will be protected adequately from the threat of intrusion or passive wiretapping for the first time. Marketing will be testing a few new Power PCs and a small wireless LAN in an effort to meet their multimedia needs.

A Lotus Notes server will also be added to expand Notes groupware capabilities across the organization enabling state-of-the-art, efficient customer support and expanding a highly profitable document intensive export business communications around the globe. It will also be the foundation for a new online business service product. Simultaneous improvements are expected to be gained in productivity, profitability, and quality. The quality of work-life will also be enhanced by providing employees with state-of-the-art tools. In short, the company expects to reap benefits far beyond the cost of additional PCs, software, and LAN connections. LAN requirements are briefly stated in Table 11.2 which follows.

TABLE 11.2 CASE STUDY LAN REQUIREMENTS.

SECURITY OR PERFORMANCE ATTRIBUTE	NORMAL BUSINESS OPERATIONS	SALES & MARKETING (PLANS, PROPOSALS, TRADE SHOWS)	BUSINESS PLANNING
Data Sensitivity	5% sensitive 95% non-sensitive	10% highly sensitive 10% sensitive 80% non-sensitive	100% Trade secrets and other highly confidential plans and data
Bandwidth	Data and voice (3 Mhz)	Data, voice, graphics, video, animation	Data, voice, graphics
Throughput and Utilization	1,500 accesses per day	120 accesses per day	100 accesses per day
Internetwork Links	Corporate HQ connection over dedicated T1 line	Market research databases	None (for data security reasons)
Office Automation: E-mail, E-fax, E-forms, Calendar, Scheduler, Directory Services	220 users	70 users	10 users
LAN Applications	Core accounting, administration systems Groupware for: customer support, project management, export management, risk management, LAN Help Desk and support, management systems support, product development, online client service	Desktop publishing of proposals and presentations Heavy graphics Multimedia video and animation presentations	LAN-ready applications Desktop publishing of proposals and presentations Quantitative analysis
LAN Utilities, Diagnostics and Administrative Tools	As required to provide high levels of dependability and security	As required to provide high levels of dependability and security	As required to provide high levels of dependability and security

One Possible Solution to the Case Study

The solution which follows in Table 11.3 is one of many which could be used to meet the needs described in our case study. All usual security safe-guards are assumed to be included without specification. A high level solution is provided as a basis for discussion.

TABLE 11.4 CASE STUDY LAN SECURITY SOLUTION.

LAN SEGMENT	LAN COMPONENT	PURPOSE OR SPECIFIC REQUIREMENT	SECURITY SAFEGUARDS, FEATURES, AND COUNTERMEASURES
Enterprise Network System	Fiber optic backbone privacy	Internetwork transmission speed and communication	Company-wide training and emphasis on security ensures awareness, accountability, adequate security procedures
	WAN Gateway server	Connect to outside internetworks, market research firms and databases and world-wide E-mail provider	Firewall against LAN intrusion via LAN-WAN gateway
	LAN Management and Administration	Centralized security management, emergency response and contingency plans, backup, LAN support	Policies, plans, procedures, training
			Online UPSs for essential electronic equipment (surge protection for other equipment), anti-virus software, automatic logoff, screen blanking, fire suppressant in server/network control rooms, and other computer rooms
			Electronic Asset Protection systems
			LAN help desk and onsite support
			Lock down and floppy drive cable locks for portable PCs
			LAN and internet analyzer; network inventory (hardware and software); monitoring, integrity, and audit software with alarms and alerts
			Contingency team leaders

continued

LAN SEGMENT	LAN COMPONENT	PURPOSE OR SPECIFIC REQUIREMENT	SECURITY SAFEGUARDS, FEATURES, AND COUNTERMEASURES
			Local LAN user support groups provide spot training, emergency support
	Intelligent router for Marketing LAN segment	Isolate Marketing LAN segment to allow: 1. High bandwidth utilization for graphics and video 2. Heavy communications traffic 3. Heavy security	Filtering communications traffic and segmenting Marketing LAN segment protects each segment from security weaknesses in other segments
Operations LAN	LAN Server	LAN server with automated setup, expert server management, disk drive duplexing, fault tolerant features	High level of hardware fault tolerance Service to include proactive parts monitoring for automatic replacement prior to failure and rapid service response
	NOS for 250 users	Accommodate 300 users in 3 LAN segments: Operations - 170 onsite 50 offsite Marketing - 20 onsite 50 offsite Business Planning - 10 onsite	Password checker ensures guess-proof passwords at time of password change Call-back system permits authorized users to access LAN from pre-authorized remote locations only
	10Base-T 300 drops	Provides maximum flexibility and ease of installation at low cost	Establish that all drops work prior to completion of work order and while vendor is on premises
Marketing LAN	5 node LAN	Support 5 MAC Power PCs	Isolate MAC LAN workstations during testing (isolation may continue after test period if security warrants)
	5 Power PCs	Evaluate Power PC supporting PC and MAC marketing applications, presentations, and demos	At Ease access control software application permits controlled shared use of Power PC by up to 10 users

continued

LAN Segment	LAN Component	Purpose or Specific Requirement	Security Safeguards, Features, and Countermeasures
	Wireless LAN for 5 Power PCs	Evaluate wireless radio frequency communications for Power PCs in rapidly changing LAN in small secure area	Spurious electromagnetic signals are not a threat in this physically secure area
	10 386 and 486 PCs	Existing PCs running Lotus 123, WordPerfect, Quark Express, etc.	Operations LAN security standards apply
	10 connections to Operations NetWare LAN	Administration and management Lotus Notes for customer support, workflow improvement	Operations LAN security standards apply
Business Planning LAN	Fiber optic cabling with 40 drops (offices, conference rooms)	Secure, fast communications to support heavy graphics, multimedia (video, animation, sound), presentations	Stand-alone LAN—no internetworking and no administrative tasks supported Password checker
	Secure Business Planning (BP) area of building to enable secure workgroup computing and networking	Internal business planning, consulting projects, and client business plans require secure processing and communications environment	Separate NICs for BP and Operations LANs in each PC permit use of either LAN but prevent non-BP and outside access to BP data In-depth security training for BP staff Treat walls, windows (coverings or glass), filters or conditioners on plumbing, and HVAC wires, cables, vents, and conduit to suppress electromagnetic signal transmission of BP and some marketing data Suppress electromagnetic emantions in area for fail-safe security
	Bulk encryption	Secure transmission of information to company HQ and client locations required	Bulk encryption enables communication of large amounts of data in secure manner
	5 486 PCs	Existing PCs on Operations LAN	Operations LAN security standards apply

continued

LAN SEGMENT	LAN COMPONENT	PURPOSE OR SPECIFIC REQUIREMENT	SECURITY SAFEGUARDS, FEATURES, AND COUNTERMEASURES
	10 connections to Operations LAN	Internetwork with Operations LAN Business operations, administration, office automation (e-mail, e-fax, e-forms, Lotus Notes)	Operations LAN security standards apply
	Lotus Notes with integrated document-voice message support	Export Management System on Lotus Notes Server contains clients' export contracts and links manufacturer, banks, agents, etc. The EMS also provides a forum for sharing export information in an easy-to-use Notes interface	Authentication of users and servers, field-level, message, and session encryption provide essential security for profitable export activities
Lotus Notes LAN server	See above	See above	Removable hard disk media for local backup and offsite storage of business classified data Physically secure disks when not in use Backup copies stored in safety deposit box and rotated every day data is changed

The Last Word on Managing Threats

Regardless of the support your organization and executives provide (or the lack thereof), it is up to the LAN manager to understand the countless threats and to protect the LAN regardless of the obstacles. There are a few more things you can do that will help you in the awesome task of securing your LAN.

Implement Readily Available Security Features First

Even when deterrents are readily available, such as the security features in the NOS, they are often not used. Even worse are the features that are implemented so poorly that they represent a tiresome burden to users but offer little protection for the LAN.

Users and even LAN administrators have been known to set up their logins so that all of their passwords are supplied automatically from disk. This does make the LAN login process easier for the user but it bypasses LAN security completely by allowing anyone to log into the LAN from any such workstation.

Consider Safeguards to Supplement Precautions Already in Effect

Take advantage of safeguards already in effect for your facility and your LAN rather than purchasing products which contain features you already have. If your operating system has virus protection, for example, you may not need to purchase a separate product to perform virus checking and removal.

Using Other Resources for Problem Resolution

There are times when even the most sophisticated LAN managers are baffled by a network problem and seek outside help from network and security professionals. *Intrusion Detection, Inc.* recently investigated an elusive message which was broadcast across a LAN occasionally in the evening. The message, "Looking for another player", would suddenly appear on LAN workstations. No one knew the source of the message or whether it was a virus, a network penetration, or some other form of security incident, so they suspected the worst. They used a network analyzer to monitor LAN traffic and identify the source of the message. It turned out that a couple of people were working late and playing *Doom*, an intriguing network game. The Doom players failed to realize that until the game has four players it continuously broadcasts messages across the LAN in an effort to locate a full complement of players. This illustrates the hazard of using untested software on a LAN. Running unauthorized software is forbidden on many LANs for precisely this reason. Games as well as applications can create hazards and security incidents such as generating a broadcast storm of messages which can result in deadlock and force a shutdown of the entire network.

Request a Security Review

In my consulting experience with some of the most prestigious organizations in the country, I have been astounded at the insecure state of our systems and networks. I have seen a total absence of internal systems controls and accounting controls on computer systems which managed assets worth billions of dollars, and little appreciation for the need to control the production of computerized data. In one such company, when a top executive asked for sales figures from sales, marketing, manufacturing operations, and finance, he got four very different figures. No wonder. The wonder was that the company ran at all.

The worst situation imaginable is being responsible for a LAN which has lax security and on one but you seems to care. You don't have to quit your job to get away from the problem. Ask you senior managers for a LAN security review. The report will spell out the problems and risks, spur management action and support for damage and get you "off the hook" for foreseeable security losses which you cannot otherwise address.

LEARN FROM THE STORIES AND THE MISTAKES OF OTHERS

Learn from the stories and examples in this book to avoid making the same mistakes others have made. Get involved with LAN security issues and do your part for security awareness by keeping your company informed. You can learn more about threats and the progress in safeguards and countermeasures by contacting one of the security resources in Appendix B. Did the examples in this book help to make the threats real for you?

Think about what you need to help you do a better job of securing your LAN. Are you having LAN security problems? What are your concerns? Would a LAN security newsletter help you to stay current? Would an on-line (confidential and secure) LAN security management service be helpful if experts were waiting to help you prepare and troubleshoot your own security plan, DRP, COOP, and risk assessments? While I cannot promise to respond, I will read every comment. My CompuServe public key is 73172.2050; and my Internet address is 73172.2050 @ compuserve.com.

Well, this book is at an end but the LAN security story is not over. Now is the time to plan the action you will take to avoid trouble on your LAN and save your organization from unnecessary losses. If you have learned one thing from this book it will have met its objective and paid for itself many times over.

APPENDIX A

GLOSSARY OF
LAN SECURITY TERMS

This Glossary has a Local Area Network security orientation. The first part of the Glossary contains acronyms. The list of acronyms is followed by definitions of Local Area Network and security terms.

Glossary

Acronyms

ACL	Access Control List
API	Application Programming Interface
ARCnet	Attached Resource Computer network
ASCII	American Standard Code for Information Interchange
AT	Advanced Technology
ATM	Asynchronous Transfer Mode
BBS	Bulletin Board System
BIOS	Basic Input/Output System
BIT	Binary Digital
BNC	Bayonet Naval Connector
BPS	Bits Per Second
CD-ROM	Compact Disc Read-Only Memory
CMOS	Complementary Metal-Oxide Semi-conductor (ROM chip)
CERT	Computer Emergency Response Team
COMSEC	Communications Security
COOP	Continuation Of Operations Plan
COTS	Commercial Off-The-Shelf
CPU	Central Processing Unit
CRC	Cyclic Redundancy Check
CRT	Cathode Ray Tube
CSMA/CA	Carrier Sense Multiple Access with Collision Avoidance
CSMA/CD	Carrier Sense Multiple Access with Collision Detection
DARPA	Defense Advanced Research Projects Agency
DAT	Digital Audio Tape
DBMS	DataBase Management System

DES	Data Encryption Standard
DIX	Digital/Intel/Xerox
DLL	Dynamic Link Library
DOD	Department Of Defense
DOS	Disk Operating System
DRP	Disaster Recovery Plan
DVM	Digital Volt Meter
EBCDIC	Extended Binary Coded Decimal Interchange Code
ECC	Error Correction Coding
EISA	Extended Industry Standard Architecture
E-Mail	Electronic Mail
EMI	ElectroMagnetic Interference
EP ROM	Erasable Programmable Read-Only Memory
ESDI	Enhanced Small Device Interface
FAT	File Allocation Table
FDDI	Fiber Distributed Data Interface
FTP	File Transfer Protocol
GB	Gigabyte
GDSS	Group Decision Support System
GUI	Graphical User Interface
HOS	Host Operating System
IDE	Intelligent Drive Interface aka: Intelligent Drive Electronics, Integrated Drive Electronics
IEEE	Institute of Electrical and Electronics Engineers
IEEE 802.0	IEEE Executive Committee Project Group
IEEE 802.1	High Layer Interface Work Group
IEEE 802.2	Logical Link Control Work Group
IEEE 802.3	CSMA/CD Work Group
IEEE 802.4	Token Bus Work Group

IEEE 802.5	Token Ring Work Group
IEEE 802.6	Metropolitan Area Network Work Group
IEEE 802.7	Broadband Technical Advisory Group
IEEE 802.8	Fiber-Optic Technical Advisory Group
IEEE 802.9	Integrated Voice and Data LAN Work Group
IEEE 802.10	Standard for Interoperable LAN Security Work Group
IPX	Internetwork Packet Exchange
IRM	Information Resources Management
IS	Information Systems Organization
ISDN	Integrated Systems Digital Network
ISO	International Standards Organization
LAN	Local Area Network
LED	Light-Emitting Diode
MAC	Media Access Control
MAN	Metropolitan Area Network
Mb	Megabits
MB	Megabytes
MFM	Modified Frequency Modulation
MHS	Message Handling Service
MIPS	Million Instructions Per Second
MTBF	Mean Time Between Failures
NDS	NetWare Directory Services
NetBIOS	Network Basic Input/Output System
NFS	Network File System
NIC	Network Interface Card
NIST	National Institute of Standards and Technology
NLM	NetWare Loadable Module
NNS	NetWare Name Service
NOS	Network Operating System

OS	Operating System
OS/2	IBM's Operating System/2 for microprocessors
OSI	Open System Interconnection or Integration
PAD	Packet Assembler/Disassembler
PDN	Public Data Network
PROM	Programmable Read-Only Memory
RAID	Redundant Array of Inexpensive Disks
RAM	Random-Access Memory
RISC	Reduced Instruction Set Computing
RLL	Run Length Limited
ROM	Read Only Memory
RSA	Rivest, Shamir, and Adelman [encryption method]
SCSI	Small Computer System Interface
SFT	System Fault Tolerant
SGML	Standardized Generalized Markup Language ISO data standard
SIMM	Single In-line Memory Module [chip]
SNA	Systems Network Architecture
SNMP	Simple Network Management Protocol
SPX	Sequenced Packet Exchange
SQL	Structured Query Language
STP	Shielded Twisted Pair [wire]
TB	Terabyte
TCB	Trusted Computing Base
TCP/IP	Transmission Control Protocol/Internet Protocol
TDDI	Twisted Pair Distributed Data Interface
TDR	Time Domain Reflectometer [network troubleshooting device]
TFT	Thin Film Transistor

TNA	The Network Archivist backup software from Palindrome
TP	Twisted Pair [wire]
TQM	Total Quality Management
TSR	Terminate and Stay Resident program
TTS	Novell's Transaction Tracking System
UPS	Uninterruptable Power Supply
USL	Unix Systems Laboratories
UTP	Unshielded Twisted Pair [wire]
w/s	Workstation
WAN	Wide Area Network
WOS	Workstation Operating System
XNS	Xerox Network System

PC-LAN Terms

A

Access

To read from or store data in, communicate with, or otherwise make use of a computer system.

Access control

Limits the use of computer resources to authorized users, or programs by means of cards, keys, passwords, physical and electronic surveillance, management controls, and operating procedures.

Access Control List (ACL)

Defines who can access files, directories, etc., and what action they can perform. NetWare 4.x NDS restricts access to all LAN objects (servers, users, printers, computers, and queues) and property rights limit access to specific properties, such as add, delete, read, compare, and write by means of the ACL.

Access time

The interval of time between the call for data by a control unit and the completion of delivery of the requested data—a factor in measuring the time it takes to read or write data to/from a disk. Access times for hard disks typically range from 8 to 60ms. Access times are significantly greater for floppy disks and CD ROM drives.

Accountability

Hold responsible for one's actions or errors. In computer systems, transactions and security violations must be traceable to individuals.

Accreditation

In government, the written, formal decision by management to approve and authorize operation of a particular automated system for processing classified information. Relative to LANs, authorization to process sensitive data based on certification by a responsible official that the system meets prespecified technical data security requirements.

Accuracy

Freedom from error.

Active wire tapping

Unauthorized attachment to a communications circuit for accessing data through capturing messages, generating false messages, or altering messages of legitimate users.

Agent

Software that is designed to perform specific tasks on data such as the "know bot" that travels databases across Europe searching for specific names and Internet addresses.

Algorithm

Abstract set of well-defined rules, processes, or instructions to the computer that solve a particular problem.

Append

       Add data or records to an existing file.

Application System

       There are two kinds of software: operating system software and application system software. Operating system software controls the working of the computer itself including such tasks as accepting information from the keyboard, storing it in memory and displaying it on the screen. Application system software—such as WordPerfect—performs tasks required to process and organize data for end users. Contrast this with system software such as the Disk Operating System (DOS) that controls PC hardware operation.

API

       Application Program Interface is a means by which an application program gains access to operating system resources, usually for data communication, data retrieval or other system services.

Archive

       To create a copy of a file, that may be stored (onsite and/or offsite) and protected for future use, record retention, or for restoring a database in the event the original file backup copy becomes unusable. In addition to protecting files from loss, archiving permits previous versions of a file to be restored, typically by date and time. Also a file attribute meaning the file has changed since the last backup.

ARCnet

       Attached Resource Computing Network. A proprietary token-bus networking architecture developed by Datapoint Corporation in the mid-1970s. It operates at 2.5 Mb/s and is relatively reliable. It supports coaxial, twisted pair, and fiber optic cable schemes. ARCnet was a popular networking architecture, especially in smaller installations, that is rarely installed today.

Array

       Items arranged in a meaningful manner. A disk array is a collection of disk drives.

ASCII

> American Standard Code for Information Interchange. A 7-bit code, intended to be the U.S. communications standard code. ASCII is used to represent data in IBM-compatible PCs and non-IBM mainframe computers.

Asynchronous Transfer Mode (ATM)

> A form of data transmission in networks based on fixed length packets (cells) that handless data, voice, and video at very high speeds.

Attach

> To establish communications with a network server.

Attributes

> A mechanism for describing properties of files and directories within a filing system. NetWare file attributes include Read, Write, Create, Delete and Execute Only (prevents files from being deleted or copied). NetWare directory attributes include Read, Write, Create, Execute and Hidden (hides information about the directory from file listings to prevent unauthorized access, deletion or copying).

Audit trail

> A record of activities that enables one to reconstruct events that occurred in processing data.

Authentication

> Verification of a workstation, individual, message or originating system or agency or location that requests access to a secure system. The purpose of authentication is to protect the system and the data it stores against unauthorized access or fraudulent use.

B

Backup

> Process of copying data, files and programs from one computer storage device to another. Backups are used to restore computer files and programs in the event the originals are destroyed or

altered by human error, software failure, viruses, hardware failures, or disasters.

Bad block table

A list of damaged blocks on a hard disk. The bad block table is usually duplicated on a label on the outside of the disk housing. Also called "media defect list." See also Hot Fix, read-after-write verification.

Bandwidth

Communications capacity, measured in bits per second (bps), of a transmission line or path through a network.

Bernoulli Box

A disk drive proprietary to Iomega Corp. that attaches to a personal computer and allows up to 150 million bytes (300MB compressed) of data to be stored on one removable cartridge.

BIOS

Basic Input/Output System. A set of computer programs, often in firmware (microcode embedded in electronic circuits used in chips and other hardware), that enables a central processing unit to communicate with input and output devices such as the keyboard, display unit, and communication ports.

Board

An electronic circuit assembly that is used in a computer to perform a specific function or set of functions, such as to control the operation of a hard disk. Also known as a card.

Boot

The process of starting a computer system. When a computer is turned on, system files—which provide operating system and disk information and prepare the machine for processing—are read into memory. (Short for "bootstrap")

Boot disk

In PCs, a diskette or disk that contains operating system files necessary for a PC to start up (or "boot"). In NetWare, a disk that contains the instructions for a workstation to attach itself to a NetWare LAN server. Users of a LAN attach to the LAN server through start up instructions in a "boot" PROM chip in the Network Interface Card and a batch file on the LAN server.

Bottleneck

Component of a network that is overloaded with more data than can be transmitted and processed in the desired time period. Bottlenecks routinely develop as network traffic (use) increases. Bottlenecks increase response time (time it takes for a network communication to be sent and for an answer to be received). Routine network monitoring and overall planning and administration help to avoid bottlenecks.

Breach

Successful defeat of system security controls.

Bridge

Device that connects two LANs that use the same datalink communications protocol such as IPS, TCP/IP or NetBIOS. External bridging requires a separate communications device or PC to connect the LANs. Bridges operate at Layer 2, the Media Access Communications (data link) layer of the OSI model. To pass data between networks with different data link communications protocols, routers should be used.

C

Cable

In networks, the media connecting workstations, servers, peripherals, hubs or concentrators, repeaters or transceivers, bridges, routers, and gateways. Popular cable media include: unshielded twisted pair (UTP), shielded twisted pair (STP), coaxial, and fiber optic. Today, about 70% of new LAN cabling installations are UTP, 20% is Coaxial cable, and 10% is Fiber Optic. UTP is preferred for ease of installation and maintenance and its lower cost. Fiber offers greater speed, bandwidth, and security. Fiber optic cable installations are on the increase as installers gain experience with the more difficult fiber LAN connections and the higher prices of interfaces and connectors decline.

Call back

Procedure for protecting data from unauthorized communications access where the caller must provide identification permitting verification of the caller's phone number (per an authorization list) that permits the called system to disconnect the dial-in communication session, and dial the authorized calling number back.

Card

See board.

CD-ROM

Compact Disk Read-Only Memory is a compact disk device that can store large quantities of information. Since the information can only be read (not changed or updated) it is used most frequently for storing large data bases to be used for reference purposes. It is distributed in the manner of other publications such as books and directories.

Certification

The evaluation of the security features and other safeguards of an Automated Information System conducted in support of accreditation. Sometimes represented by a written statement of risk assessment and an inventory of the [classified or sensitive] system components. Management approval of a certified system for operation is called accreditation.

Classified

Information that requires special protection because of its sensitivity, proprietary nature, or significance to the national interest, which has been assigned a security classification.

Clearance

Certification given to a person that permits viewing data that has been classified at or below a particular level.

Client/Server

A computing architecture used with Local Area Networks in which a front-end (client portion) interacts with the user and the back-end or server (sometimes called the database engine) provides computation-intensive processing. The result of distributing tasks according to computing resource requirements for processing speed, memory, disk speed, disk capacity and input/output equipment optimizes overall throughput. Client/server systems permit security functions to be centralized at the server for greater control.

CMOS (Complementary Metal-Oxide Semiconductor)

ROM chip powered by a battery which stores boot configuration, system clock, and possibly boot/resume passwords and disk information.

Coaxial Cable

A copper-core cable widely used in networks that follow the Ethernet standard in the U.S. Coax uses two conductors: a central, solid wire core surrounded by insulation which is surrounded by a braided wire conductor sheath. Coaxial cable was the preferred cabling media for LANs because it accommodates high bandwidth, is resistant to interference, and offers low electromagnetic emissions compared to unshielded twisted pair (UTP) wiring. See also twisted pair.

Code

In cryptography, use of substitution to conceal the meaning of data.

Cold site

In a Disaster Recovery and Continuation of Operations Plan, the alternate processing facility containing only the hardware necessary to recreate operations after a disaster. Software, files, procedures, and staff must be brought into a cold site when the Plan goes into effect.

Communication link

Physical connection of locations to permit transmission and receiving of communications.

Communications

The act of exchanging information including exchange by spoken word, letter, thought, telephone, telegraph, facsimile, sign and body language. In computers, implies transmission of data. See datacomm.

Common Carrier

Authorized communications service provider such as AT&T, Sprint and MCI.

COMSEC

Communications security that is concerned with (1) denying sensitive information that may be derived from telecommunications to unauthorized persons, or (2) ensuring the authenticity of such communications.

Compartmentation

Security technique that employs separation of data into identifiable compartments to permit limiting access to data in different compartments to users with corresponding access requirements and appropriate authorizations.

Compression

See data compression.

Compromise

Unauthorized disclosure or loss of sensitive or classified information.

Computer Emergency Response Team (CERT)

An organized team of 14+ at the Software Engineering Institute of Carnegie-Mellon University. Established to respond to Internet security incidents including attacks by network hackers and crackers. CERT provides information and assistance to penetration victims as well as incident advisories and preventative safeguard measures.

Confidentiality

Restriction of information access to authorized users.

Configuration

In LANs, physical arrangement of server, workstations, communications devices, cabling, and software in such a way as to meet the specifications required for network operation.

Contingency Plan

> See Disaster Recovery Plan and Continuation Of Operations Plan.

Controller

> An electronic device that interfaces and controls a component of the computer such as a hard disk drive. See SCSI, ESDI, Disk Controller.

Controller card

> An electronic circuit board that contains the electronics to control a component of the computer, such as a hard disk drive.

Cracking

> As in network cracking; highly motivated, expert network penetration activities, usually performed for profit. Contrast with hacker activities.

Crash

> A crash is a hardware or software failure that usually results in the computer being inoperable or "down" for some period of time. A crash is often the result of a software malfunction and can sometimes be "fixed" by restarting the computer. A hard disk or head crash normally damages the hard disk and usually requires physical repairs and data recovery efforts.

Crosstalk

> In communications, unintentional intrusion of data or voice transmission signals from another communications line due to proximity of two or more sets of lines. A phone call in which you hear extraneous voices is an example of crosstalk.

Cyberpunk

> Term used in science fiction to describe a hacker.

D

Data Communications

> The exchange of information between two or more computers. Communication of data in this country is usually done over

telephone lines although transmission is also accomplished via satellite, microwave or shortwave, Public Data Networks and privately-owned networks. Our present public telephone system is slow but is constantly changing. The use of fiber optic cable in new network links to replace existing copper wire expands our communications capacity—for data and voice.

Data Compression

Compacting data by eliminating blanks and redundancies that allows more data to occupy a smaller physical space. Hard disk data may be compressed, using Stacker 4.0 for example, to effectively more than double the amount of disk storage space. Besides saving storage space, compression makes data more secure since data is not readable in its compressed form (although it can be decompressed without difficulty).

Data Density

The amount of data—usually expressed in bits per inch (BPI)—of data stored on a track of a disk.

Data encryption

Use of key(s) to transform data so it cannot be read without being unencrypted.

Database

Collection of related information (data) in a computerized system. Databases are generally stored on disk. They are accessed by programs and Data Base Management Systems (DBMS).

Data Base Management System (DBMS)

Software such as Approach, DB2, dBASE IV, Oracle, and Q&A, that is used to accept, store, manage, control, process, query and report related information in a data base to create an application system.

Datacomm

Data communications.

Dedicated

A device that has only one function. For example, a dedicated server cannot also be used as a workstation in a network.

Dedicated line

Leased or private communications line. See also dial-up line.

Device driver

In PCs, a program that provides the instructions for DOS, an operating system, to control non-standard devices such as a mouse, a non-standard keyboard, or a tape unit used for backups.

Dial-up line

Telephone line that is used to transmit data and is accessed by a modem that converts digital data signals into analog signals for transmission over telephone lines.

Digital

Number-oriented. Data is stored in computers and newer communications devices in digital form as opposed to analog which is measurement-oriented.

Digital Volt Meter

Network test device that measures voltage (volts), resistance (ohms), current (amps), and continuity in cabling.

Directory caching

A copy of the File Allocation Table and the directory entry table are stored in the network file server's memory. A file can then be located and read very quickly in memory, which is faster than locating and reading it on disk.

Directory hashing

A performance feature that indexes disk file locations to reduce the time needed to locate a file stored on disk.

Directory rights

Restrictions that limit access to a particular directory.

Directory structure duplication

NOS feature that protects data from failures in network hardware. A hard disk directory and file allocation table contain the file address needed by the NOS to store and retrieve data. Duplicate copies of both the directory table and the file allocation table are maintained on separate areas of the hard disk. If the primary copy is lost or destroyed, the secondary copy can be used.

Directory verification

NOS feature that protects data from failures in network hardware. Each time the server is turned on, the NOS performs a consistency check on duplicate sets of directory and file allocation tables to verify that the two copies are identical.

Disk Access

The process of locating data on disk for retrieval, writing or updating. Disk access time is a critical factor in measuring computer throughput. Disk access time is measured in milliseconds (typical rates for PC hard disks are between 8 and 60ms). Disk access time can be improved through more efficient file organization, disk caching, physical data layout on disk, and efficient programmed instructions for file operations and disk management.

Disk Array

Multiple hard disk drives used together to provide large amounts of storage capacity and/or fast transfer rates.

Disk Cache

A special area in memory or on a disk controller used for storing data at the time it is being read from or written to the disk. Data in the cache may then be retrieved directly from the cache without the delay of positioning the read/write heads to locate and retrieve data where it is stored in a permanent location on disk. Disk caching improves disk input/output performance, lowers access times, and usually improves transfer rates.

Disk Capacity

Total amount of data that can be stored on a physical disk device. Capacity is usually measured in millions of bytes (MB or Megabytes).

Disk Controller

Device used to connect and control the operation of a disk device such as a hard disk or a floppy disk drive. The controller typically performs low-level, time consuming functions of managing the data format on disk, disk access and data transfer so the operating system can focus on other processing. In disk controllers, the software routines and instructions may be embedded in integrated circuits (called *firmware*) to maintain their integrity, and conserve processing memory and program storage space on disk.

Advanced intelligent drives with built-in controllers including the Enhanced Small Device Interface (ESDI), Integrated Drive Electronics (IDE), and Small Computer System Interface (SCSI, called "scuzzy") and may control many devices and perform a wide array of input/output functions. Advanced intelligent controllers may contain powerful microprocessor chips or integrated circuits, extensive logic, large amounts of RAM for caching, and ROM to store all the necessary software instructions.

Disk mirroring

Network feature in which data on one hard disk is duplicated on a second hard disk on the same channel. Disk writes to the original hard disk are also written to the second hard disk. If the primary disk fails, the duplicate disk takes over automatically. If the channel fails, data can be lost. See disk duplexing for greater protection.

Distributed processing

A processing mode that enables multiple computers to cooperate in the completion of tasks, typically in a networked environment. Each computer that contributes to the completion of the total task does so by completing subtasks independently of its peers and reporting the results as its subtasks are completed.

DOS

Disk Operating System. IBM's Disk Operating System for PCs is called PC-DOS; Microsoft's Disk Operating System for PCs is called MS-DOS; Novell's Disk Operating System for PCs is called Novell DOS.

Download

To send files from a fileserver to a workstation, send files from a mainframe to a LAN fileserver or workstation, or send fonts from a fileserver to a network printer.

Downsize

In managing information resources, move functions once per-formed on expensive mainframe (and less frequently on mini) computers to less costly microcomputers linked via LAN. Downsizing is possible because of vast improvements in com-puter and communications technology within the last decade. The recession has given impetus to the search for lower-cost methods of employing scarce resources and downsizing repre-sents opportunities for enormous savings.

Driver

See device driver.

E

EBCDIC

Extended Binary Coded Decimal Interchange Code. The char-acter set used to translate binary numbers used in mainframe computers into numbers, alphabetic characters and special characters used in English communications. See ASCII.

EISA

Extended Industry Standard Architecture. Advanced bus design that processes 32-bits of data at a time and (like IBM's Microchannel) supports straightforward, stable, seamless integration of multiple processors and intelligent controllers. Advanced bus designs are necessary to handle the throughput demands of faster microcomputers and LAN applications. It is an upward compatible extension of the ISA or AT bus design.

Electromagnetic emissions

Stray signal emitted by electronic equipment and cables which can be intercepted and decoded thus compromising the security of a computer or LAN.

Electronic Mail

NOS or LAN application system for sending and receiving messages electronically on a network. E-mail generally allows attachment of spreadsheets and documents to messages. Intelligent e-mail allows users to customize message handling with respect to: priority criteria; different handling for different senders/recipients; filing, faxing, routing, retention requirements.

Elevator seeking

A NOS performance improvement feature that allows the disk read-write head to pick up files in the direction it is traveling across the disk rather than picking them up in the order they were requested.

Emanations

Electromagnetic emissions from electronic devices and network wiring. Emanations may be analyzed to disclose information.

Encryption

Encoding of data before transmission or storage to prevent its unauthorized use. Encrypted data must be deciphered (unencrypted) before it can be understood by people.

ESDI

Enhanced Small Device Interface, is a hard disk interface standard capable of transferring data at ten million+ bits per second. ESDI controllers were frequently used in high-end 386+ PCs to control hard disk devices at one time. IDE, SCSI, and SCSI-2 interface is used more often today. Unlike the MFM design, the ESDI drive has the data separator built-in, but the controller is on a separate board. See also SCSI, IDE.

Ethernet

Data communications protocol and data access standard developed by DEC, Intel and Xerox that uses copper-core cable to transmit data at the rate of 10 Mb/sec. Ethernet is vulnerable to interference and eavesdropping compared to FDDI, the fiber optic network standard. 10Base-T is a variation (IEEE 802.3 standard) on the Ethernet protocol and data access standard that communicates at a maximum rate of 10Mb/sec using a star topology, and an unshielded twisted-pair network cabling scheme.

External drive

A disk or tape drive that is located outside of the System Unit and has its own power supply and enclosure.

F

Facsimile

Also "fax". A method of transmitting images using digital or analog signals that differ from signals used in voice and data transmissions. Fax boards are used in PCs that permit faxing documents between PCs, or PC and Group 3 fax machines over a network. A Faxserver consists of communications software and facsimile transmission board(s) that may be collocated in the e-mail server. Fax servers permit workstations on the LAN to send faxes from their PCs and receive faxes at a central point, through pooled modems.

Fault tolerant

Characteristic of computers that continue to process data despite hardware or software failures. See System fault tolerant.

FCONSOLE

NetWare utility used to access the network server and fine tune its performance. It is a virtual console utility that allows the operator to control a server from any station on the network.

FDDI

Fiber Distributed Data Interface is a fast-emerging token-ring LAN standard for 100 Mbps (Megabit per second) data transmission over fiber-optic cable that promises multivendor compatibility.

Fiber Optic

Glass or plastic cable media capable of transmitting data, sound, graphics and video. Fiber optic cable is particularly well-suited to LANs because intrusions are easily identified, taps are difficult to install, electromagnetic emissions are limited, it supports transmission speeds in excess of 100Mb/sec and offers the bandwidths to support data, sound, graphics, video and multimedia communications.

Unlike Ethernet LAN cabling media, fiber optic cable is very fast, flexible, not vulnerable to physical and electromagnetic interference and signal radiation, does not corrode or conduct electricity and cannot be tapped easily. Fiber offers broadband capabilities, thus is widely used in 100 Mbps backbone networks to connect Ethernet LANs. It is somewhat more expensive than coaxial cable, and twisted-pair wiring. Installation and expansion is more difficult. It is feasible to use fiber optic cable to connect desktop computers to fiber optic networks now that many fiber-based LAN installations are complete.

File Allocation Table (FAT)

Table directory used by MS-DOS to locate files on a disk. A FAT keeps track of file locations in a particular volume. A table located on disk cylinder 0 that contains information about the order and allocation of sectors on the disk to the files the disk contains. The NOS divides each volume into blocks and stores files in these blocks. If the file consists of one or more blocks, the file may be stored in blocks that are not adjacent. The FAT keeps track of all the block numbers where parts of one file are located. To retrieve a file, the NOS searches through the FAT until it finds the FAT entries and corresponding block numbers for the requested file.

File handles

In DOS, refers to the number of files DOS can manage in RAM at one time.

File sharing

An important feature of networking that allows more than one user to access a file at the same time or in rapid succession.

File Transfer Protocol (FTP)

A TCP/IP protocol that provides data transfer service from operating systems to the TCP (transmission control protocol) for encapsulation and transmission. It includes access control and encryption options.

Fileserver

In Local Area Networks, a computer that controls the network and manages network resources. Fileservers store files and data bases and perform file sharing and other network services for workstations on the network. A dedicated fileserver is used only for that purpose; a non-dedicated fileserver may also be used as a workstation.

Firmware

Software etched in electronic circuitry and embedded in hardware such as a Read Only Memory (ROM) chip. Firmware is generally used for system software that should not be changed except by the hardware manufacturer. It can result in more efficient computer systems since instructions embedded in hardware can be removed from the operating system software. This results in a smaller, more efficient operating system that then requires less memory.

Fragmentation

Fragmentation is the separation of files into non-consecutive sectors on a hard disk that results in slow disk access time.

Frame Relay

A new narrow-band wide-area switching standard designed to handle high-speed LAN-WAN internetworking. Said to be the "last gasp for narrow-band communications".

G

Gateway

Gateways use software-based intelligence to permit communications between networks with dissimilar data coding and protocols such as a LAN (IPX, ASCII) and an IBM mainframe (SNA, EBCDIC). Departmental LANs are often connected to a backbone LAN that is connected to a WAN gateway. Users are able to communicate with Public Data Network host computers, mainframe computers, upload and download files from other computers, and share e-mail across incompatible networks through network gateways. Gateways operate at the highest level (7) of the OSI model.

Gigabyte (GB)

A unit of measure for memory or disk storage capacity. A Gigabyte is one billion bytes.

Global backup

Backup of all information on a hard disk including directories and files on all disk drives.

H

Hacker

A person who knowingly attempts to perpetrate unauthorized penetration of computer systems or networks. The hacker's purpose ranges from ill-advised pursuit of technical challenges and recognition to intentional infliction of damage or destruction to the penetrated system. Also known as cyberpunk and technopath.

Hardware

The physical, electronic parts of a computer such as the display screen, system unit, chips, and keyboard are hardware. Contrasted with hardware, the instructions that tell the hardware what to do are called software. Instructions to the computer are frequently packaged into [software] programs. Sets of programs that work together are called [software] systems.

Head Crash

In computers with disk drives, when a read/write head strikes the disk surface, a head crash occurs that may damage the magnetic storage medium. In PCs, the heads may be moved to a safer place by executing a program such as SHIP or PARK before the computer is moved or bumped, to avoid damage to the hard disk.

Host

A computer on a network that provides services to other computers beyond simply storing and forwarding information.

Hot Fix

A NetWare feature in which a small portion of a hard disk's storage space is set aside as a Hot Fix redirection area. When read-after-write verification determines that there is a bad data block on the disk, Hot Fix redirects the data to be stored there in the Hot Fix redirection area. Hot Fix marks the defective block as bad so the server will not attempt to store data at that location.

Hot Site

Alternate processing LAN facility fully equipped and ready for backup file restore and continuation of computer or LAN operations.

Hub

A communications hub is the control point of the network and connects servers and nodes via LAN cabling. The hub is responsible for concentrating and strengthening weak messages, transmission control, error correction, and other features of a particular LAN protocol. Many hubs are increasingly intelligent and may have integrated security, bridging, routing, and LAN management capabilities.

I

IEEE

Creates networking standards for cabling, electrical topology, physical topology, and access schemes.

Integrity

In computers and communications, correctness, completeness and accuracy of data and processing of data.

Interface

The connection and its specification between two systems, computers, communications devices, or components.

Interleaved

A logical sector arrangement on a disk for optimization of processing and data transfer.

Interoperability

The concept of connectivity of computing hardware and software from multiple vendors whereby differences between software and hardware from different manufacturers is transparent to the end user.

Internet

A large network originally sponsored by DARPA (Defense Advanced Research Projects Agency). The Internet interconnects many U.S. government agencies, corporations and academic institutions. It has expanded to provide as many as 20 million users with a rich set of services including e-mai, multimedia, and the *World-Wide Web* of commercial services through connectivity to many other networks and computers.

Internetwork

Communications between two or more networks connected by an internal or external device such as a bridge, router or gateway. Internal devices are located on a board in the server; external devices are located in a PC or other hardware device attached to the LAN.

IPX

The communications protocol (developed by Xerox, known as the XNS standard) that is optimized for the local workgroup and is used in Novell's NetWare. IPX allows the exchange of message packets on an internetwork.

ISO

Information Systems Organization typically responsible for corporate data processing including data centers, system planning and development, database management, data administration, and computer operations.

K

Key disk

A disk with embedded codes (the key). Key disk can be used to authenticate system users and to protect software from being copied. The key disk must be present in the floppy disk drive (or installed permanently on the hard drive) for the authentication to take place.

L

Lines

In communications, the copper wires or fiber optic cables used to carry voice and data transmissions. The term "transmission lines" is sometimes intended to include satellite and microwave radio communication links in which there are no physical communication lines.

Load

To load an application means to start it and involves bringing at least some of the software and some of the files into memory so an executable program can be run. With respect to LANs, load is used to describe the quantity of communications messages and other traffic which the network must handle.

Local Area Network (LAN)

Type of data communications network that is intended to allow computers to communicate and share files over a limited geographical area such as a floor, department, building, or campus. LANs connect personal computers and electronic office equipment, enabling users to communicate, share resources such as data storage, files and printers, and to access remote hosts or other networks.

One LAN typically has at least one file or network server—and may have additional specialty servers for gateways, etc.—and may have anywhere from a few to hundreds of users. LANs are often dedicated to serving one workgroup or department and may be interconnected to other LANs within an organization, using a high speed "backbone". See Network.

Choices made in the configuration of LANs represent design decisions and trade-offs. A typical LAN configuration includes the follow five components:

LAN COMPONENT	TYPICAL CHOICE FOR 10BASE-T LAN
Network topology	Star-wired configuration of workstations and server
Network access method	CSMA/CD (Carrier Sense Multiple-Access with Collision Detection)
Operating system	Novell NetWare 3.11
Communications protocol	Ethernet 10BASE-T IEEE 802.3 standard
Cabling media	Unshielded, Teflon-coated (plenum insulation) twisted-pair.

LocalTalk

Shielded twisted pair cable introduced by Apple.

Logic bomb

A type of computer virus (more precisely, rogue program) that may exist in a passive state in a computer or storage device until activated by a particular date or event. Also known as a Time Bomb. An example is the Michelangelo, an especially destructive logic bomb that activates on Michelangelo's birthday (March 6th) each year.

Login

Process of identifying oneself to a computer security system in order to gain access; usually it includes entering an authorized unique userid and password. Users must go through a login procedure to gain access to the LAN.

Login script

A set of instructions that directs your workstation to perform specific actions when you log in to the network. The network supervisor can create a system-wide login script (which is the same for all users on the network) that instructs all workstations to perform the same actions upon login. Your individual login script executes after the system-wide login script. It specifies your individual drive mapping.

Logout

Exit from a system such as a network to which one previously logged in. LAN users either logout manually before turning the power off in a workstation or they may be automatically logged out.

M

Metropolitan Area Network (MAN)

Relatively new networking technology used to connect LANs in separate locations allowing high-speed communications (including image).

Mean Time Between Failures (MTBF)

A performance statistic or specification of significance in testing and evaluating computers and technological devices. MTBF indicates the mean (or statistical average) time a component can be expected to work continuously, based on tests conducted by the manufacturer.

Medium

The magnetic coating on the surface of a disk or tape on which data is recorded and stored. Also, the type of disk, tape or other device substance used to record or transmit data.

Memory-resident

A program that remains in the computer's memory once it has been loaded. Memory-resident software can usually be accessed quickly by pressing a series of keys (called "hot keys") on the keyboard. Also known as Terminate and Stay Resident or TSR.

Microprocessor

A single integrated circuit chip that is designed to process data in a computer. Microprocessors are "computers on a chip".

Middleware

All encompassing term for system-level software that performs services (database management, security, SQL protocols, directory names, workflow routing) permitting clients and servers to work across distributed networks and protocols (regardless of differences) facilitating client/server application development.

Modified Frequency Modulation

One encoding method used for storing data on disks. Early PCs used this storage method. Newer disks used RLL (Run Length Limited coding) that stores 1.5 times the data in the same space and offers faster data transfer rates.

Multitasking

Running more than one program (or performing more than one type of operation) in a computer at the same time. UNIX and OS/2 operating systems allow multitasking. PC software that claims to provide multitasking usually alternates processing cycles between two or more different processes so that the user is aware that the dual (or multiple) operation is taking place. In true multitasking, multiple operations should be transparent to the computer user.

N

NetBIOS

Network Basic Input and Output System. An IBM peer-to-peer communications interface that operates on OSI Transport and Session layers (4 and 5). NetBIOS provides an entry point into a LAN that supports communications using multiple communications standards and cabling media.

NetView

IBM high-end network monitoring software for Systems Network Architecture (SNA) networks.

NetWare

The network operating system developed by Novell, Inc. The NetWare operating system is loaded when the server is booted; it controls all system resources and the way information is processed on the network. It provides file, print, communication and backup services using printer, disk, tape backup, modem, and fax resources on the network.

NetWare Directory (NDS)

A new NetWare object-oriented, hierarchical, globally distributed directory service that tracks LAN resources (*e.g.*, users, groups, servers, volumes, directories, computers, and printers) through a system of objects, properties, and values. NDS gives NetWare an enterprise orientation where users log into the LAN rather than a server at a time.

NetWare Loadable Module (NLM)

Software that can be added to the NetWare operating system to provide additional function to a network server. NLMs can be dynamically loaded or unloaded from the server without having to take the network down.

NetWare shell

The NetWare program loaded into the memory of each workstation on the network. The NetWare shell builds itself around DOS to intercept the workstation's network requests and route them to a NetWare fileserver.

Network

A communications system that sends and receives data and messages, typically over a cable. A computer network enables computers to communicate with each other, share peripherals (such as hard disks and printers) and access remote hosts or other networks. LANs usually connect only PCs and minicomputers and are distance limited, whereas WANs usually connect mainframe, mini and microcomputers and may be physically connected across the globe.

Network adapter

The hardware installed in workstations and fileservers that enables them to communicate on a network.

Network File System (NFS)

A distributed file system network protocol developed by Sun Microsystems now used by NetWare.

Node

A location (or drop) on a network with a connection for a workstation, printer, or other device.

Nondedicated

A device that performs multiple simultaneous functions. For example, a nondedicated network server runs the network and also performs as a workstation.

O

Operating system

There are two kinds of software: operating system software and application system software. Operating system software controls the workings of the computer itself including such tasks as accepting information from the keyboard, storing it in memory and displaying it on the screen, while application systems software performs tasks required to process data for end users. DOS has been the primary operating system used in PCs. Availability of more powerful microcomputers (such as the 386, 486, 860 and Pentium) that offer more than the typical PC 640k maximum standard memory, opens the door for UNIX, OS/2, Pick, and other operating systems that could not be used with the 640k memory limitation.

OS/2

IBM's newest operating system for PC ATs and more powerful micro computers which supports multitasking.

Open System Inter-connection (OSI)

A reference model for network communications consisting of seven layers that describe the communications activity that takes place when systems communicate with each another. The model was developed by ISO (International Standards Organization) and consists of seven layers with definitions for electrical characteristics, communications standards, and software applications.

Oscilloscope

A network test and measurement device that measures signal voltage and attenuation. Graphically displays short circuits, open circuits, crimps, kinks, and impedance mismatches on cable segments.

P

Packet

The unit of information by which the network communicates. Each packet contains data, sending and receiving station identities, error-control information, a request for services, information on how to handle the request, and any necessary data that must be transferred.

Packet assembler/ disassembler (PAD)

Device or program used to create packets of data for transmission over a CCITT X.25 packet data network and to remove data from the received packets. The kind commonly used in PC and LAN communications is a CCITT X.29 PAD, used for packetizing and depacketizing asynchronous ASCII data.

Packet switching

Data communications switching method that divides data into individual envelopes called packets for transmission. Packets contain data plus addressing, sequencing and routing information.

Passwords

A password (sometimes called passphrase) is a unique code-word used to gain access to protected files or networks. LAN users must enter a unique userid and password when they log into the network. Passwords are verified to ensure that the individual logging into the LAN is the individual who owns the userid. Choosing hard-to-guess but easy-to-remember passwords is key in thwarting would-be network crackers. Some LAN applications such as WordPerfect provide password protection for files. Groupware applications such as e-mail and Lotus Notes offer an additional level of password protection.

Public Data Network (PDN)

A network operated by the government or a private agency that provides data transmission services to the public.

Port

Hardware physical location available for accessing devices such as disk drives or printers.

Power supply

A box that contains components to convert electrical current into voltages required by the computer.

Private network

Network installed and operated by a private organization for users in that organization.

Protocol

The rules that govern the language of data communications. Many protocols (such as the X.25 standard) exist to provide the following rules for different data communications situations:

1. The code set (typically, ASCII or EBCDIC) used to translate data as stored in computers into human language.

2. Synchronous (fast, efficient, uses constant time slice and is used in mainframe and WAN communications) or asynchronous transmission (used in PC and LAN communications).

3. Transmission control, error detection and correction method such as CSMA/CD.

Protocol suite

A collection of networking protocols that provides the communications and services needed to enable computers to exchange messages and other information, typically by managing physical connections, communications services and application support.

R

Recovery

The process of returning a computer system to the point before a crash or malfunction.

Read-after-write

NOS hardware verification feature that protects against loss of data as a result of hard disk and network hardware failures. When NetWare, for example, writes data to a block on the hard disk, it reads back the data and compares it to the original data still in memory. If the data from the disk matches the data in memory, the data in memory is released. If the data does not match, Hot Fix marks that block on the disk as bad and redirects the data to another location on the hard disk.

Record locking

A network feature that prevents two users from writing simultaneously to the same record in a file on the fileserver.

Repeater

Device that amplifies communications signals from one segment of network cable and passes them to other parts of the network. Repeaters extend the distance a LAN cable can be run.

Rights

A security feature that controls the directories and files a user can access and limits actions the user is allowed to take on those directories and files. Rights are assigned to directories and files by the LAN Administrator.

Risk Assessment

Process of determining the value of assets to be protected, their vulnerability, the nature and likelihood of threats, and the effectiveness of potential safeguards. Threats include environmental hazards, equipment failure, employee error that can lead to compromise, damage, or loss of equipment or data.

Router

A device that connects two or more networks and routes data dynamically between them based on the data destination and routes available. Routers can generally manage communications between different data protocols such as NetWare's IPX and TCP/IP. A NetWare Router, (formerly known as an internal or external bridge), for example, can connect networks that use different network adapters or media as long as both networks use the same protocols. Routers operate at Layer 3, the Network Layer of the OSI model. If a router is located in a server, it is called an internal router, although most routers are stand-alone devices. Router devices perform bridging and routing functions.

RSA

RSA is the most widely used public key encryption system. RSA was developed by three MIT professors, Drs. Ronald Rivest, Adi Shamir, and Leonard Adelman. This public key encryption method is suitable for protecting the privacy of network messages because it uses a pair of keys for each user, a public key that is known to all, and a private key that is secret. RSA is used by software manufacturers and developers world-wide.

S

Small Computer System Interface (SCSI)

(pronounced "Scuzzy"). Disk drive control technology that allows a single SCSI adapter card to control multiple devices such as hard disks, floppy disks, optical disks, tape drives, and scanners without taking data processing power away from the Central Processing Unit (CPU). Before SCSI each device had to have a dedicated controller that occupied one slot in the system unit. With SCSI, the controller functions are built into each device. The SCSI adapter along with the device driver software manages the input/output operations (such as copying a file from disk to tape) and data management functions (such as eliminating fragmentation of the hard disk). SCSI-2 drives support data transfer rates up to 20 MB per second.

Secure Dial-in

Secure or "authenticated" call-in requires positive identification of the caller. Mainframe systems and secure LANs use authenticated call-in or call-back systems to prevent unauthorized access to their LANs. Call-backs usually pre-authorize calling phone lists. When a call is received from an approved number (the system may also require entry of an access code), the system hangs up and dials the number back. Only then is a user allowed to login to the LAN.

Security

In computers and communications, protection of system resources from unauthorized loss, destruction, or disclosure. Security activities seek to safeguard resource availability, data and process integrity, and the privacy of confidential data.

Server

A computer on the network capable of recognizing and responding to client requests for services. These services can range from basic file and print services to support for complex, distributed applications. For example, a distributed database management system can create a single logical database across multiple servers. See also network server and client server.

Shareware

Software that is made available to potential users through bulletin boards and computer users groups. Shareware is typically licensed to a user at a nominal fee if after trying the program at no obligation, the user wishes to become an licensed user.

Spoof

The act of unauthorized penetration of a computer system or network and modifying or adding spurious information while pretending to be an authorized user.

STU-III

Secure Telephone Unit, third generation, which safeguards voice communications over telephone lines against interception.

Streaming

Streaming occurs during a tape backup operation, when data is transferred continuously (usually with the help of a buffer) and more data is available than the tape drive can record. The tape drive does not start and stop while streaming.

Surge protector

> An electronic device that offers some protection against voltage increases that might damage the computer circuitry.

System Fault Tolerance (SFT)

> System fault tolerance is the ability of a system to suffer malfunctions (primarily in hardware) without the loss of data or termination of processing normally associated with such a malfunction. There are several levels of hardware and software system fault tolerance but the primary method employed is redundancy (or duplication). One kind of redundancy is duplication of data on multiple storage devices so that if one storage device fails, the data may be accessed from the other device. This protects the data and also allows the system to continue to function, whereas without fault tolerance the system would lose access to the data and would fail, "crash" or "go down".

> A system crash typically requires technical experts to spend hours or days to determine the cause, more hours with hardware repair technicians brought in to correct the problem, and at least several more hours to restore the system (databases, files, and applications) to some point before the failure occurred. Often the end users would then spend more hours redoing some work. A system failure is a very expensive, time consuming, and stressful experience for all concerned.

> The ability to tolerate faults should be aimed at the network components that are most likely to fail. Most failures are in cabling, followed by failures in hard disks. Redundant cabling is only being used for the most critical networks because of the costs involved.

Systems Network Architecture (SNA)

> IBM's network architecture, defined in terms of its functions, formats, and protocols. SNA is IBM's interpretation of the OSI 7-layer data communications model. SNA came into use long before LANs did and is in wide use in the large installed base of IBM computers and software products.

T

T1

The standard for high speed digital transmission in the U.S. T1 specifies 1.544 Mbps (Million bits transmitted per second) and contains 24 lines of 64 kbps each. The cost of a T1 line is determined by the network congestion along its route as well as its length. For example, a T1 line from Washington to New York costs $6,500 per month compared with a T1 from Virginia to Texas which costs only $1,000 per month. The average T1 line costs from $3,000-5,000 per month.

TCP/IP

Transmission Control Protocol/Internet Protocol. A protocol and related applications developed for the U.S. Department of Defense as part of ARPANET research in the 1970s and 1980s specifically to permit different types of computers to exchange information. TCP/IP is currently mandated as an official Department of Defense protocol and is used by many manufacturers in the UNIX Internet community. TCP/IP is emerging as the internetworking standard on all network types.

Technopath

Person who knowingly devises and unleashes virus-type programs designed to destroy data or disrupt the use of computer systems and networks.

Tempest

The investigation, study, and control of compromising emanations from computers and communications equipment resulting from DOD specifications.

Thicknet

Thick broadband coaxial cable used in networks.

Thin Film Transistor (TFT)

Technology used in flat panel display screens. TFT screens are light, can produce brilliant color, emit few electromagnetic signals, are easy on the eyes, and are expensive.

Thinnet

Thin baseband coaxial cable used in networks. Also called cheapernet because it is less expensive than thick coaxial cable.

Throughput

Measure of the work a computer can perform in a given period of time. Throughput is a complex function of keyboard time, program execution, disk access, file storage and transfer, and presentation of output on a display screen or hard copy (printer-type) device and is affected by factors such as internal computer processing speed, disk access and data transfer times, disk caching, and data blocking. Intensive data entry, data base update, or computational processing operations are usually used to measure throughput. The measurement is sometimes referred to as a benchmark.

Time bomb

Type of computer virus or rogue program that replicates its destructive capability and typically remains dormant until some predetermined event triggers its execution of destructive (or at a minimum, unwanted) program instructions. The predetermined event can be attainment of a date, such as in the Michelangelo time bomb that is activated on March 6th.

Topology

The physical layout of network components (but primarily of computers and cables). There are three main LAN topologies: star, ring and bus. Token Ring uses a ring topology; 10BASE-T uses a Star topology.

Transaction Tracking System (TTS)

NetWare feature that protects data from failures in network hardware. TTS protects the integrity of databases by backing out incomplete transactions that result from a failure in a network component.

Trap door

Point of entry into a computer system that avoids security safeguards and results in vulnerability to intrusion. Traps doors are typically devised by programmers to provide quick and simple access for future program modification and testing. An example of vulnerability intrusion is the Morris worm, which was introduced into the Internet network in 1988 through trap doors in variants of the UNIX operating system on Sun and VAX computers.

Trojan Horse

A type of computer virus that is introduced without the user's knowledge and is hidden in programs that are stored in computer storage devices.

Trusted Computing Base (TCB)

The computing platform of hardware and software, as well as management procedures and controls that together ensure the security of a computer system. Guidelines provided by the National Security Agency's Defense Computer Security Center are the basis for security classes A through D, where A2 is the highest possible security class and D indicates insecure or not yet evaluated, for assignment of security ratings to commercial products. At the basic level of security, C1, users must identify themselves at login and confirm their identity by providing their unique, protected password. NetWare is rated C1 and is working towards a C2 rating—as are Banyan Vines and Windows NT—whereby users are identified and the means are provided to hold individuals responsible for their actions.

Twinaxial cable

A cable similar to coaxial cable except that there are two center conductors. Twinaxial cable is used with IBM 5250 class terminals.

Twisted-pair

Ordinary, inexpensive telephone-type copper wire commonly used in LANs which transmit data in the 1-10 Mbps range. Copper wire emits electromagnetic signals when a signal is passed through on an electric current, but the twisting of the wire neutralizes some of the emissions and susceptibility to interference or crosstalk. Several grades of twisted-pair wire are used in LANs, from the unshielded twisted-pair (UTP) that

exists in buildings (called inside wire) to the more expensive
Type 1 shielded twisted-pair wiring specified by IBM for use in
Token Ring networks operating at 16 Mbps transmission
speeds. Emerging twisted-pair standards and products for
LANs include: *TDDI* (Twisted Pair Distributed Data Interface,
often called CDDI) standard that would specify transmissions
of 100 Mbps over twisted-pair, and wiring with eight or nine
times as many twists per foot which may carry data at speeds
of 16-100 Mbps. The principal competition for twisted-pair in
new LAN cabling installations is the older coaxial cable and
more recently, fiber optic cable. Fiber optic cable is superior in
every respect, except that is more expensive to install and more
difficult to expand to encompass additional workstations.

U

Uninterruptible power supply (UPS)

A power unit that provides power from batteries for a short
time when the normal power supply is interrupted. Some
devices supply power continuously and others provide power
only when the power fails. UPS devices permit an electronic
device, such as a file server, to shut itself down "gracefully"
without loss of data.

UNIX

Operating system developed by AT&T Bell Laboratories in the
'50s. UNIX supports multiple concurrent users, multitasking
(multiple programs running simultaneously), and networking.
Despite efforts to standardize the UNIX platform, there are
already several proprietary versions (Sun Solaris, UnixWare,
SCO UNIX) and since UNIX is an open system, the source
code may be purchased from Novell by any software house to
develop a new UNIX version.

UPS monitoring

A NOS feature that protects LAN data from power faults and
UPS hardware failures. A third-party uninterruptible power

supply (UPS) provides power to the server either all the time or just during power fluctuations and outages. For example, NetWare's UPS monitoring feature monitors the status of the UPS attached to the server.

User

In networks, any person who attaches to a server or host.

User accounts

A security feature in which each user on the network has a user account. User accounts determine user's login names, the groups the users belong to, and what file and directory rights users have. User accounts are maintained by the LAN Administrator.

Userids

Userids should identify an individual to the NOS and LAN applications. Userids are usually published information and follow a naming pattern within a given organization or LAN workgroup.

Virus

A destructive program written to damage or destroy information or otherwise disrupt the operation of a computer system. Using software provided by software manufacturers and reliable developers is recommended but is no longer a completely reliable preventative measure against viruses. Virus-type programs are differentiated by computer professionals. A short list follows:

■ *Rogue program*, meant to encompass the genre of destructive self-replicating programs that may be inadvertently introduced into a computer by an unsuspecting user or purposely introduced for destructive ends.

■ *Creeper*, a demonstration virus-type program introduced into the ARPANET in the '70s that displayed the message "I'm the creeper, catch me if you can" on display screens.

■ *Logic bomb*, a kind of Trojan Horse that remains dormant until a predetermined event triggers it to activate its destructive (or unwanted) program instructions. The predetermined event can be execution of a transaction or entry of a piece of data.

- *Time bomb*, a kind of logic bomb that remains dormant until a predetermined time or date triggers it to execute its destructive or unwanted program instructions. The predetermined event can be attainment of a date, such as in the Michelangelo time bomb that is activated on March 6th.

- *Trojan Horse*, a program which performs action unintended by the user. An example is a program that acts in place of a logon routine to capture login IDs and passwords so a perpetrator can masquerade as the user to penetrate the system at another time.

- *Virus*, program code that "infects" other programs by adding itself to other "host" programs.

- *Worm*, an independent program that can propagate itself into other machines, usually through a network.

Note that there is no one "correct" or definitive list or description of virus-type programs, thus the information contained in this Glossary is a simplified statement of prevailing wisdom on the subject accumulated over the past twenty years. Low-cost antivirus-type programs are available that scan computer memory, floppy disks, and hard disks and remove viruses.

Volume

A volume is the highest level in the NOS directory structures—it is the same level as a DOS root directory. A volume represents a physical amount of hard disk storage space.

W

Waveform

Graphic display of a communications signal used in testing and troubleshooting data transmission, equipment and cable. A sudden shift, for example, may indicate a cable short, open, kink, damage, or tap.

Wide Area Network (WAN)

A network that typically uses common carrier facilities (such as AT&T or MCI long distance) to connect communications devices over wide areas. WANs typically do extensive error checking and packaging to ensure the integrity of the data transmitted thus they add overhead that lowers overall network throughput and consumes bandwidth. WANs usually operate at slower speeds and tolerate more errors than do LANs.

Wiretapping

Unauthorized attachment to a communications circuit for accessing data through capturing messages, generating false messages, or altering messages of legitimate users.

Workgroup manager

Workgroup manager is a user classification in NetWare 386. Workgroup managers have supervisory control over any user or user group they create on the LAN.

Workstation (w/s)

In networks, any microcomputer attached to a network in order to share files, peripherals, and software. Also, a powerful, expensive, single-user microprocessor computer with large-scale disk capacity and high performance characteristics (such as 32-bit bus, math co-processor, graphics support, etc.) are typically used for engineering, financial engineering and analysis, and multimedia processing.

Worm

A destructive computer virus-type program that progressively fills up memory or hard disk space to slow the operation of a computer until it can no longer function. Other forms may destroy stored data. See also [computer] virus.

X

X.25

Interface standard between Data Terminal Equipment and Data Circuit Terminating Equipment for a terminal operating in packet mode on Public Data Networks.

APPENDIX B

HOTLINES AND OTHER SECURITY RESOURCES

 he following hotlines, bulleting boards, and other resources provide network and computer security information and a degree of support for those who are responsible for LAN security.

ORGANIZATION	**INFORMATION/SERVICES PROVIDED**
CERT Coordination Center (412) 268-7090 Fax: (412) 268-6989 Internet: cert @ cert.org	Internet security incident advisories, information, and assistance in network emergency situations. 24-hour hotline.
Computer Virus Industry Association Virus Information Bulletin Board (408) 988-4004	Virus forum Anti-virus shareware
COM-SEC Online Information System and Security Bulleting Board Service for NCSA, ISSA, EDP Auditors Assn. (415) 495-1811 BBS: (415) 495-4642	Professional educational on-line system offers: IS security information Member e-mail service IS and network security on-line forums Security conferences for professionals Computer crime studies
CSI Computer Security Institute and Network Bulleting Board Service (415) 905-2370	Computer security education and training Members hotline Conferences and seminars Buyers guide *Computer Security Alert* newsletter
Information Systems Security Association (ISSA) (714) 250-4772	Professional association for IS security education and information
National Institute of Standards and Technology (NIST) U.S. Department of Commerce Customer Service: (703) 487-4660	Federal Information Processing Standards (FIPS) and other published security reference materials
National Institute of Standards and Technology (NIST) Computer Security Bulleting Board BBS: (301) 948-5717	Virus information Computer security resource center and the National Computer Systems Laboratory (NCSL) information Security conferences sponsored by NIST and government agencies

ORGANIZATION	INFORMATION/SERVICES PROVIDED
National Computer Security Association (NCSA) (800) 488-4595	Research and product evaluations Antivirus shareware Tutorials and security training programs Information security catalog Newsletter Telephone support
Office of Management and Budget (OMB) Publications (202) 395-7332	Executive branch reports, publications, and Executive orders of the President
U.S. General Accounting Office (GAO) (202) 512-6000	Reports and Congressional studies on waste, fraud, abuse, internal control, and other problems in government agencies and topics of concern to Congress and the general public

APPENDIX C

LAN SECURITY
AND SAFEGUARD PRODUCTS

AN security product information is presented in this Appendix. The first list presents the products alphabetically and show the manufacturer or vendor on the right. The list of contact information by company name follows.

PRODUCT	MANUFACTURER/VENDOR
\<LOCK> security software for DOS/Windows, PCs and LANs	Secure Systems Group International, Inc.
AccuTrack Cable Design and Management System	AT&T
Alarm Products (Spider, Fly, Alarm Box)	B-SAFE Industries, Inc.
ARCserve Lan backup systems	Cheyenne Software, Inc.
AT&T Gretacoder for secure data transmission in X.25 Networks	AT&T
AT&T Surity™ for securing local and wide-area Networks	AT&T
Assure® Security for PCs and Networks	Cordant, Inc.

Bernoulli® Disk Drives
    Floptical Disk Drives
    Tape Backup Drives
	Iomega™

BindView Network Control System (NCS)	The LAN Support Group, Inc.
BookGuard™	Sensormatic® Electronics Corp.
Cable-trap (secures PC cables)	Qualtec Data Products, Inc.
CD-ROM drive lock	Qualtec Data Products, Inc.
Comnet III network capacity planning and analysis software	CACI Products Company
Computer Equipment Insurance	Safeware, The Insurance Agency, Inc.
COOP preparation and planning services	Electronic Data Industries (EDI), Inc.
COOP in Lotus Notes	PCs 'R' Us

PRODUCT	MANUFACTURER/VENDOR
DACS	Mergent International
DatArray for disk fault tolerance without proprietary hard disk or controller cards	Blue Lance, Inc.
Data encryption hardware	Racal-Datacom, Inc.
Data Recovery Services recovers data from failed and corrupted disks	Ontrack Data Recovery, Inc.
DataLock® Access Control Keyed Disk	AZTEC Security Products
DataMate® Theft Deterrents for computers and office products	Qualtec Data Products, Inc.
Disaster Recovery Services	Comdisco, Inc. Sun Gard REcovery Service, Inc.
Disk Technician Gold	Disk Technician Corporation
DRP preparation, planning, and review services	Electronic Data Industries (EDI)
Expert Sniffer Analyzer™ Software	Network General
Network test and measurement equipment	Tektronix
Fiber optic cable, FDDI assemblies and connectors	Fiber Wave Technologies
File-lok floppy disk drive lock	Qualtec Data Products, Inc.
Firewalls/Routers	Cisco Systems, Inc.
Flectron metallized fabric blocks electromagnetic emissions	Monsanto APM
Floppy Disk Drive Lock	Secure-It, Inc.

PRODUCT	MANUFACTURER/VENDOR
FraudFighter	Complimentary Solutions, Inc. (CSI)
Network Advisor expert system problem isolation for local area networks	Hewlett Packard
IBM Netview	IBM
IBM Security Architecture for information systems security	IBM
Inergen™	Ansul Fire Extinguishing Agent
InfoKey remote user authentication	LeeMah
InocuLAN® anti-virus protection for Novell LANs	Cheyenne Software, Inc.
INSIGHT expert system server management software	Compaq
Integrated Security Systems: Inventory, Access Control, Closed Circuit Television (CCTV), and Electronic Asset Protection (EAP)	Sensormatic® Electronics Corp.
Integrity MasterTM—Detects file corruption, changes, and viruses	Stiller Research
InterLock UNIX LAN segment access control	ANS Systems, Inc.
Kablit™ Anti-Theft and Tampering products for PCs and office equipment	Secure-It, Inc.
Kane Security Analyst™ network security assessment	Intrusion Detection Inc.
LAN Pharaoh Network monitor and LAN analyzer	Azure Technologies

PRODUCT	MANUFACTURER/VENDOR
LAN test and measurement hardware tools and network analyzers	Tektroniks
LANalyzer® for Windows software analyzes, monitors and troubleshoots Ethernet and token ring LANs	Novell, Inc.
LAN Desk® Manager	Intel®
Langard	Command Software Systems, Inc.
LAN PC Adapter Cards	Racal-Datacom, Inc.
LAN/WAN protocal analyzers	Hewlett Packard
LAT Armor™ UNIX login and password break-in protection LAT TermServ™ UNIX dial-in protection LAT UniShred Pro™ removes classified data from hard disks	Los Altos Technologies (LAT) Security Software
Living Disaster Recovery Planning Systems	Strohl Systems
Locking Pads (PCs, printers)	Secure-It, Inc.
Lok-Kit lock-down plate kits	Qualtec Data Products, Inc.
Lotus Notes (VAR)	PCs 'R' Us
LT Auditor network auditing LT Stat documents NetWare bindery LT HelpDesk manages LAN service and support activities	Blue Lance, Inc.
Motion alarms	B-SAFE Industries, Inc.
NETcat 800 Lan Trouble Shooter hand-held diagnostic LAN tool	Datacom Technologies
Net/DACS	Mergent International

PRODUCT	MANUFACTURER/VENDOR
NetOFF™ logs off inactive users lessening network traffic	Citadel Computer Systems, Inc.
NETremote+TM4.0	Brightwork Development, Inc.
NetWare NOS	Novell, Inc.
Network Advisor	Hewlett Packard
Notebook cable lock	Secure-It, Inc.
Norton Utilities 8.0 diagnoses, recovers, and repairs DOS files, compressed drives, and hardware; Windows utilization monitor; 200 NDOS commands	Symantec®
Norton Antivirus For Netware centralized server security	Symantec®
Norton DiskLock 3.0	Symantec®
NSO Network Security Organizer network management, server risk analysis, auditing, electronic software distribution, anti-virus	Thompson Network Software
Origen™	Preferred SYSTEMS®
Password Coach password checker	Baseline Software
Password Genie password generator	Baseline Software
PC/DACS for DOS or OS/2	Mergent International
PC-Lok	Qualtec Data Products, Inc.
Physical Anti-Theft Devices	Qualtec Data Products, Inc.
PK-ZIP	PKWare, Inc.
ProLiant, ProSignia, SystemPro Servers	Compaq Computer Corporation

PRODUCT	MANUFACTURER/VENDOR
RC-88 LAN protocol analyzer and RC-100 WAN analyzer	RADCOM
RSA Public Key Algorithm	RSA Data Security Inc.
Routers/firewalls	Cisco Systems, Inc.
SafeBoot™ SmartDisk	Fischer Intl. Systems, Corp.
SAFEcomply™	SAFEware™
SafeNetTM offsite storage and backup rotation program	SafeSite®
SECURE card	Datamedia Corporation
Security reviews, strategies, standards, security plans and risk assessment	Electronic Data Industries (EDI)
Security plans, policies, plans, standards, and procedures	PCs 'R' Us
Security Awareness Programs	SAFEware™
SEcured GAteway SYStem (SeGaSys) secure telemaintenance and network management	Microframe
Site/DACS	Mergent International
Locking Fileserver Security Station server and workstation cabinets	Data-MATE®, Inc.
SCO Unix	Santa Cruz Operation
SmartDisk™ SafeBoot boot protection	Fischer International Systems Corporation
Smart House security products	Smart House, L.P.

PRODUCT	MANUFACTURER/VENDOR
SmartStart automated NOS load and configuration on Compaq servers	Compaq Computer Corporation
Sniffer LANanalyzer hardware	Network General
SSO/DACS	Mergent International
Steelguard Heavy Duty Security System	Qualtec Data Products, Inc.
Storage Express™	Intel®
Sun Solaris (UNIX)	Sun
Surge Suppressors	American Power Conversion
Systimax®	AT&T
TellTag® EAP detects tampering and removal from protected areas (sounds an alarm)	Sensormatic® Electronic Corporation
TraqNet secures data lines	LeeMah
Tricord servers	Tricord
Uni-Kit screw-on lock down kits	Qualtec Data Products, Inc.
Uninteruptible Power Supplies	American Power Conversion
UnixWare	Novell, Inc.
Vi-Spy anti-virus	RG Software Systems, Inc.
Vines	Banyan
Watchdog Armor Director PC	Fisher International Systems Corporation
Wiretap Detector Alarm System for single communication lines	Security Call™

LAN SECURITY
AND SAFEGUARD PRODUCTS

Contact information for LAN security product manufacturers, suppliers, and vodors is listed alphbetically below.

American Power Conversion
132 Fairgrounds Road
West Kingston, RI 02892
Phone: (800) 800-4APC
Fax: (401) 789-3180
Products: Surge Suppressors
Uninterruptible Power Supplies

ANS Systems, Inc.
100 Clearbrook Road
Elmsford, New York 10523
Phone: 1 800-456-8267
Products: InterLock

Ansul Fire Protection
One Stanton Street
Marionette, WI 54143-2542
Phone: (715) 735-7411 (800) 346-3626
Products: Inergen™ Fire Suppressant Systems

AT&T Network Systems
505 North 51st Avenue
Phoenix, AZ 85043
Phone: (800) 344-0223 x 3102
Products: AccuTrack Cable Design and Management System
Systimax® Structured Cabling System

AT&T Security Products
  Guillford Center
  P.O. Box 25000
  Greensboro, NC 27420-5000
  Phone: (919) 279-7000
  Products: AT&T Surity™
          AT&T Gretacoder

AZTEC Security Products
  7441 E. Burherus Drive, Suite 600
  Scottsdale, AZ 85260
  Phone: (602) 483-7144, (800) 333-4002
  Fax: (602) 483-7996
  Contact: Ron Junier or Linda Elliott
  Products: DataLock® Access Control Keyed Disk Drive Lock

Austwins Zwinger
  P.O. Box 383
  Furlong, PA 18925
  Phone: (215) 598-0443
  Fax: (215) 598-0489
  Products: Pure-bred Rottweilers and imports

Azure Technologies
  63 South Street
  Hopkinton, MA 01748
  Phone: (508) 435-3800
  Fax: (508) 435-0448
  Products: LAN Pharaoh

B-SAFE Industries, Inc.
  P.O. Box 153-H
  Scarsdale, NY 10583
  Phone: (914) 723-2553
  Fax: (914) 723-2925
  Product: Banyan

Baseline Software
 P.O. Box 1219
 Sausalito, CA 94966-1912
 Phone: (415) 332-7763 or (800) 829-9955
 Products: Password Coach
        Password Genie

Banyan Systems, Inc.
 120 Flanders Road
 Westboro, MA 01581
 Phone: (508) 898-1000
 Products: Vines NOS
        Enterpise Network Services (ENS)
        StreetTalk

Blue Lance, Inc.
 1700 West Loop S., Suite 1100
 Houston, Texas 77027
 Phone: (713) 680-1187
 Fax: (713) 622-1370
 Products: LT Auditor
        LT Stat
        LT HelpDesk

Brightwork Development, Inc.
 766 Shrewsbury Avenue
 Jerral Center West
 Tinton Falls, NJ 07724
 Phone: (800) 552-9876 or (908) 530-0440
 Fax: (908) 530-0622
 Product: NETremote+™ 4.0

CACI Products Company
 3333 North Torrey Pines Court
 LaJolla, CA 92037
 Phone: (619) 457-9681
 Fax: (619) 457-1184
 Product: Comnet III

Cheyenne Software, Inc.
Three Expressway Plaza
Roslyn Heights, NY 78150
Phone: (516)484-5110 or (800) 243-9462
Fax: (516) 484-3446
Products: ARCserve LAN backup systems
InocuLAN® server based anti-virus program

Citadel Computer Systems, Inc.
9800 Northwest Freeway, Suite 610
Houston, TX 77092
Phone: (713) 686-6400
Contact: Michael Berman
Product: NetOFF

Cisco Systems, Inc.
Menol Park, CA

Comdisco, Inc. Disaster Recovery Services
6111 North River Road
Rosemont, IL 60018
Phone: (800) 321-1111

Command Software Systems Inc.
1061 E Indiantown Road, Suite 500
Jupiter, FL 33477
Phone: (407) 575-3200 or (800) 423-9147
Fax: (407) 575-3026
Product: Langard

Compaq Computer Corporation
P.O. Box 692000
Houston, TX 77269-2000
Phone: (713) 370-0670 or (800) 345-1518
Products: ProLiant Servers
INSIGHT
SmartStart

Complimentary Solutions, Inc. (CSI)
4250 Perimeter Parks, Suite 200
Altlanta, GA 30341
Phone: (404) 936-3700
Fax: (404) 936-3710
Product: TELEMATE Fraud Fighters (anti-telephone signal hacking)

Cordant, Inc.
11400 Commerce Park Drive
Reston, VA 22091
Phone: (703) 758-7000, (800) 843-1132
Fax: (703) 758-7320
Products: Assure® Security for PCs and Networks

Data-MATE®, Inc.
46 Bridge Street
P.O. Box 408
Nashua, NH 03061-0408
Phone: (603) 882-5142 (800) 258-1768
Fax: (603) 882-4192
Product: Locking Fileserver Security Station

Datacom Technologies
1001 31st Place West
Everett, WA 98204
Phone: (206) 355-0590 or (800) 468-5557
Fax: (206) 290-1600
Product: NETcat® LAN Trouble Shooter

DataMedia Corporation
20 Trafalagar Square
Nashua, NH 03063
Phone: (603) 886-15780
Product: SECURE card

Disk Technician Corporation
1940 Garnet Avenue
San Diego, CA 92109
Phone: (800) 847-5000
Product: Disk Technician™ Gold

Electronic Data Industries, Inc. (EDI)
7575 Chrisland Cove
Falls Church, VA 22042
Phone: (703) 207-0992
Fax: (703 207-0999
Products: Security reviews, strategies, standards, Security Plans, Risk
        Assessment, DRPs and COOPs

Fiber Wave Technologies
540 Clinton Street
Brooklyn, NY
Phone: (718) 802-9011 or (800) 280-9011
Products: Fiber optic cable
        FDDI assemblies and connectors

Fischer International Systems, Corp.
4073 Mercantile Avenue
Naples, FL 33942
Phone: (813) 643-1500 or (800) 237-4510
Contact: Laura Sullivan
Fax: (813) 643-3772
Products: SafeBoot
        SmartDisk
        Watchdog PC
        Watchdog Director
        Watchdog Armor

Hewlett Packard
T&M U.S. Marketing Organization
5301 Stevens Creek Blvd
P.O. Box 58059, M/S 51LSC
Santa Clara, CA 95051-8059
Phone: (408) 345-8618
Fax: (408) 345-8626
Contact: Dennis Gonden
Products: Network Advisor
LAN/WAN protocol analyzers

IBM United States
Department EU6
1133 Westchester Avenue
White Plains, NY 10604
Phone: (800) 426-1457
Product: IBM Security Architecture

Intel® Intel Corporation
P.O. Box 10266
Portland, OR 97210-9879
Phone: (800) 538-3373 ext. 1247
Products: LANdesk® Manager
Storage Express™

Intrusion Detection, Inc.
217 East 86th Street, Suite 213
New York, NY 10028
Phone: (212)427-9185
Product: Kane Security Analyst™

Iomega Corporation
1821 West Iomega Way
Roy, Utah 84067
Phone: (801) 778-3261
Fax: (801) 778-3450
Products: Bernoulli® Tape Drives
Bernoulli® Disk Drives
Bernoulli® Floptical Disk Drives

LeeMah DataCom Security Corporation
3948 Trust Way
Hayward, CA 94545-3716
Phone: (510) 786-0790, (800) 331-2734
Fax: (510) 786-1123
Contact: Steve Kruse, Senior Security Consultant
Products: InfoKey (Remote User Authentication for Secure Dial-In)
TraqNet (Secures data lines)

Los Altos Technologies, Inc.
Phone: (415) 988-4848
Fax: (415) 988-4860
Products: LAT TermServ™
LAT Unishred™
LAT Armor™ Security Software

Mergent International
70 Inwood Road
Rocky Hill, CT 06067
Phone: (203) 257-4223
Fax: (203) 257-4245
Products: PC/DACS for DOS or OS/2
Net/DACS
SSO/DACS
Site/DACS
Domain/DACS

Microframe
21 Meridian Road
Edison, NJ
Phone: (908) 494-4440 or (800) 395-7450
Product: SeGaSYS (The secured gateway system for remote and tele-
maintenance)

Monsanto Advanced Performance Materials (APM)
3481 Rider Trail South
St. Louis, MO 63045
Phone: (800) 843-4556
Product: Flectron metallized fabric for blocking
electromagnetic emissions

Network General
4200 Bohannon Drive
Menlo Park, CA 94025
Phone: (800) 846-6601
Products: Expert Sniffer Analyzer™ Software
Sniffer LAN analyzer hardware

Novell®, Inc.
890 Ross Drive
Sunnyvale, CA 94089
Phone: (408) 747-4000
Fax: (408) 747-4361
Products: LANalyzer® or Windows
Novell DOS™ 7.x
NetWare NOSs

Ontrack Data Recovery, Inc.
6321 Bury Drive, Suite 15-19
Eden Prairie, MN 55346
Phone: (612) 937-5161 or (800) 872-2599
Fax: (612) 937-5750
Contact: Pam Bednar
Product: Data Recovery Services

PCs 'R' Us
P.O. Box 155
Brielle, NJ 08730
Phone: (908) 262-9230
Fax: (908) 262-9240
Products: Lotus Notes Business Partner and VAR
Lotus Notes template and secure custom applications including: Security Plans, DRP, COOP, LAN Policies, Standards, and Procedures

PKWARE, Inc.
7545 North Port Washington Road
Glendale, WI 53217
Product: PKZIP compression software

Preferred SYSTEMS, Inc.
250 Captain Thomas Boulevard
West Haven, CT 06516
Phone: (800) 222-7638 or (203) 937-3000 ext.613
Fax: (203) 937-3032
Product: Origen™

Qualtec Data Products, Inc.
47767 Warm Springs Blvd.
Fremont, CA 94539
Phone: (800) 628-4413
In CA: (415) 490-8911
Contact: Maureen Wilner, Sr. Sales Representative or Dawn Stratton
Miller, Marketing Manager
Products: Physical Anti-Theft Devices

Racal-Datacom, Inc.
155 Swanson Road
Boxborough, MA 01779
Phone: (508) 263-9929 or (800) LAN-TALK
Fax: (508) 263-8655
Products: LAN communication components
Data encryption hardware

RADCOM
900 Corporate Drive
Mahwah, NJ 07430
Phone: (201) 529-1100
Fax: (201) 529-5777
Contact: Avi Zamir
Products: RC-88 LAN Analyzer
RC-100 WAN Analyzer

RG Software Systems, Inc.
6900 E. Camelback Road, #630
Scottsdale, AZ 85251
Phone: (602) 423-8000
Fax: (602) 423-8389
Product: Vi-Spy anti-virus

RSA Data Security Inc.
100 Marine Pkwy., #500
Redwood City, CA 94065
Phone: (415) 595-8782
Fax: (415) 595-1873
Product: RSA Public Key Encryption Algorithm

Safesite®
Post Office Box 330
N Billerica, MA 01862
Phone: (508) 663-7100 or (800) 255-8218
Fax: (508) 870-5406
Product: SafeNet (offsite storage and rotation of file server
backup tapes)

Safeware, The Insurance Agency Inc.
2929 N. High Street
P.O. Box 02211
Columbus, OH 43214
Phone: (614) 262-0559 or (800) 848-3469
Fax: (614) 262-1714
Product: Computer Equipment Insurance

SAFEware™
12030 Sunrise Valley Drive, Suite 300
Reston, VA 22091
Phone: (703) 391-6051 or
Fax: (703) 391-2731
Products: Security Awareness Programs
SAFEcomply

SDSC SmartDisk Security Corporation
4073 Mercantile Avenue
Naples, FL 33942
Phone: (813) 263-3475
Fax: (813) 643-6357
Product: SmartDisk SafeBoot

Secure Systems Group International, Inc.
100 Nobel Court, Suite 300
Alpharetta, GA 30202
Phone: (404) 475-0833
Fax: (404) 475-0833
Product: <LOCK>

Secure-It, Inc.
18 Maple Court
East Longmeadow, MA 01028
Phone: (413) 525-7039 (800) 451-7592
Fax: (413) 525-8807
Contact: Harry Themistos, Marketing Representative
Product: Kablit™ Anti-Theft Product
Notebook cable lock

Security Call™
Post Office Box 33194
Los Gatos, CA 95031-3194
Phone: (408) 226-3110
Product: Wiretap Detector Alarm System

Sensormatic®
Electronics Corporation
500 Northwest 12th Avenue
Deerfield Beach, FL 33442-1795
Phone: (305) 420-2000
Contact: Pat Bolling, Direct Marketing
Products: TellTag®
BookGuard™
Access Control
Closed Circuit Television (CCT)
Electronic Asset Protection (EAP)

Smart House, L.P.
401J Prince Georges Boulevard
Upper Marlboro, MD 20772
Phone: (301) 249-6000
Product: Smart House

Stiller Research
2625 Ridgeway Street
Tallahassee, FL 32310
(800) 622-2793 outside USA (708) 397-1221
Fax: (708) 397-0381
Product: Integrity Master™ (detects file or program corruption and
viruses)

Strohl Systems
500 N.Gulph Road, Suite500
King of Prussia, PA 19406
Phone: (800) 634-2016 or (215) 768-4120
Fax: (215) 768-4135
Product: Living Disaster Recovery Planning Systems

Sun Gard Recovery Services, Inc.
1285 Drummers Lane
Wayne, PA 19087
Phone: (610) 341-8700 or (800) 247-7832
Fax: (610) 341-8739
Contact: Donna Baun
Product: Disaster recovery services, facilities, and hotsites

Symantec® Corporation
10201 Torre Avenue
Cupertino, CA 95014-2132
Phone: (800) 441-7234
Fax: (408) 255-3344
Products: Norton Antivirus for Netware
The Norton Utilities 8.0
The Norton DiskLock 3.0

Tektronix
P.O. Box 1197
Redmond, OR 97756
Phone: (800) 833-9200
Products: Network test and measurement equipment

The LAN Support Group Inc.
2425 Fountainview, Suite 390
Houston, TX 77057
Phone: (800) 749-8439
Fax: (713) 977-9111
Product: BindView NCS

Thompson Network Software
(A division of Leprechaun Software International, Ltd.)
P.O. Box 669306
Marietta, GA 30066
Phone: (404) 971-8900
Fax: (404) 971-8828
Product: NSO Network Security Organizer

Tricord Systems, Inc.
   3750 Annapolis Lane
   Plymouth, MN 55447
   Phone: (612) 557-9005
   Fax: (612) 557-8403
   Product: Power Frame Enterpise Server

X-10 USA
   91 Ruckman Road
   Closter, NJ 07624
   Phone: (201) 784-9700
   Product: X-10 computer-controlled home security and energy manage-
      ment components

APPENDIX D

SAMPLE STANDARDS AND
PROCEDURES FOR LAN USERS

A sample set of standards and procedures for LAN users follows. They are based on a typical LAN which is configured with a NetWare 3.x NOS and a Compaq SystemPro server. Topics included in the sample standards and procedures are:

1. LAN Userids and Mail Ids
2. Directories, files and printers
3. LAN Printing
4. Virus Prevention
5. Trouble Identification
6. Trouble Reporting

7. Storing files on the LAN Server

8. File Transfers

9. Requesting Changes such as New LAN Applications

10. Records Retention on the Server

1. LAN Userids and E-mail Ids

A LAN Userid is required to use the LAN and a cc:Mail id is required to use the E-mail application. The authorized users are listed in the LAN Inventory and lists of users in the E-mail User Guide.

If you are not an authorized LAN user and wish to use E-mail or other LAN applications or files, contact your LAN User Support group or the LAN Administrator.

2. Directories and Files

Files and applications are grouped on the server for efficiency and ease of user access. Users can view only files for which they have access rights. The directories, subdirectories, and files of note on the main LAN server are shown in Table D.1 which follows:

TABLE D.1 DIRECTORIES ON THE MAIN LAN SERVER.

DIRECTORIES SUBDIRECTORIES	DIRECTORY CONTENTS
LOGIN	Login files: bootconfig, image, etc
SYSTEM	Hidden from users; contains NetWare programs
PUBLIC	NetWare commands and utilities
MENU.SYS	Hidden from users; contains menu files
\DOS7	Novell DOS 7.0 files

continued

DIRECTORIES SUBDIRECTORIES	DIRECTORY CONTENTS
MAIL	
MAILBOX 00000001	User's Mailbox is the NetWare Id, eg:
PRINTCON.DAT	User's print configuration file
LOGIN	User's network login script
WPXXX}.set	WordPerfect defaults
APPLICAT	
MENU.SYS	Menu files for server applications
LOCAL	Menu files for local applications
NS	Network Scheduler programs
CALENDAR	Calendar files
USERS	User, group, printer and log files
CCMAIL	
EXE	Notify, messenger, mail, snapshot
ADMIN	Post Office Administration
POM	Post Office information
GATEWAY	Gateway to PDN, SNA, etc.
WP51	WP5.1 programs
MACRO	Macros
LEX	Dictionary and thesaurus
PRINTER	Printer files and fonts
GRAPHIC	Graphics
STYLE	Formatting styles library
LEARN	Online tutorial
SETUP	Set up file for WP5.1 defaults

continued

DIRECTORIES		
SUBDIRECTORIES		**DIRECTORY CONTENTS**
FONTS		Font files for WP5.1
LOTUS		Lotus 1-2-3 files
WPFONTWR		Hidden; Bitstream programs to make fonts
DATABASE		DBMS programs
TNA		Network Archivist files for backup and archive
MESSAGE		
USERFILE		Area for user Home directories and user data
USERHOME		User Home directories here (eg: DOEJ)
XXX		Private directories
PUB		Public shared directories
PUB.NDX		WP Index to contents of public directories
README		PUB Directory rules—a DOS file
LAN, SUPPORT, TQM		Public directories
BRAINS		Public shared conference for brainstorming
PRIVATE		Private directories
BACKUP		
UPGRADE		

ACCESS TO DIRECTORIES

Access to directories and files can be limited in most LANs by implementing NOS access control security features. Users can only view and process directories and files to which they have been granted access rights. NetWare Rights either permit or prevent users from accessing and processing files. In USERFILE directories, including USERFILE\PUB, users have right of RWCEMFA. A directory/file *owner* (the creator) may also grant rights to other users. NetWare attributes apply to files and directories and override user access rights. Attributes may further limit your ability to use applications and files. Detailed information on rights and attributes is contained under the heading Novell's NetWare Access Rights to Directories and Files in the chapter on software.

FILE EXTENSION NAMING CONVENTIONS

These are useful in establishing order and structure on network servers. The following conventions are used for naming files. To create a file on the LAN server, be sure you are in a directory to which you have Write access rights.

FILE EXTENSION	TYPE DOCUMENT
BRF	Brief
CHT	Chart
CMT	Comment
GUI	Guideline
LTR	Letter
LST	List
MEM	Memo
MTH	Methodology
NOT	Note
OPN	Opinion
PIC	Lotus graphic file
PLN	Plan
PRN	Lotus Spreadsheet graph print file
PRO	Procedure
QST	Questionnaire
REV	Review
RPT	Report

continued

FILE EXTENSION	TYPE DOCUMENT
STD	Standard
SMY	Summary
TES	Testimony
WK1	Lotus Spreadsheet
WK	Work file
WPG	WordPerfect Graphic
WPM	WordPerfect Macro
Lxx	List (xx = list number*)
xxx	Form (xxx = form number)
Lists and Forms to follow.	

Note that users can only view and access directories and files to which they have been granted access rights. Should you require access to additional directories or files, contact your LAN User Support group or the LAN Administrator.

3. LAN Printing

Any workstation on the LAN is capable of printing to any other workstation all existing. LAN printers are attached to workstations, thus are considered by NetWare to be "Remote" printers.

You can print directly to a printer attached to your workstation through your LPT1 port, just as you did in DOS. You can also route your printed output through the LAN to any LAN printer by changing your routing or specifying the name of a Print Queue within the application itself (this routing feature only works for WordPerfect at present).

The following information on LAN print jobs, printers, and LAN print queues is needed to route printed output to a network printer.

PRINT JOB	PRINTER	QUEUE NAME	WORKSTATION
SERVR1P1	SALES-HPLJ3P-P1	SALES-HPLJ3P-Q1	Alana
SERVR1P2	LEGAL-4019-P2	LEGAL-4019-Q1	Armondo
SERVR1P3	ADMIN-HPLJII-P3	ADMIN-HPLJII-Q1	Andrew

To route printing within WordPerfect only, select *Print Options, Select Printer, Port. Select LPT1, 2,* or *3* to correspond with your print routing setup (or choose *Port, Other,* and type a Queue Name preceded by server name "SERVR1\"). This routing takes precedence over all other print output routings for the WordPerfect application.

If you need assistance with print routing, refer to the LAN Tutorial in your Training Plan, call the Help Desk, or see your LAN User Support group.

4. Virus Prevention

Using software from a PC, Bulletin Board, or other source which is infected with a virus may result in spreading the virus to your PC, the network server, and other LAN workstations. Although Anti-virus software is on the LAN, note that *no* existing virus protection software has been proven to be 100% effective against all viruses, worms, Trojan Horses, logic bombs, etc.

Because there is the possibility that new and unknown virus-type programs may be developed for which there is no known antidote, we will use several simple mechanisms to prevent virus attacks on the LAN.

■ The most effective prevention against viruses is for network users to control and be responsible for the diskettes they use on network-connected PCs and to be virus-aware. Should this system fail, the floppy drive will be removed from the PC used by the person who introduces the virus. It is a drastic measure which is justified because of the potential for data and data integrity loss, and because getting rid of a virus and restoring data integrity is difficult and time-consuming.

■ "Scanning" diskettes used on other PCs will help to prevent the introduction of viruses into the network. Diskettes which were used on any other uncontrolled PC (at home or in another unit) may harbor a virus-type program. All LAN workstations have anti-virus software and diskettes can also be scanned at designated stand-alone PCs.

■ Individuals and workgroups will be granted access to directories and files based on their "need-to-use" the programs and the data which will prevent unauthorized access and also protect against virus infections. The determination of directory and file access requirements will be made by the LAN Administrator, LAN User Support group, and the Executive Director, where necessary.

■ Some virus-type programs attach themselves to existing programs. As a precaution, all programs will be write-protected on the LAN.

■ The last protective measure against virus-type programs is to monitor network usage to identify unusual occurrences. While LAN management and network audit software is used for this purpose, experience has shown that most network problems are noticed first by LAN users. Thus, informed network users are the best source of problem alerts and will likely provide the most useful information about trouble on the network from this and other sources.

5. Trouble Identification

Trouble on the LAN is usually indicated by an unusual event such as unusually slow response time. When an unusual event occurs, notify your LAN User Support group as soon as possible. If there is a serious problem, an early warning can prevent unnecessary damage.

6. Trouble Reporting

Trouble on the LAN should be reported to your LAN User Support group or the LAN Administrator. If the problem is urgent, notify your LAN

User Support group or the LAN Administrator *immediately*. If the problem is not quickly resolved and requires further action, it will be documented in the Trouble Log file for follow up.

7. Storing Files on the LAN Server

Users can store files and programs in their Home directories and in the PUB Public directory. However users have a limited amount of space on the server. The amount of space allocated to a user varies from 3 million to 30 million bytes of storage which can be adjusted should the need arise. If you wish to store files elsewhere on the file server, the LAN Administrator will need to know how large the files are, what their purpose is, and who requires what kind of access to the files. The Server Change Request will guide you in terms of the information required.

8. File Transfers

Files can be freely transferred between Home directories and subdirectories of the PUB public directory. Transferring files to non-public directories must be done by the LAN Administrator or a person with the NetWare rights to store files in that directory.

9. Requesting Changes Such As New LAN Applications

Applications which are destined to be used in a production mode should be discussed with LAN Administration well in advance of their cut-over date because of the number of planning activities which must be completed prior to installing a new system on the LAN. Application sponsors should know:

1. Who will "own" (be responsible for) the application and the data it uses

2. How the application will be used

3. Who the users will be and what functions they will perform

4. What data will be input, processed, output

5. Who will support the application

6. What is required to operate and support the application.

10. Records Retention On the Server

Application data elements should be defined in the data dictionary and the data administration requirements should be established prior to development of a LAN application. Retention of records in the LAN environment is the responsibility of the owner (i.e. originator or user) of the data.

Lack of understanding of record retention in LANs embarrassed Oliver North during the inquiry about the Iran-Contra affair. He believed all incriminating evidence was destroyed when he deleted his files and E-mail messages. What he didn't understand is that in LANs data is retained on the server, even after it has been deleted, until a Purge takes place. After files are physically deleted they are available for "Salvage" until the Purge removes them completely. The server will be purged of deleted files every 6 months, although more frequent purging may be necessary as time goes on. Users will be given 30 days notice prior to a Purge so wanted files can be salvaged. You should note that *NetWare automatically purges* deleted files when more disk space is required during normal processing.

Even after a file has been deleted and purged from the server, it may exist on a backup tape and may be recoverable through your backup and recovery procedures. Only the LAN Administrator has access to information contained in server backup files, so any needs you have which necessitate file recovery from backup tapes should be addressed to your LAN User Support group or the LAN Administrator.

APPENDIX E

STANDARDS AND PROCEDURES FOR LAN ADMINISTRATION

Standards and procedures assist the LAN Administrator in managing and operating the network. Sample LAN Administration standards and procedures are briefly summarized below.

1. Facilitate LAN printing
2. Add new users
3. Delete User IDs and Passwords for Terminated Employees
4. Reset passwords
5. Troubleshoot problems
6. Report problems
7. Back up network servers

8. Perform routine server maintenance

9. Monitor, audit, and analyze LAN usage

10. Document and analyze LAN problems

11. Recover LAN applications and data [after a disaster]

12. Continue LAN operations offsite

1. Facilitate LAN Printing

The following tasks are performed to facilitate printing on the LAN.

TASK	NETWARE COMMAND/APPLICATION	DESCRIPTION
Display Printer Status	PSC PS=SERVRS1 STAT	view printer status on workstation
	PSERVER	view status on console
	PCONSOLE	check printer, queues, servers, users, operators
Define new LAN printer	PCONSOLE	define print queue, server, printer
	PRINTER	connect print server
Print to LAN printer from DOS	PRINTDEF	define printers
	PRINTCON	setup print jobs for routing through LAN
	PSERVER	Unload, then load SERVRS1
Re-route queue to other printer	PCONSOLE	printer config, queues, printers, insert/delete queue
Switch LAN printer to private	PSC SERVRS1 PRI[vate]	printer control

continued

TASK	NETWARE COMMAND/APPLICATION	DESCRIPTION
Control printer/ server	PCONSOLE	add/change/view print servers, printers, queues, users, operators, notify list
	PSC	PAUse, ABort, STOp, STARt, CancelDown, SHare
Customize printing	PRINTDEF	print setup; custom forms, etc.
	PRINTCON	
	PCONSOLE	

2. Add New Users

The following tasks are performed to add new users to the LAN.

TASK	COMMAND/APPLICATION	DESCRIPTION/NOTES
Add userid to LOGIN.DAT file	Edit LOGIN.DAT	insert user, eg: {DOEJ{SERVR1}1
Add user NIC and Login Script file to BOOTCONF.SYS	Edit BOOTCONF.SYS	insert NIC and Image
Create Login Script file, if unique PC or LAN printer	DOSGEN	create Image.SYS file
Enter in NetWare LAN	SYSCON	full name [eg:Doe, Jr, John J]; password; space limit of 3MB; note NetWare ID; set Trustee rights
Update the LAN Inventory	Lotus 1-2-3	update Z:\PUBLIC\LAN\ LANINVEN.WK1

continued

Task	Command/Application	Description/Notes
Send user's full name to Post Office Manager	cc:Mail	PO Manager records name in all Offices
Enter user in cc:Mail	cc:Mail	fullname, L [local]
Verify ids, passwords and applications		login as user to test
Give pledges, ids, passwords to users		

3. Delete User IDs and Passwords for Terminated Employees

Delete user IDs, passwords, and LAN connection information for employees who are terminated before they leave the building.

4. Reset Passwords

Forgotten passwords can be reset to a standard password using SYSCON. The user should change the password as soon as possible.

5. Troubleshoot Problems

The following tasks are performed to troubleshoot problems with the LAN.

Task	Command/Application	Description/Notes
Troubleshoot Problems in	LAN Trouble Checklist	Check cables, change log, trouble log, etc.)

continued

TASK	COMMAND/APPLICATION	DESCRIPTION/NOTES
NetWare		
	MONITOR	Check Connections, Resources, etc.
	PSERVER	Check printer usage
Troubleshoot problems with other tools	LANalyzer, Network Advisor, LT-Auditor, etc.	Use all necessary methods and tools to determine cause of trouble
Document trouble	Lotus Notes	Update Trouble Log

Trouble on the LAN is usually indicated by an unusual event such as particularly slow response time. When an unusual or noteworthy event occurs, the Help Desk, the LAN User Support group, or the LAN Administrator should be notified as soon as possible. If the problem is serious, an early warning can prevent unnecessary damage or loss.

Network problems should be documented in the Trouble Log by the LAN Administrator. The LAN Help Desk is an in-house clearinghouse for LAN problems and support. The idea of the central Help Desk is to prevent redundant problem solving initiatives from consuming scarce LAN workgroup resources.

6. Report Problems

Report significant LAN problems to the LAN Help Desk and the LAN Administrator via E-mail. Request a receipt so you will know when the message was received by a responsible person. The LAN Administrator and LAN Manager will be contacted by beeper by the Help desk. The LAN Administration staff will complete a follow up trouble report in Lotus Notes which you should review as soon as possible.

7. Backup Network Servers

The following backup procedures are followed using The Network Archivist (TNA) software and Palindrome backup tape unit.

TASK	NETWARE COMMAND	DESCRIPTION/NOTES
Run Daily LAN Server Backup	Login ARCHIVIST	Boot ARCHIVIST PC with backup boot disk prior to Login
	ARCHIVIST Password	
	TNA	F2 for Tape Status, or F4 to start Backup (insert tape in Palindrome unit)
	LOGOUT	Reset or reboot ARCHIVIST workstation

8. Perform Routine Server Maintenance

Updates to the NetWare Operating System and LAN applications on the server are applied within the month after they are received. Updates are not applied immediately because it is wise to allow time for implementation problems to surface before making the changes on the server your users rely on. Even a small problem can result in the loss of valuable LAN services.

Routine server maintenance is performed at least every two months during non-business hours. If the LAN performance is slow or unexplained system errors occur, the maintenance procedure is done as soon as possible. The following four utilities are run during routine maintenance:

LAN UTILITY	PURPOSE
VREPAIR	Correct volume problems after many additions and deletions
BINDFIX	Maintains integrity of NetWare Bindery
CHKSTAT	Reports the integrity of the Post Office database
RECLAIM	Reorganizes Post Office database

9. Monitor, Audit, and Analyze LAN Usage

LAN usage is monitored routinely for early warnings of situations such as viruses and attempted network penetrations which could be hazardous to the health of the network.

The following tasks are performed to ensure that the LAN is performing as expected.

TASKS	PROGRAM/APPLICATION	DESCRIPTION/NOTES
Monitor LAN Usage	MONITOR	Check LAN connections, users and NICs logged in, resources in use, environmental conditions in the server room, change logs, trouble log, PCs, etc.
	PSERVER	Check printer usage
Document unusual findings	Lotus Notes	Compose a LAN Status entry describing any unusual situation in detail to assist in identifying errors before they result in loss of LAN service

10. Document and Analyze LAN Problems

LAN problems should be documented as soon as possible after they occur. Trouble with the network is recorded in the Lotus Notes Trouble Log. This log is reviewed constantly and is used to identify performance trends, problems, and opportunities for quality improvement in LAN operations.

11. Recover LAN Applications and Data

In the event of a disaster which results in damage to the server or network data, the DRP in the Security Plan will go into effect. The purpose of the DRP is to minimize loss of data, equipment, and network services and to recover essential applications and files so that critical processing can be resumed as quickly as possible.

Applications are scheduled for recovery based on their priority, the urgency of the information they process, and the period of down time which is considered tolerable by the application users. If the normal site is accessible and equipment is operable, recovery of data and applications will take place there. If our normal site is inaccessible, or the equipment cannot be made operable within tolerable application down times, recovery will take place offsite at the designated alternate processing location. Backup files, disaster recovery plans and procedures are stored at the alternate location for this purpose.

12. Continue LAN Operations Offsite

If applications must be available *before* normal operations are expected to be resumed, the COOP in the Security Plan will be put into effect. When normal network operations can be resumed onsite, the most recent server backup will be restored on the server, the COOP activities will cease, and LAN processing activities will resume as usual.

APPENDIX F

FOR FURTHER READING

Bowen, Nicholas and Pradhan, Dhiraj, *Processor and Memory Based Checkpoint and Rollback Recovery*, IEEE Press, Computer, February 1993.

Bowsher, *Medical Devices: The Public Health at Risk*, USGAO Report GAC/T-DEMO, 1990.

Carroll, John M., *Computer Security*, 2nd edition, Butterworths, MA, 1987.

Cerullo, M. and McDuffie, S., *Computer Contingency Plans and the Auditors: A Survey of Businesses Affected by Hurricane Hugo*, Computers and Security, 1992.

CRN/The Gallup Org. (September 1993 Gallup survey for Resellers News).

David, Jon, *LAN Security Standards*, Computers and Security, 11, 1992.

Didio, Laura, *User's Guide to Safe Computing*, LAN Times, September 14, 1992.

Fields, Davis, *Why Client/Server Computing*, third edition, Parallan Computer, 1990.

Gilooly, Caryn and Brown, Bob, *Novell Users Face Threat to Security, Network World*, October 5 and 12, 1992.

Hains, David, *PC Security Threatened By New Wave Operating Systems*, Computer Control Quarterly, V.10, 1992.

Haneson, Nancy G. and Turner, Clark S., *An Investigation of the Theriac-25 Accidents*, Computer, 1992.

Harler, Curt, *How to Prevent Wily Hackers from Plundering Your Phones*, Communications News, January 1992.

Harris, David, PC Security Threatened by New Wave Operating Systems, Computer Control Quarterly.

Heinlein, Edwin B., *World Trade Center—A Retrospective*, Computers and Security, 12, 1993.

Highland, Harold Joseph, *Disaster Recovery at the World Trade Center*, Computers and Security, 12, 1993.

Hoffman, Lance J., *Rogue Programs: Viruses, Worms and Trojan Horses*, Van Nostrad Reinhold, NY, 1990.

IntelliQuest study for 3M, Computing, October, 29, 1992.

Menkus, Belden, *The Lessons of the Great Chicago Flood of 1992*, Computers and Security, 11, 1992.

Miller, Mark A., *LAN Protocol Handbook*, M&T Books, NY, 1990.

Panettier, Joseph C., *Guardian of the NET*, Information Week, May 23, 1994.

Peterson, A. Padgett, *Tactical Computers Vulnerable to Malicious Software Attacks*, Signal, November 1993.

Poor, Alfred, *Safe Stations for Networks*, PC Magazine, October 15, 1991.

Ranger, Night, *Hacking Voice Mail Systems*, Communications News, January 1992.

Stiller, Wolfgang, *Defeating Viruses and Other Threats to Data Integrity*, Stiller Research, FL, 1992.

Wood, C.C. and Banks, W.W., *Human Error: An Overlooked but Significant Information Security Problem*, Computers and Security, 12, 1993.

INDEX

377

V

W

X

Z